Sloppy Craft

Sloppy Craft

Postdisciplinarity and the Crafts

Edited by
Elaine Cheasley Paterson and
Susan Surette

BLOOMSBURY VISUAL ARTS
LONDON • NEW YORK • OXFORD • NEW DELHI • SYDNEY

BLOOMSBURY VISUAL ARTS
Bloomsbury Publishing Plc
50 Bedford Square, London, WC1B 3DP, UK
1385 Broadway, New York, NY 10018, USA
29 Earlsfort Terrace, Dublin 2, Ireland

BLOOMSBURY, BLOOMSBURY VISUAL ARTS and the Diana logo are trademarks of
Bloomsbury Publishing Plc

First published in Great Britain by Bloomsbury Academic 2015
This edition published by Bloomsbury Visual Arts 2019
Reprinted 2023

A catalogue record for this book is available from the British Library.

The Library of Congress has cataloged the Bloomsbury Academic edition as follows:
Sloppy craft : postdisciplinarity and the crafts / edited by Elaine Cheasley Paterson and
Susan Surette.
pages cm
Includes bibliographical references and index.
ISBN 978-1-4725-3488-0 (hardback)-- ISBN 978-1-4725-2900-8 (pbk.) 1. Handicraft--
Philosophy. 2. Avant-garde (Aesthetics) 3. Amateurism. 4. Ugliness in art. I. Paterson, Elaine
Cheasley. II. Surette, Susan.
TT14.S66 2015
745.5--dc23
2014049237

ISBN: HB: 978-1-4725-3488-0
PB: 978-1-3501-5769-9
ePDF: 978-1-4742-4897-6
eBook: 978-1-4725-3307-4

Typeset by Fakenham Prepress Solutions, Fakenham, Norfolk NR21 8NN

To find out more about our authors and books visit www.bloomsbury.com
and sign up for our newsletters.

To all makers and teachers using craft processes, concepts, tools, or materials, as well as those who value and talk about them.

CONTENTS

LIST OF ILLUSTRATIONS

Figures

Plate Section

NOTES ON CONTRIBUTORS

Editors

Elaine Cheasley Paterson is Associate Professor of Craft History at Concordia University, Montreal, Canada. She holds an MA in Canadian Art History from Concordia University (Montreal, 1999) and a PhD from Queen's University (Kingston, 2004), where she was a Social Sciences and Humanities Research Council and FCAR (*Fonds pour la formation des chercheurs et l'aide à la recherche*, Government of Quebec) scholar and recipient of the Bader Fellowship in Art History. Her current funded research concerns women's cultural philanthropy in early twentieth-century British, Irish, and Canadian craft guilds of the home arts movement. She is particularly interested in establishing connections among the main umbrella organizations for craft revival in each of these countries, specifically between the internationally known Home Arts and Industries Association, London (1884) and both the Irish Industries Association, Dublin (1886) and the Canadian Handicrafts Guild, Montreal (1905). She has presented this research at many international conferences, including in Britain, Ireland, and the United States. Her writing and teaching are focused on the relationships between material culture and feminist theory, with an emphasis on the decorative arts and craft history. Some of her publications include "Crafting a National Identity" in *The Irish Revival Reappraised* (2004); "Decoration and Desire in the Watts Chapel," *Gender and History* 17:3 (2005); "Gender and Canadian Ceramics: Women's Networks" in *On the Table: 100 Years of Functional Ceramics in Canada* (Gardiner Museum catalog, 2006); "Judy Chicago's Rainbow Shabbat at the MMAQ" in *Chicago in Glass – en Verre* (2010); "'Meet me in St. Louis': Emigration and Craft Revival in nineteenth-century Ireland and Canada," *Canadian Journal of Irish Studies* (forthcoming, 2016); "Crafting Empire: Intersections of Irish and Canadian Women's History," *Journal of Canadian Art History* (2014); a special issue of *Cahiers métiers d'art / Craft Journal* on Craft and Social Development (Fall 2012) (co-edited with Gloria Hickey); as well as review articles for *RACAR*, *The Canadian Journal of Irish Studies*, and *The Journal of Stained Glass* (London). She is a member of the editorial board of *Cahiers métiers d'art / Craft Journal* (Montreal), a member of the Centre for the Study of Canadian Women Artists and the Quebec Quilt Registry Project at Concordia, a Research Fellow of the Institute for Studies in Canadian Art and also sits on the board of Centre des textiles contemporains de Montréal/Montreal Centre for Contemporary Textiles and TRAMES, la galerie (CMTC). Her curatorial work has focused on contemporary Quebec craft.

Susan Surette is a professional artist established in the field of Canadian crafts for over 35 years, and currently a postdoctoral fellow at NSCAD University. Her ceramics are found in corporate, public, and private collections. She has participated in national juried craft shows, as well as group and solo exhibitions. In her recently completed PhD in the Department of Art History at Concordia University (2014), she examined Canadian ceramic relief murals executed in the quarter-century between 1960 and 1985. Her theoretical interests currently involve material culture studies, decorative arts, and craft theory. She has taught undergraduate courses at Concordia and Nova Scotia College of Art and Design universities on ceramic and textile history and a graduate course on decorative art at Concordia. Her publication history includes "*The Story of Life*: A Ceramic Mural by Lorraine Malach," *Journal of Canadian Art History* (Autumn 2012); "Social Engagement: The Interface of Passion and Commitment Between Judy Chicago and the MMAQ," *Chicago in Glass – en Verre* (2010); "Créativité, Éthique et Comportement" in *Itineraire: Rendez-vous 2009 en métiers d'art* (2010); "Jordi Bonet's *Hommage à Gaudí*: Sensual Matters," *Cahiers métiers d'art / Craft Journal* (Spring 2010); "Review of *Maurice Savoie: Art, Architecture, Industrie, Exhibition at Musée des maîtres et artisans du Québec, December 17, 2008–March 1, 2009*, curated by Céline Le Merlus," *Cahiers métiers d'art / Craft Journal* (Autumn 2009); and "I Am a Blind Tourist: A Look at the Pines of Oka," *Cahiers métiers d'art / Craft Journal* (Summer 2007). Publications based on her MA thesis (Art History, Concordia University, 2003) include "Invoking the Land: the Evocative Vessel," *Utopic Impulses: Contemporary Ceramics Practice* (2007); "Domesticated Wilderness: Landscapes On and In Functional Ceramics," in *On the Table: 100 Years of Functional Ceramics in Canada, Gardiner Museum of Ceramics, Feb. 15–April 22, 2007*, curated by Rachel Gotlieb and Sandra Alfoldy; and "Landscape as Language in Canadian Ceramics: A Reading of a National Collection," *Craft: Perception and Practice* 2 (2005). She has presented papers at the 2012 Canadian Women Artists History Initiative conference, the 2011 Association of Art Historians conference and at several Universities Art Association of Canada (UAAC) sessions since 1998, and has co-chaired double sessions at UAAC with Denis Longchamps ("The Embodiment of Craft") and Elaine Paterson ("Post-disciplinarity and Sloppy Craft—A Critical Engagement") in 2009 and 2011 respectively. She also serves on the editorial board of *Cahiers* *métiers d'art* / *Craft Journal* (Montreal). Susan Surette's research has been supported by Social Sciences and Humanities Research Council and FQRSC (*Fonds de recherche du Québec – Société et culture*) grants, J. W. McConnell Graduate Memorial Fellowships and the Renata Hornstein Graduate Fellowship in Art History.

Foreword

Anne Wilson is a Chicago-based visual artist who creates sculpture, drawings, performances, and video animations that explore themes of time, loss, and private and social rituals. Her artwork embraces conceptual strategies and handwork using everyday materials—table linen, bed sheets, human hair, lace, thread, glass, and wire. In 2012, Wilson participated in the *Global Threads* exhibition at the Whitworth Art Gallery in Manchester, UK. Her 2011 solo exhibitions include *Rewinds* at the Rhona Hoffman Gallery and *Local Industry* at the Knoxville Museum of Art. In 2010, Wilson's work was part of *Hand+Made* at the Contemporary Arts Museum Houston, and her solo exhibition *Wind/Rewind/Weave* was presented at the Knoxville Museum. She participated in *Out of the Ordinary* at the Victoria and Albert Museum in London in 2007–8. Her work was part of *Alternative Paradise* at the 21st Century Museum of Contemporary Art in Kanazawa, Japan, in 2005–6. The Contemporary Arts Museum Houston hosted a major solo exhibition of Wilson's art in 2004, and *Anne Wilson: Unfoldings* was presented at MassArt, Boston, in 2002, and at the University Art Gallery at San Diego State University in 2003. She was included in the 2002 Biennial at the Whitney Museum of American Art in New York and her solo exhibition entitled *Anne Wilson: Anatomy of Wear* was presented in 2000 at the Museum of Contemporary Art, Chicago. Wilson's art is in the permanent collections of the Metropolitan Museum of Art, New York; the Art Institute of Chicago; the Museum of Contemporary Art, Chicago; the Detroit Institute of Arts; the Museum of Glass, Tacoma; the Victoria and Albert Museum, London; and the 21st Century Museum of Contemporary Art in Kanazawa, Japan, among others. Wilson is the recipient of grants from the Driehaus Foundation, Artadia, the Tiffany Foundation, the National Endowment for the Arts, and the Illinois Arts Council. Her work is represented by the Rhona Hoffman Gallery, Chicago, and Paul Kotula Projects, Detroit. She is a professor at the School of the Art Institute of Chicago.

Part one

Joseph McBrinn MA (Glasgow), PhD (Dublin) was educated and has worked in Ireland, Scotland, and France. He has held teaching positions at the Schools of Art and Design in Dublin and Belfast and has written and lectured widely in Britain, Europe, Scandinavia, and North America on Irish design and craft. His most recent research centers on the intersection of masculinity and craft, culminating in the book *Men and the Culture of Sewing*. He sits on the Executive Committee and Board of Trustees of the Association of Art Historians (AAH) and serves on the editorial boards of the *Journal of Modern Craft* and *Irish Arts Review*.

Elissa Auther is the Windgate Research Curator at the Museum of Arts and Design and the Bard Graduate Center. Her book *String, Felt, Thread: The Hierarchy of Art and Craft in American Art* (2010) focuses on the broad utilization of fiber in American art of the 1960s and 1970s and the changing hierarchical relationship between art and craft expressed by the medium's new visibility. She is co-editor with Adam Lerner of *West of Center: Art and the Counterculture Experiment in America, 1965–1977* (2012). In addition, she co-directs "Feminism & Co.: Art, Sex, Politics," a public program at the Museum of Contemporary Art, Denver that focuses on issues of women and gender through creative practice.

Elyse Speaks is a postdoctoral fellow in Gender Studies at the University of Notre Dame. She completed her PhD in art history at Brown University, and writes primarily on contemporary sculpture and gender. Recent publications include essays in such journals as *Art Journal*, *Sculpture Journal*, and *Women's Studies*. She also has an essay in the anthology *Sculpture and the Vitrine* (2012).

Denis Longchamps is Chief Curator at the Art Gallery of Burlington, Ontario, and formerly Manager of Exhibitions and Publications at the Rooms Provincial Art Gallery, Newfoundland. He received his PhD in art history in 2009 from Concordia University where he was the administrator of the Gail and Stephen A. Jarislowsky Institute for Studies in Canadian Art from 2006 to 2011. Longchamps also taught art history at Concordia University and at Dawson College in Montreal. He has contributed essays, articles, and reviews to magazines and journals such as *Espace-Sculpture*, *Ceramics Monthly*, *Ceramics Art and Perception*, and the *Journal of The Picturesque Society*. Recent curatorial projects include *Crafting Paradox* (2011, the Rooms Provincial Art Gallery, St. John's) and *Guilty Pleasures* (2011, upArt Contemporary Art Fair, Toronto). He is the publisher and managing editor of *Cahiers métiers d'art / Craft Journal* (craftjournal.ca).

Part two

Sandra Alfoldy is Professor of Craft History at Nova Scotia College of Art and Design (NSCAD) University, Halifax, Nova Scotia, and Associate Curator of Fine Craft at the Art Gallery of Nova Scotia. She received her PhD in craft history from Concordia University in 2001, and completed her post-doctoral fellowship at the University of Rochester in 2002. Her current research focuses on the relationship between craft and architecture in post-war Canada, and the historical tensions between Canadian studio craft and industrial design. She is the author of *Crafting Identity: The Development of Professional Fine Craft in Canada* (2005), editor of *Neocraft: Modernity and the Crafts* (2007), and co-editor of *Craft, Space and Interior Design: 1855–2005* (2008). Her most recent book, *The Allied Arts: Architecture and Craft in Postwar Canada*, was published in spring 2012 by McGill-Queen's University Press. Dr. Alfoldy co-curated the 2007 traveling exhibition *On the Table: 100 Years of Functional Ceramics in Canada*, and was the chief curator of the *Canadian Fine Craft* exhibition at the 2009 Cheongju International Craft Biennale in South Korea, and the *Canadian Fine Craft* exhibition at the 2010 Olympic Winter Games. In 2007 she organized the international Neocraft: Modernity and the Crafts conference at NSCAD University.

Juliette MacDonald is an Associate Head of Design at Edinburgh College of Art, University of Edinburgh. Her research interests focus on both historical and contemporary craft and design with a particular emphasis on issues of socio-cultural identity and nationalism. She writes on consumerism, craft and design theory and practice and has articles and reviews published in various journals including the *Journal of the British Society of Master Glass Painters*, the *Journal of Design History*, and the *Journal of Culture and Cloth*, as well as two chapters in *Exploring Visual Culture* (2005) and a chapter on craft in the expanded field in *Parallax Views: Interpreting Ceramics* (2011).

Gloria Hickey is a curator and writer living in St. John's, Newfoundland and Labrador, with more than 250 published craft-related articles. She holds a Masters degree in Philosophy of Art from the University of Toronto (1981) and has curated major exhibitions—including a retrospective of Michael Massie's silverwork—for several institutions including the Canadian Clay and Glass Museum, the Kitchener Waterloo Art Gallery, the Koffler Gallery, and the Rooms Provincial Art Gallery of Newfoundland and Labrador. She has also published a chapter in the book *The Culture of Craft* (1997) and has edited two books published by the Canadian Museum of Civilization— *Common Ground: Contemporary Craft, Architecture and the Decorative Arts* (1999) and *Making and Metaphor: A Discussion of Meaning in*

Contemporary Craft (1994). She is a two-time winner of the Betty Park Award for Critical Writing, hosted by the *Surface Design Journal*, and received the 2010 award for Cultural Leadership in the Atlantic Region. In 2011 she was the inaugural winner of the Critical Eye, an Excellence in Visual Arts award for critical writing given by Visual Arts Newfoundland and Labrador.

Elizabeth Kalbfleisch holds a PhD in Visual and Cultural Studies from the University of Rochester, NY. She has taught art history and women and gender studies at several Canadian universities and published essays on aspects of contemporary Aboriginal art. Her research addresses interculturalism in Aboriginal art and craft from the Reservation Era to the present. She was a Research Fellow (2011–12) at the Canadian Museum of Civilization where she studied settler and Aboriginal traditions of knitting in Canada.

Part three

Eliza Au received her BFA from the Nova Scotia College of Art and Design (2005) and her MFA from the New York State College of Ceramics at Alfred University (2009). Au's work is ceramic based and centers on the process of slipcasting. In recent work she has expanded her practice to include other materials, including paper, metal, glass, and wax. She has taught at the Nova Scotia College of Art and Design and the Emily Carr University of Art and Design, and in 2011 was Emerging Artist in Residence with the Pilchuck Glass School. In autumn 2012 she took up a teaching post at the Alberta College of Art and Design.

Jean-Pierre Larocque is Associate Professor of Ceramics in the Faculty of Fine Arts, Concordia University, Montreal. Larocque received his Bachelor of Fine Arts from Concordia (1986) and his Master's in Fine Arts from the New York State College of Ceramics at Alfred University (1988). Prior to joining Concordia University, Jean-Pierre lived and worked in Montreal as a self-supporting artist for ten years. From 1990 to 2000 he taught full-time at a number of institutions across North America including Emily Carr University of Art and Design in Vancouver, the New York State College of Ceramics at Alfred University, the University of Athens in Georgia, the University of Michigan in Ann Arbor, and California State University, Long Beach, Los Angeles. In 2004, Larocque was commissioned to create a large solo exhibition for the reopening of the Gardiner Museum of Ceramics in Toronto. Entitled *Jean-Pierre Larocque: Clay Sculpture and Drawings*, the exhibition, accompanied by a catalog, opened in 2006. A film of the project was presented at the International Festival of Films on Art later that year. His work was featured in *Raw/Medium/Rare/Well Done*, the ceramics exhibition in the FOFA Gallery in March 2009.

Kelly Thompson is Assistant Professor of Fibres in the Faculty of Fine Arts at Concordia University, Montreal. She received her BFA from the California College of Arts and Crafts (1984) and her MA in Visual Arts from CSA, Australian National University (1994). Thompson has lived and worked in California, Australia, New Zealand, and the UK. This nomadic life has informed her research as an artist involved in contemporary fibers/ textiles as an expanded field in art discourses. Her art practice explores visual touch, signs and traces of order, mapping, surface and structure relationships in objects and installations. Before joining Concordia, she was head of the textiles program at Goldsmiths, University of London, and spent a decade as a senior lecturer and program manager at the School of Art, Otago Polytechnic in Dunedin, New Zealand. Research interests are explored through intersections of digital imagining and material engagement with traditional weave and fibers construction, print, dye, and jacquard technologies. Themes include notions of location, mobility and identity; travel and material culture read through postcolonial theory; and textiles as cultural signifiers and embedded with narrative content. Other interests include the analysis of language employed within travelogs, global, geopolitical, and environmental contexts. She is active in arts education and pedagogy in both formal and informal communities and her artwork has been exhibited in group and individual exhibitions internationally.

Conor Wilson studied ceramics in Bristol and Cardiff and has worked and exhibited since in a variety of contexts—public art, performance, sculpture, and ceramics. He was awarded a Jerwood Contemporary Makers prize in 2010 and his work is held in many private and several public collections, including that of the Museum of Fine Arts, Houston, and the World Ceramic Exposition Foundation, Republic of Korea. Wilson has also worked as a freelance lecturer in the theory and practice of art and design. After 25 years as a maker, his attention has shifted slightly, from the production of objects to the value of skill and specialized material investigation. This shift led to his current research into making, writing, and the sites at which they occur, as an AHRC-funded PhD candidate at the Royal College of Art, London. He recently published "You Can Use Clay, But You Can't Do Ceramics: Some Thoughts on Why Ceramics isn't Sculpture," *Interpreting Ceramics* 14 (2012).

Peter Wilson started in ceramics at high school and has been developing and refining his work ever since. His first exhibition was in 1977 and he has exhibited both nationally and internationally since then. He has undertaken a research fellowship in Faenza, Italy, visiting professorships in Lahore, Pakistan, and residencies in Rufford in the UK and in Canada at Burlington. He is a regular contributor to the major ceramic journals on a variety of topics. Wilson currently teaches at Charles Sturt University in Bathurst, Australia, and works from his studio in the same city. In his work he values a strong sense of design and craftsmanship and appreciates the inherent "effects of the fire" that are unique to ceramics.

Postscript

Glenn Adamson, Director of the Museum of Arts and Design, New York City, and formerly Head of Research at the Victoria and Albert Museum, London, works closely with colleagues within the museum and in collaboration with scholars and institutions worldwide. He holds a PhD in art history from Yale University, and was previously curator at the Chipstone Foundation in Milwaukee. Dr. Adamson co-curated (with Jane Pavitt) the exhibition *Postmodernism: Style and Subversion, 1970 to 1990*, which opened at the V&A in 2011. He has also written widely on craft history and theory, in such books as *Thinking Through Craft* (2007), *The Craft Reader* (2010), and *The Invention of Craft* (2012); and has edited numerous publications including the triannual *Journal of Modern Craft*, the volume *Global Design History* (co-edited with Giorgio Riello and Sarah Teasley, 2011), and *Surface Tensions* (co-edited with Victoria Kelley, 2012).

ACKNOWLEDGMENTS

The editors would like to express their appreciation to the contributors of *Sloppy Craft: Postdisciplinarity and the Crafts* for their hard work in developing the essays for this volume and for providing the illustrations of the works, including their own, that make this book as visually engaging as it is thought-provoking. We are thankful to Gloria Hickey and Denis Longchamps for their early conversations about sloppy craft which helped inspire the original conference panel; to the organisers who welcomed our sloppy craft discourse within the Universities Art Association of Canada conference; and to the Social Sciences and Humanities Research Council of Canada and *Le Fonds de recherche du Québec – Société et culture* for the financial support of this project.

The research assistance provided by our graduate students Barbara Wisnoski, Akycha Surette, and Jason Klimock was much appreciated as was their perseverance, careful attention to detail, thoughtful comments and constant enthusiasm.

We are also indebted to Bloomsbury commissioning editor Rebecca Barden for taking this project on and for the guidance she and her editorial staff (especially Abbie Sharman) provided to see it to completion. Our thanks to the Bloomsbury anonymous peer reviewers who provided encouragement and helpful suggestions for the final form of the book.

We would also like to express our gratitude to Concordia University for making our academic home a most welcoming one to the crafts in all their scholarly permutations and a particular thanks to our peers in the Department of Art History and the Faculty of Fine Arts whose support and encouragement mattered.

As editors, we are proud of the bridge-building scholarship presented here (between disciplines and pedagogical approaches as well as among scholars, artists and educators). We are also particularly pleased with those accomplishments achieved while the book came to fruition—most especially Noah Grey (born at the advent of the project) and a brilliant doctorate on Canadian ceramic murals, successfully defended at its close.

Finally, each editor would like to thank their families for their continued support and patience: Susan—to my husband Richard and daughter Akycha who as fellow craftspeople and critics engaged with me in lively conversations on this topic; and Elaine—to my amazing Mark who has spent countless hours playing with our sons, Jack, Owen, and Noah, so that I could work on this project.

Foreword: Sloppy craft— origins of a term

Anne Wilson

School of the Art Institute of Chicago

A great deal of theoretical acumen and energy are now focused on the concept of "craft." Terms like "conceptual craft," "neocraft," and "postcraft" expand the discursive space for discussion and debate about the ever-increasing number of ways of making. Art historical and cultural platforms such as feminism, queer theory, multiculturalism and non-Western aesthetics, and the art fabric movement all play critical roles in deepening our understanding of the many meanings of craft.

History—*it was a critical, content-driven decision to work "sloppy"*

I first introduced the term "sloppy craft" in conversation with Glenn Adamson at a Victoria and Albert Museum symposium called "Fabrications: Craft in the 21st Century," held on November 23, 2007.[1] This symposium was organized by Adamson in conjunction with the eight-artist exhibition entitled *Out of the Ordinary: Spectacular Craft*, curated by Laurie Britton Newell.[2] The symposium included practitioners, curators, art historians and critics engaged in the production of visual works—from outsourcing using high production values in large work teams to solo studio practices. In talking with Adamson on one panel in front of the symposium audience, I told an anecdote about visiting the studio of my then graduate advisee, artist Josh Faught, at the School of the Art Institute of Chicago. In a spirited and somewhat light-hearted manner, I used the term "sloppy craft" in conversation with Faught as I was referencing an aspect of his new work that I felt was exceptionally intelligent and formally progressive. I wanted to underscore the criticality of Faught's decision to make work in this way. The rough craft of his weave and crochet was a critical choice driven by the content of his work, certainly not by any lack of knowledge or skill to make work with a neater, more refined technical aesthetic. That was my point—his was a critical, content-driven decision to work "sloppy."

Following the V&A symposium, the term "sloppy craft" quickly entered craft discourse. The editor of the well-respected UK magazine *Crafts* was in the audience for the symposium and emailed me asking if I would write about my use of this term. I declined at that time. In the April 2008 issue of *Crafts*, "sloppy craft" was proposed to be a movement, as per the heading above Adamson's essay title "When Craft Gets Sloppy—Young craftsmen like Josh Faught are at the forefront of the sloppy craft movement. Glenn Adamson discovers why the haphazard has become so hip."[3]

On October 10, 2009, I participated in another public discussion at the invitation of Namita Gupta Wiggers, then curator of the Museum of Contemporary Craft in association with the Pacific Northwest College of Art in Portland, Oregon.[4] The panel description read: "A term coined by Anne Wilson at the School of the Art Institute of Chicago, 'sloppy craft' is described by craft theorist Glenn Adamson as the 'unkempt' product of a 'post-disciplinary craft education.'" The panel, comprised of myself, artist Josh Faught, sculptor Nan Curtis (Pacific Northwest College of Art) and artist Jessica Hutchins, came together to "discuss this rising—and controversial—approach to conceptual craft practice."[5] At this event I proposed the idea of a "false binary," an idea elaborated later in this text.

Why?—*the haphazard has become so hip*

The term "craft" has historical alignments with refined skill, mastery of technique and a striving for perfection. These terms and goals, of course, have enormous variance, aesthetically and culturally. To many, however, "sloppy" feels like the antithesis of what good craft should be. "Craft" and "sloppy" set up a binary of opposites that draws attention to itself and defies and possibly flips established hierarchies of value. It is this provocation that fueled interest in the term.

Although this binary is of particular relevance within a craft discourse, it should be noted that a more relaxed aesthetic had entered many genres of contemporary art at about the same time. The New Museum's 2007 exhibition *Unmonumental: The Object in the 21st Century* identified a more informal aesthetic within many kinds of sculptural practices that somewhat aligned with what has been termed the "provisional" in painting discourse.[6] As well, many artists were using craft media work within the liberal idea of the postdisciplinary, a position less conforming to traditional boundaries of established genres and disciplines. Many artists create work in multiple mediums, embracing a fluidity in acknowledging multiple historical lineages, materials, and processes.

There are numerous theories as to why this turn to a more informal aesthetic. Certainly, as in Faught's work, the content of the art is a primary driver. However, I would assert that it is also the ubiquity of computer screens, the infiltration of digital media into so many aspects of life and the availability of seemingly easy perfection that demands its opposite—the wish for a more sensorial experience, materiality and the mark of the hand, privileging foible and imperfection, irregularity and uncertainty.

I see no inherent value in either sloppiness or perfection in the way a thing is crafted. I advocate employing craft as appropriate to content or to a particular conceptual structure of work. And it seems useful to always consider a breadth of approaches that may expand the rubric of craft, of how things are made. Adamson, in his book *Thinking Through Craft*, analyzes numerous platforms for consideration.[7] Interestingly, the V&A Museum itself has a lovely text, carved in stone, arching over the grand entry doors, that says: "The excellence of every art must consist in the complete accomplishment of its purpose."[8]

False binary—*there are many "sloppy" aesthetics*

> To let threads be articulate again and find a form for themselves to no other ends than their own orchestration, not to be sat on, walked on, only to be looked at, is the raison d'etre of my pictorial weavings.[9]
>
> Anni Albers, writing in 1959

In the evolving use of the term since 2007, I've noted that the interpretation of "sloppy craft" presents a challenging false binary, often implying that work has to be either "well crafted" or "sloppy." To position sloppy craft in this way is reductive and non-inclusive to a range of aesthetics that may well fall between the two poles, or be positioned in a different intellectual or emotional register entirely where such language is limiting.[10]

We know from the early teachings and modern weavings of Anni Albers that the use of fiber has many aesthetic directions within art. I think of the monumental and highly expressive collaborative fiber sculpture of Ritzi and Peter Jacobi from Germany and the richly textural, woven fiber pieces of Grau Garriga from Spain, both works from the 1970s. Is this work "sloppy craft"? I think not. This work extends from other contexts and different historical lineages within a European painting and sculpture perspective. But this work does have properties of gestural abstraction, and rich, irregular surface textures respond to deep ideological and historical knowledge of art and culture and contribute significantly to critical discourse within visual art production. Similarly, there is much contemporary artwork now that also may not be well served by an essentializing or polarizing definition of "sloppy craft."

It is my hope that the different voices in this volume will identify and complicate the multiple ways in which "sloppy craft" expands and meanings evolve within a postdisciplinary discourse.

Notes

1   "Fabrications: Craft in the 21st Century", held on November 23, 2007 at the Victoria and Albert Museum, London, originally available from http://www. vam.ac.uk/vastatic/microsites/1637_outoftheordinary/events.php. See also, http://www.vam.ac.uk/content/articles/p/past-exhibitions-and-displays-2007/ (accessed October 14, 2013).

2   *Out of the Ordinary: Spectacular Craft* exhibition held at the V&A Museum, London, from November 13, 2007 to February 17, 2008, curated by Laurie Britton Newell with exhibition catalog featuring essays by Glenn Adamson and Tanya Harrod: http://www.vam.ac.uk/vastatic/microsites/1637_ outoftheordinary/exhibition.php (accessed October 14, 2013).

3   Glenn Adamson, "When Craft Gets Sloppy," *Crafts* (UK), March/April 2008: 36.

4   Namita Gupta Wiggers was subsequently appointed Director and Chief Curator of MoCC (May 2012) and after ten years at the MoCC stepped down from the position in 2014 to pursue independent projects.

5   The entire panel discussion "Open Conversation: Sloppy Craft" is available online from http://museumofcontemporarycraft.org/exhibitions/programs (accessed October 14, 2013).

6   Laura Hoptman, Richard Flood, Massimiliano Gioni and Trevor Smith, *Unmonumental: The Object in the 21st Century* (New York: Phaidon and New Museum, 2007), in Raphael Rubenstein, "Provisional Painting," *Art in America*, May 2009, http://www.artinamericamagazine.com/features/ provisional-painting-raphael-rubinstein/ (accessed October 14, 2013).

7   Glenn Adamson, *Thinking Through Craft* (London: Berg, 2007).

8   "One of the last things to be completed was the inscription around the main door arch, which was adapted from Sir Joshua Reynolds: 'The excellence of every art must consist in the complete accomplishment of its purpose.'" Excerpt from V&A website: http://www.vam.ac.uk/content/articles/a/ architectural-history-of-the-v-and-a-1899-1909-webb-completes-the-new-building/ (accessed November 20, 2011).

9   *Anni Albers: Pictorial Weavings*, exhibition catalog at MIT New Gallery (Cambridge, MA: MIT, 1959).

10 Thanks for my conversations with Josh Faught and Mike Andrews, 2012–13.

Introduction

Elaine C. Paterson and Susan Surette

Sloppy Craft: Postdisciplinarity and the Crafts draws together theory, practice, and pedagogy in this in-depth examination of "sloppy craft." This volume critically explores and analyzes the post/interdisciplinary implications of "sloppy craft" within a twenty-first-century context where the future of craft practice is, once again, at a crossroads.

The following collection of essays is the first scholarly project to bring together an international selection of artists, historians, theorists, and educators to clarify the possibilities and limitations of the idea and practice of sloppy craft within an increasingly interdisciplinary (or even postdisciplinary) contemporary art and craft environment. The central issues emerging through these contributions from Canada, the United Kingdom, the United States, and Australia implicate both contemporary art and contemporary craft. Key concerns are the lingering importance of traditional concepts of skill and the implications of this on a twenty-first-century interest in interdisciplinarity, as well as considerations of activist, performance, amateur, queer and Aboriginal practices as these relate to a postdisciplinary craft milieu.

Sloppy craft is perceived as an accessible term to most readers interested in craft, evoking images of perhaps unsuccessful experiments with materials and processes. While this is certainly one aspect of sloppy craft, it has also recently assumed the role of social critic, and in doing so has illuminated shared concerns of the art and craft worlds, while posing questions that elicit disagreement among these worlds. Behind these concerns are the concepts of postdisciplinarity, skill, and hybridity. We hope the critical approach to these concepts underpinning the chapters in this book will appeal to a large scholarly audience in the fine arts, crafts, and education, but especially to academic communities devoted to the study of both contemporary craft and art. This book also aims to serve as a valuable tool for teaching within the university milieu as well as appealing to an audience who make and consume craft objects and teach craft materials and processes. We believe readers will find something in these collected writings of value to scholarship in fields as varied as Aboriginal studies, queer theory, performance art, as well as fine art, material culture, and craftivist, Indie craft and DIY interests. Enlarging the discussion around sloppy craft will be useful not only to makers and academics, but will serve institutions dedicated to professionalism, such as crafts councils and guilds, and curators of contemporary craft and galleries collecting works grounded in hybrid practices as expressed within the sloppy craft paradigm.

Sloppy craft: Disruptive/disrupting craft discourse

Myriad views of scholars, curators, makers, and amateur enthusiasts have drawn upon the rich history and complex discourse of craft. Each has teased out particular aspects of craft, which in turn have drawn out other attendant strands. We believe this is tied to anthropologist Webb Keane's interpretation of material semiotics. Keane suggests qualities inherent in an object are bundled together with others, and when one of these qualities is pulled into the limelight because of cultural conditions, it brings others along, inflecting previous meanings of them.[1] How then might sloppy craft inflect other "bundled" concepts of craft in this current context? In artist Anne Wilson's terms, the craft qualities pulled into view are materials and processes or skill, rather than, for example, the concept of containment as foregrounded by ceramist Paul Mathieu.[2] Several other emergent strands of enquiry within the crafts are briefly worth noting here. These diverge from popular understandings of craft and engage with the bundled qualities of craft within the context of sloppy craft.

In recent curatorial writing, craft has been deployed as a verb—a series of actions or performances, rather than a noun—an object made of wood, clay, fiber, metal, glass, paper, etc. In 2012, writing for *American Crafts Magazine*, critic Lisa Radon described this shift as a "radical reconsideration" of the word craft.[3] According to former Director of the Museum of Contemporary Craft (MoCC) Namita Gupta Wiggers, this focus on process rather than outcome emerges from a desire to take into account how people experience their lives and where materials come from within the global economy. She also considers how materials are manipulated by the studio maker as well as by any sweated laborer and how craft forms connections among people.[4] MoCC guest curators Shannon Stratton and Judith Leemann turned to this approach when they engaged with craft as methodology in their 2010 exhibition *Gestures of Resistance*. This show fused craft production with active performance in ways that engaged with "gesture, ritual and extended time-based ways of working."[5] Drawing together activist concerns, crafter micro-economies, audience and maker engagement, collaboration and exchange, they threw open the doors of craft while exploring respectfully many of its conceptual limits.

Yet craft in performance is not a recent phenomenon, attested to by Kalbfleisch's chapter in this volume. Indeed an emphasis on process has preoccupied makers for some time, particularly beyond the confines of the geographical and ideological West. While the dematerialization of the craft object seems to have come decades after that of the art object, the performative aspects of craft have long been theorized in meaningful ways. One example is the 1965 translation to English of Yuichiro Kojiro's *Forms in Japan* which has many parallels to the later *Verb List Compilation: Actions to Relate to Oneself, Material, Place and Process* (1967–8) by Richard Serra, an American sculptor related to the Process Art movement of the 1960s.[6] Kojiro's attempt to develop a classification system for the traditional crafts of Japan included the action-based headings: Forms of Union [such as tying, binding, weaving]; Forms of Collection [such as gathering, heaping, felting]; Forms of Arrangement [such as pairing, scattering, discarding]; Forms of Fluidity [such as dropping, flowing, smearing].[7] Stratton and Leemann acknowledge that both of these texts informed their approach to "performative craft" developed for *Gestures of Resistance* where the emphasis was placed squarely on the actions of the makers rather than the material outcomes of their processes. In this way the objects were markers of time rather than space.[8]

British designer and woodworker David Pye and writer Peter Dormer's foundational views for craft, as "workmanship of risk" (rather than certainty) and "tacit knowledge" (rather than distributed), inflect design historian Mike Press's argument for craft as a form of knowledge, one which can contribute to solving problems in and making connections with other specialized fields, drawing upon and contributing to their knowledge and expertise.[9] For Press, craft knowledge is "too important and too unique to be limited to the domain of the handcrafted object. This knowledge provides a key to humanizing technology and addressing the politics of work and consumption." If considered in this way, Press claims, craft offers interdisciplinary "creative strategies and approaches that open up new possibilities of form, meaning, and significance in our digital culture."[10] Similarly, Swedish craft theorist Love Jönsson discusses craft in broad strokes invoking making, materials or finished object but, as with Press, he also makes a case for craft as a form of knowledge—useful in negotiating a digital world and applicable to many fields. Jönsson concludes craft might alter our appreciation of digital technology (in which he includes a user-led Web, file-sharing and open-source software) as it is harnessed by craftspeople for their own purposes. Among his suggestions are mixing it with age-old traditions, or subverting its applications and giving digital technology new symbolic values.[11]

In articulating its ever-changing position within the wider cultural field, craft might incorporate issues of design, making, distribution, consumption, and use, as many of the contributors in this volume contend. They acknowledge as well how these issues are subject to any number of physical, mental, social, political, or cultural interventions.[12] Taking craft for granted within the idea of sloppy craft is to ignore this exciting and ever-expanding body of writing and scholarship, curatorial methods and making within the crafts in the twenty-first century. By revealing many of these strands, the contributions to this volume enliven and enrich the discourse of craft.

While other recent publications have cast a glance at the current phenomenon of sloppy craft, none has taken on the challenge of thoroughly investigating and questioning its history, practice, contradictions, and possibilities. This investigation is particularly important in light of the changing pedagogical practices in post-secondary institutions and the consequent shifts in art and craft practice reflected within all levels of society, as evident in public, private, and corporate collecting practices. Many post-secondary institutions are de-emphasizing material-based practices, are turning to internet teaching even for material-based disciplines, or are faced with an inability to assure their students will graduate with enough expertise in a wide range of skills necessary to function as professionals in their fields. More and more people are embracing craft practices, not as professionals, but as joyful amateurs, excited by the physical and social processes of making, rather than by the goal of producing a highly finished product. As well, museum curators and collectors with a keen eye for the avant-garde are opening up their spaces and pocket books to conceptual works based on craft media and processes.

The goal of this book is to present a multitude of perspectives on the notion of sloppy craft in order to address these intersecting and interdisciplinary communities of academics and makers of all ilks who are interested in craft media and/or techniques. This collection offers a variety of perspectives and a rich compilation of voices with which to unpack the idea of sloppy craft (as initially intended by Anne Wilson) and its inclusion within the concept of postdisciplinarity (as suggested by Glenn Adamson). In undertaking this task, the editors have included a wide array of craft techniques, materials, processes, and authorial voices so that each individual author or artist could animate the slant they chose in relation to the concepts of sloppy craft and postdisciplinarity. These contributions to concerns and issues surrounding sloppy craft underscore the variety, individuality, interconnectedness, and dissent characterizing the current state of the discourse.

Sloppy craft: A background

At first glance the term sloppy craft is an oxymoron. Coined in 2007 by Art Institute of Chicago artist and educator Anne Wilson (author of the Foreword), this term was her response to the purposeful, rather messy technique used by her student, Josh Faught, in his politically motivated textile works. Writing for *Crafts* in 2008, Glenn Adamson, then Head of Research at the Victoria and Albert Museum, London, and now Director of the Museum of Arts and Design in New York City, popularized Wilson's term. Adamson highlighted the use of calculated sloppy technical execution along with its appearance in traditional craft materials as part of contemporary conceptual art/craft practices. In the same article he also suggested the term postdisciplinarity, rather than multi- or interdisciplinarity, to refer to this crossover approach.

Given the impressive professional credentials and staggering cultural capital of both the artist/educator, Wilson, and critic/curator, Adamson, responsible for introducing these terms, it is not surprising they quickly gained a foothold in academic discussions of craft. In a 2010 issue of *Fiberarts* magazine American scholar Elissa Auther described sloppy craft as "a new aesthetic" in fiber arts, and *Studio: Craft and Design in Canada* focused on the disciplinary debate, including post-, trans-, multi-, and cross-disciplinarity in their 2012 issues. The creative potential of breaking down traditional boundaries in contemporary art and craft has been explored recently in a variety of ways by Maria Elena Buszek through an edited collection of essays, *Extra/Ordinary: Craft and Contemporary Art* (2011), Glenn Adamson in *Thinking Through Craft* (2007), and Howard Risatti in *A Theory of Craft: Function and Aesthetic Expression* (2007). These publications are representative of an early twenty-first century paradigm shift in both the craft and art worlds concerning practice and theory—a shift signaled by the term sloppy craft itself. However, dissent from this new paradigm has also emerged. In 2011 cultural historian Christopher Frayling noted "craftsmanship is definitely in the ether [but] as an idea ripe to be 'reclaimed', 're-evaluated' and 'redefined'—an idea that should shed its tendency to speak its name with a cringe."[13] The chapters and discussions in this book offer meaningful insight into and contribute substantively to this complex and contentious debate.

American art historian Maria Elena Buszek's assemblage of essays from various artists, scholars, critics, and curators analyzes what she calls the "insistence" of the craft world on its "romance" with craft media and the corresponding romance of the "so-called art world ... with the conceptual."[14] *Extra/Ordinary* casts a light on crossover practices where contemporary art practitioners employ craft materials because of the "sociohistorical underpinnings of a medium," and turn to craft practices to highlight them as conceptually "subversive" or "poignant."[15] Buszek does acknowledge that few of the emerging crossover artists who use craft materials obsess over conventions of "craftsmanship or are completely ... involved in the actual making of their work in craft media."[16] Moreover, citing art historian Jean Robertson, she suggests craft criticism has failed to keep up with the critical content and conceptual aspects in work using craft media and processes, a gap she contends both *Extra/Ordinary* and Adamson's *Thinking Through Craft* have finally filled.[17] Indeed, Adamson first hints at the idea of postdisciplinarity within a craft context in this 2007 book—an idea which coalesces, by his 2010 *Craft Reader*, into the notion of an "undifferentiated field of practice" where artists can freely define and redefine themselves.[18]

In discussing strategies for the presentation of postdisciplinary craft in contemporary settings, Adamson claims the emphasis has been on issues of labor and obsession (or extreme process) rather than skill and, arguably, Buszek's approach falls within these parameters.[19] For Buszek, craft is primarily based on traditional craft media or processes, rather than the concept of skill that would then overlap with other practices and materials involved in painting and sculpture, for example. In *Extra/Ordinary*, skill is always a subtext, while media and processes are the main thrust. On the other hand, Adamson argues craft itself (and by extension craftsmanship) is an idea that should be viewed as a series of processes at the conceptual limit of art, where skill emerges as "the most complete embodiment of craft as an active relational concept rather than a fixed category."[20] Related to this is Richard Sennett's opinion that "the craft of making physical things provides insight into the techniques of experience that shape our dealings with others. Both the difficulties and the possibilities of making things well apply to making human relationships. Material challenges like working with resistance or managing ambiguity are instructive in understanding the resistance people harbor to one another or to uncertain boundaries between people."[21] In the same vein, Paul Greenhalgh has observed "skill—regardless of how one characterized it—was part of the infrastructure of making which empowered communities and allowed for the creation of a free, creative society. Skill as an actual phenomenon was far less important than what it represented on the ideological plane. For the craftsperson it was to do with empowerment, for the avant-garde fine artist it was to do with constraint."[22] In this volume, Alfoldy maintains there is a "power" to learning a skill which has been overlooked in current theorizing of sloppy craft. These essays take up Adamson's "challenge" to always see craft "as a problem to be thought through again and again," without accepting his argument that the "modern object" made by "'traditional' craftspeople" is worthy only for historical analysis rather than critical attention.[23]

Craft and skill have traditionally been conceptually aligned. Adamson points out American architectural theorist Charles Jencks understood skill as open-ended, a way of thinking through problems in situations "necessary to expedient bricolage,"[24] and in fact sloppy craft does contain elements of bricolage, especially evident in the work of artists Josh Faught, Allyson Mitchell or Mike Kelley. In this sense skill is problem-solving and while such sloppy craft projects may contain the notion of skillful manipulation of materials and tools, they are not bound to them. Adamson also brings to our attention that British architect and historian Kenneth Frampton conceived craft skill "as a way of being within society," in which the maker "engages with the internal forces of material [that] provide a set of constraints [whereby] the material becomes cultural."[25] In this sense skill is implicated in the processes that emerge at the interfaces between materials, the hand and tools. Several of the chapters in this volume take up this notion of craft as a way of being in the world, relating it to the failures of the craft amateur in the case of Alfoldy and McBrinn, or based in community practices as with Hickey and MacDonald. It inflects inter-cultural exchanges as discussed by Kalbfleisch, and alluded to by Adamson when he argues: "[S]kill ... both includes and excludes. The manner in which it performs this action ... is only effective within a certain cultural perspective."[26]

Skillful manipulation of materials might be the expertise of the craft-person, taking much time and energy to acquire, but artists consider the skillful manipulation of ideas to be their purview. American art and craft theorist Howard Risatti sees this attitude in the philosophy of R. G. Collingwood, who implied "skill is related to craft (to non-art, mindless production), while art is inventive and not dependent upon skill, which he argues is secondary to art."[27] But both these views are culturally contingent views of skill (craft) and idea (art). If skill is set up as a way of achieving "cultural authority"[28] within a material discipline, then working within that discipline without the requisite skill has the potential to mount a challenge to this authority. The need to be highly skillful in using materials may have excluded some artists from expressing a number of their ideas in craft materials; but other ideas, usually framed as social critiques, can be effectively expressed in these same materials using less skill involving material and tool manipulation. At the same time the handcrafted object, usually functional, made through the virtuosic manipulation of materials and tools, is too often subject to exclusion from art institutions on the questionable assumption that more skill implies less intellectual content. Such an erroneous presumption perpetuates the body/mind split prevalent in Western epistemology that is now being challenged. In the same light, sloppy craft is also culturally dependent, an observation borne out in the chapters, and particularly evident in Longchamps's close study of the skill-fully "sloppy" aesthetic and cultural critique in the work of Laurent Craste (see cover image).

The contemporary concern with skill, the interest in hybrid practices and the tension when these come together in a work or practice are not new concerns for the craft world, having historical roots stretching back to Walter Crane's 1892 observation that crossover practices could be creatively stimulating.[29] The professionalization of the twentieth-century studio craft movement has been incumbent upon the acquisition of skill by its members, and hence the trivialization or even demise of skill raises serious questions. The notion of skill, itself, is however also culturally contingent, as Adamson has observed, "continually transformed and displaced into new activities."[30] British author George Sturt writing in the

1920s was elegiac in describing the wheelwright's skill, as was American potter Hal Riegger writing in 1972 about knowledge required to fire pots successfully without a kiln. Within different contexts, discussions around skill and craft have engaged craft theorists, practitioners and teachers over the last several decades, including: David Pye, *The Nature and Art of Workmanship*, 1968; the provocative 1982 essay by Christopher Frayling and Helen Snowdon, "Skill: A Word to Start an Argument With"; Peter Dormer, *The Culture of Craft*, 1997; Howard Risatti, *A Theory of Craft: Function and Aesthetic Expression*, 2007; and Glenn Adamson, *Thinking Through Craft*, 2007, where skill is discussed as one of the defining characteristics of craft. In this current collection, the maker/teachers add their voices to this list, explaining the very real challenges they confront along with creative opportunities for integrating interdisciplinarity while seeking to transmit material skills.

Sloppy craft: Creativity and constraints of sloppiness—a framework

While the tension between hybridity and skill is not new, the widespread adoption of strategies involving traditional craft materials and techniques in conceptual practice is a more recent phenomenon. This academic collection of essays examines issues related to the relationship between the professional and amateur, and the social and political implications on identity when skill is devalued within certain practices. It also addresses the opportunities and limitations of sloppiness as a new artistic convention, the importance of disciplinary boundaries and the challenges of teaching and working within inter-, multi- or postdisciplinary environments.

The variety of international contributors, including scholars (art historians, craft theorists, curators), educators, and makers (artists, studio craftspeople, crafters), brings a wide spectrum of opinions and approaches to sloppy craft. By highlighting three particular themes within the general term sloppy craft, presented in three distinct yet interlocking parts, this collection encourages readers to become aware of the nuances inherent within the term and within the multiple practices that are enveloped by it. The final part, in particular, is unusual in that it seeks to represent a conversation on aspects of sloppy craft and postdisciplinarity among artist-educators to complement and complete the rigorous academic texts in the first two parts.

Part one: Explorations of postdisciplinarity through sloppy craft

In her Foreword to this volume, Anne Wilson suggests that the coupling of "sloppy" with "craft" sets up an enticing "binary of opposites" that demands attention and provokes discussion and may even flip hierarchies of value. The first part in this volume includes chapters that use sloppy craft in this original context—to describe a consciously deskilled aesthetic (as coined by Wilson and elaborated on in her Foreword)—yet weave into this initial understanding parallels with queer theory, gendered labor and processes of reskilling.

In his initial forays into postdisciplinarity, most notably in his 2008 contribution to *Crafts*, Glenn Adamson acknowledges that craft is challenging, given its continued relationship to certain modes of making, many of which, he contends, retain their value in the cultural field precisely because of their difficulty and requisite skills. Indeed, when craft is understood as skilled production, which is often the case, craft theorists Liesbeth Den Besten and Jorunn Veiteberg propose deskilling as a methodology for questioning the nature of craft itself.[31] This strategy is explored by Denis Longchamps and coupled with reskilling in the context of Canadian craft practices as these relate to a sloppy craft aesthetic. For Adamson, the postdisciplinary world that sloppy craft inhabits is one in which "no one activity has any more right to be called art than another" and makers are free to call themselves whatever they like, or to not call themselves anything at all.[32] This questioning of identity—self-imposed or culturally constructed—is Irish scholar Joseph McBrinn's point of entry into discussions of sloppy craft within a textile or fiber context.

The *dematerialization* of the craft object accompanies many current considerations of craft and, while not new, has been used recently to position craft as a methodology, as a form of knowledge, as a performance. Given this turn, it is worth noting how second-wave feminist art strategies may be read as informing much contemporary "performative craft" showcased in exhibitions such as *Gestures of Resistance* and *Hand+Made*. As Elissa Auther and Elyse Speaks explain in this part, several of these are also woven into the "sloppy" work of Josh Faught in a moment of recuperation.

Within this volume, our own discussion of sloppy craft may be read as inflected by, for instance, the concept of "maintenance labour" (or activities that make things possible, such as cooking, cleaning, ironing, mending and so forth) introduced by conceptual feminist artist Mierle Laderman Ukeles, who insisted in her "Manifesto for Maintenance Art, 1969!" that this labor underpinned the ideals of modernity (progress, change, individual creation).[33] In a twenty-first-century context then, does "craft" do the maintenance work required to make sloppy craft exciting and relevant in a contemporary art and craft context? Is it a continued striving for skilled production by studio craftspeople which gives the combination of sloppy and craft its avant-garde edge? Is the emphasis on the conceptual within a fine arts world needed in order for critical craft to be best expressed in sloppiness rather than skill, in performance/action/activism rather than object/material/virtuosity? Or might the maintenance work itself, craft in all its permutations, become the focus of this enquiry—where sloppy craft is one among many possibilities?

The chapters in this first part explore and explode the notion of sloppy craft as it was introduced by Anne Wilson and Glenn Adamson, through novel contributions to this constellation of meanings of craft, which include: discourses on skill, deskilling, and reskilling; process, materials, and materiality; concerns for gendered labor, sexuality, and identity; and interest in professionalism and global economies, and how they do or do not relate to a discrete object.

Taking as a starting point the complex relationship between amateurism and sewing from which sloppy craft emerges, McBrinn asks us to consider "sewing amateurishly as a performative and queer act." In his chapter, "'Male Trouble': Sewing, amateurism, and gender," he traces a lineage for sloppy craft within textile history to Victorian era "slopwork"—the making of inexpensive cloth for starvation wages almost exclusively by women in sweated labor conditions and which continues today within the context of the globalized textile industry. He further suggests how the making of contemporary sloppy craft carries some resonance of this history and intersects with these current labor practices. As the wider system of global art production slowly co-opts craft making skills and cloth as signifiers and transmitters of social meaning, McBrinn posits "there is a growing engagement with textiles and textile history as a means to explore the construction of masculinity and to extend feminism's critique of the fixity of all subject positions." His discussion of contemporary artists, such as Gavin Fry and Fernando Marques Penteado, among several others, is framed by the important British exhibitions *Men of Cloth* (Manchester, 2010) and *Boys Who Sew* (London, 2004). McBrinn argues by "engaging directly with the feminine and amateur associations of needlework, many gay men in particular find a language that can contest masculinity as a normative, fixed category of being and deconstruct its implicit heterosexism and homophobia." The interconnections among sewing, amateurism, and gender are examined by McBrinn as a means through which to investigate the textile origins of the term sloppy craft and bring to light the crucial place that gay, or queer, self-identification plays within the work of artists such as Fry, Penteado, and, in particular, Josh Faught, the original "sloppy" crafter.

In "Sloppy craft as temporal drag in the work of Josh Faught," Elissa Auther and Elyse Speaks reflect upon studio craft, feminist and conceptual art, and queer theory to contextualize the sloppy craft aesthetic and lay the groundwork for its broader relevance within contemporary culture. Focusing on Faught's recent installation *Longtime Companion* (2012)

Auther and Speaks address the concern raised in this volume by McBrinn—how might Faught's "queer self-identification" (McBrinn) play out through his decision to work "sloppy"? Drawing on the idea of temporal drag, as outlined by Elizabeth Freeman, whereby a "usable past" may be productively "harnessed" for the present, Auther and Speaks explore how the past(s) "puncture the present" in Josh Faught's fiber works to demonstrate a continued utility. Faught remakes objects in ways that call attention to their departure from the original values invested in them (in most cases those associated with perfected craft skills) by developing a "unique style of loose, pieced, asymmetrical or irregular weavings with a variety of surface embellishments" from pockets to fringes, sequins to loose threads, greeting cards to self-help paperbacks. Through his process, Faught renews the affective character of these fiber remnants in order to create "fissures" in the material artifact that are "always partial traces of lifestyles that sit uncomfortably within the historical [and often contemporary] record." Auther and Speaks argue convincingly that this unconventional manipulation of fiber, one which flouts traditional craft skills, may be seen as embracing the politics of queer theory in material form. In this way "craft's central codes are activated, performed or even amplified, and at the same time scrambled in order to draw out its associations with the decorative, the abject, and other codes of alterity." Building upon scholarship at the intersection of craft and queer theory (by artists such as L. J. Roberts), Auther and Speaks advocate a "queering of craft" through strategies embodied in sloppy craft.

Shifting away from textile and fiber through "An impression of *déjà vu*: Craft, the visual arts and the need to get sloppy," Canadian craft curator and writer Denis Longchamps presents the ceramic work of French-Canadian artist Laurent Craste. Craste's deconstructed porcelain forms are used to reinterpret the recognizable object and its attendant histories, including those of French Sèvres porcelain and so-called sloppy craft within the Quebec craft scene. Longchamps suggests the processes of deskilling and reskilling are at play in Craste's transgression of the notion of "la belle ouvrage" (a work done well), a notion underpinning most craft education in Quebec and elsewhere. Grounded in John Roberts's claim from *Intangibilities of Form* (2007), that reskilling is a "rupture that dislocates and delegitimizes established competencies," Longchamps argues from a craft perspective that "deskilling occurs when makers distance themselves from a technical mastery of their craft medium and engage in a form of reskilling" by which they express the critical content of their work. Indeed, each piece is perfectly honed by Craste using the porcelain-making traditions of his art education, and then assaulted with crowbars, wrenches, axes, and other stereotypical tools of working-class trades in order to deform, but not destroy, the original historical piece. Craste's work pushes the boundaries of ceramic craftsmanship, according to Longchamps, without rejecting it: "his sculptures, with their layered meanings, concepts, and technical mastery, are evidence of a highly skilled artist and ceramist."

In this close study of Craste's work within the context of the Quebec craft scene (including the glasswork of François Houdé, among others), Longchamps argues that skill remains important, even when artists are "getting sloppy." In much the same way as Faught's work is considered as a "consciously deskilled aesthetic" by Auther and Speaks, Longchamps interprets Craste's work as taking this "strategy of sloppiness" to another level through a process of reskilling. In this case Craste is consecrating the object through the conceptual nature of both his skilled actions in building and supposedly unskilled destructive actions, which are, in fact, highly skilled destructive gestures.

Part two: The implications of sloppy craft

The second part of this book presents chapters that problematize sloppy craft, challenging the notion of it as a casual approach to making with an antagonistic relationship to the history of fine craft's privileging of skill, precision, and physical finish. Linking several recent strands of enquiry within the crafts—performance and dematerialization as well as knowledge and interdisciplinarity—Wiggers claims the performance of craft is a transaction between the viewer and the producer in which the former gains knowledge of how an object is made.[34] But what of the finished object as embodying the knowledge of the making process? This is where the amorphous, grassroots Do-It-Yourself (DIY) understandings of craft might offer meaningful contributions to curatorial, academic, and professional discourses for craft.

The longstanding relationship between the amateur and craft has been reimagined in the now ubiquitous (thanks to Etsy) DIY "crafter." DIY craft has been variously described as a "remix" of 1970s craft revivals, a "mash-up" of capitalist and communist economies, as accomplishment without professional help (and, by extension, its costs), and as nostalgically ironic, often offering biting sarcasm in the face of the presumed role of domestic creativity. It is linked to a wide range of grassroots political activism, as well as grounded in a social network created to draw makers and consumers closer together. These "crafters," largely women, are defined by their eclecticism, if nothing else, and are often motivated by a desire for creative and economic freedoms without seeking validation within traditional art methodology and the sites of art or, for that matter, craft.[35]

Speaking at the *Think Tank: European Initiative for the Applied Arts* conference *SKILL*, Liesbeth Den Besten reflected on the ways "young craftspeople" are tending to neglect skill, "to purposely abuse proper craftsmanship, like finishing, durability or use"[36] which begs the question, left unanswered by Den Besten, is it possible to produce craft without being skilled at it? If so, would this outcome be sloppy and how might this interact with the sloppy craft proposed by Wilson and Adamson? The chapters in the second part of this book tackle these questions through a series of nuanced reflections on the differences between a lack of skill and a strategy of deskilling. At the same time, they broaden their scope to explore the intersections of performance, interdisciplinarity, grassroots communities, and activism as a platform from which to unpack the implications of sloppy craft within the wider contexts of Scottish urban renewal, the DIY market, studio craft communities, and intercultural craft practices.

The wonderfully anecdotal contribution "Doomed to failure" of Canadian craft historian Sandra Alfoldy unravels the many implications of the unintentional resemblance between the work of amateur Do-It-Yourselfers and the sloppy craft of professional artists, as these relate to the economic interests of the DIY craft market and those of the professional artistic community. In an unconventional twist on the scholarly explications of sloppy craft presented to this point, Alfoldy characterizes sloppy craft instead as a "purposeful approach to failure" where intent suggests a degree of expertise underpinned by an ability to differentiate between "good and bad technical skills." Focusing her discussion on amateur or hobby craft (whose greatest constituency remains women), Alfoldy opens with the questions: "but what if sloppy craft is completely accidental? What if it is genuinely sloppy, without aesthetic affectation or purpose?" She then launches into an exploration of the lived reality of the accidental sloppy crafter, whose results rarely achieve the perfectionism advocated in the glossy images of DIY publications, blogs, YouTube tutorials or television shows.

Locating common ground between the accidental and purposeful sloppy crafter in their mutual rejection of the perfected, "triumphant object" sought by both studio and hobby craft of the twentieth century, Alfoldy examines this dismantling of "modern world craft standards." She argues this rejection of studio craft standards may be misinterpreted as falsely suggesting studio craft has achieved parity with fine art. Indeed, Alfoldy suggests the current borrowing of craft by contemporary sculpture or its placement within gallery spaces as sloppy craft, for instance, reduces the idea of craft to materials alone, while also preventing the craftsperson from exhibiting their conceptual skills unless they enter the cultural arena as a sculptor. In this context, "craft is marginalized as merely the skilled manipulation of materials, making it an easy target for appropriation" since, according to Alfoldy, "the mindfulness or conceptual nature of its materiality has never been fully recognized." She argues that left out in this equation is the power of learning a skill—in this context, that which enables the professional crafter to escape being "doomed to failure in the treacherous arena of public taste." Yet, as an increasing number of women stop to question their pursuit of flawless crafts, she concedes both hobbyists and artists can relate to the power of sloppy craft within the spaces of art galleries. When situated in this space, sloppy craft has the potential to enact a reversal of this perfectionism, yet Alfoldy claims instead its elite role only further serves to alienate the *accidental* sloppy crafter. As hobby craft becomes rooted in domestic perfection, sloppy craft inhabits the conceptual realm, moving further away from accessible ideas of craft. In her cautionary chapter, Alfoldy warns us that this recent constituency of craft, that of sloppy craft, will result in professional studio craft being marginalized, as traditional in its approach to craft, not cutting-edge or conceptual enough for the spaces of the gallery, while accidentally sloppy hobby crafters remain marginalized within the crafts in spite of these visual parallels to a sloppy craft aesthetic.

Taking up the discussion of the amateur maker initiated by Alfoldy in "The value of 'sloppy craft': Creativity and community," Scottish design historian Juliette MacDonald frames craft practice as a social endeavor. Using social anthropologist Tim Ingold's approach to thinking about creativity as a generative and iterative process, she assesses the value of sloppy craft in relation to community in Glasgow, Scotland. As with Alfoldy, this chapter concentrates on amateur craft processes, yet MacDonald offers the more optimistic view of craft as a "power tool for the disenfranchised." Her intent is to explore the possibilities of craft as a process rather than thinking of craft as a perfect end product. Here, MacDonald looks at craft as a shared phenomenon in these case studies of community rebuilding projects. The amateur crafters enrolled in these Scottish programmes engaged with the diverse craft processes of stained glass, joinery, stone masonry, roofing, and pointing through workshops which provided opportunities to learn about traditional crafts, the intricacies of building and, most importantly for MacDonald, to participate in rebuilding. She contends these craft processes "embody an approach where value lies not in the end product but within the potential for freedom of thought and creativity which lie beneath the surface of the artifact, no matter how ugly or sloppy one might consider that artifact to be." Drawing on the work of Ingold on creativity, agency, and materiality, as well as that of psychologist Mihaly Csikszentmihalyi's on flow—the complete absorption of the creative mind in an activity as it relates to happiness—and sociologist David Gauntlett's *Making is Connecting* (2011), MacDonald mounts a convincing argument for the ways in which contemporary collaborative craft practices—whether domestic (though performed in public), amateur or professional—demonstrate a potential for complex webs of meaning and connection to community and locale, linking sloppiness to processes of sharing and renewal.

Casting the scholarly net even wider, Canadian craft scholar, critic, and curator Gloria Hickey suggests sloppy craft might embrace many social currents, such as think global/act local, feminism, gender politics, social justice, and ecological concerns. Thus she examines what she views as sloppy craft's historical precedents to contextualize current postdisciplinary craft practices. Her chapter "Why is sloppy and postdisciplinary craft significant and what are its historical precedents?" stems from a belief that the "advent of postdisciplinary craft has created a profound gap between the contemporary practice of craft and how scholars understand it." She suggests that small, active communities of crafters are "hotbeds of cross-fertilization which produce wonderful hybrid makers and practices." As with MacDonald in the Scottish context, Hickey contends the consequences of this are evident not simply in "products and techniques but in community attitudes, [and] local educational institutions" where a grassroots focus generates "postdisciplinary practitioners." Given the diverse results of a sloppy craft practice, Hickey seeks to focus her enquiry by asking not what sloppy craft *is* but rather how sloppy craft *behaves*. In order to answer this question, she analyzes Canadian Rachel Ryan's *Modern Day Nativity*, among others, for the ways in which craft is "messy" because it expresses that "life is messy." Another tack offered by Hickey is to look at collecting practices, patrons, and institutions mandated to acquire according to specific media. She argues that postdisciplinarity in the crafts connects with "a socially engaged public" who are "interested in being more than a passive audience or a collecting public." By focusing her attention on craft communities already living a postdisciplinary practice, thinking of the effects, not results, of sloppy craft and exploring how institutions may adapt to a postdisciplinary environment for the crafts, Hickey draws her historical lineage into a current, twenty-first-century context.

As an important counterpoint to the contexts presented in the other chapters of this book, Elizabeth Kalbfleisch's "From Maria Martinez to Kent Monkman: Performing sloppy craft in Native America" interrogates the stakes of sloppy craft, specifically its postdisciplinary and performative aspects. Through a discussion of craft objects within the space of North American Aboriginal performance art and performance within the space of Aboriginal craft, Kalbfleisch presents the possibilities for sloppy craft outside the dominant culture, a topic as yet unexplored and thus essential to this volume dedicated to a broad examination of this discourse.

Aboriginal art (historically craft-based in a European art world context, with current work often referencing this craft lineage or embracing it by creating works of craft) is gaining a stronger foothold within the global art establishment, in spite of a historical lineage of ethnographic craft with its potentially marginalizing effect. Ironically, urban professional crafters and artists alike have now started to develop a "rather breathless enthusiasm" for a sloppy craft aesthetic. The deskilled look implies a rejection of the technical virtuosity and polished finish of traditional craft practices, including those most prized as the epitome of Aboriginal art (basketry, weaving, blackware pottery, fine beadwork, etc.). Situating sloppy craft within this context of contemporary North American Aboriginal art, Kalbfleisch focuses on the relationship between postdisciplinary craft and performance in the work of "current art world star" Swampy Cree multimedia artist Kent Monkman (b. 1965). As with Hickey, a concern for contextualizing this relationship by looking to a history of Aboriginal craft demonstrators (Pueblo potter Maria Martinez and Abenaki basket weaver Anna Panadis) underpins Kalbfleisch's effort to test the limits, and the potential, of the discourse emerging around sloppy craft.

Indeed, Kalbfleisch concludes that certain contemporary Aboriginal art practices can be usefully theorized as sloppy craft and supports this claim with her unusual and exciting take on the theatrical performance props of Monkman. She suggests many Aboriginal artists, including Monkman, engage with sloppy craft for its "refusal of the boundaries of studio craft and 'high' contemporary art." She further considers what negotiations an artist must take on when delving into the realm of the crafted object—with the stakes for Aboriginal artists remaining high given their struggle to have their art accepted, valued, and displayed as contemporary art, rather than ethnographic specimen, often aligned to craft. Kalbfleisch explores Monkman's interests in this intercultural history, the traffic in Aboriginal handicrafts and cultural appropriations of indigeneity by settlers, through the performance aspect of sloppy craft as practiced by this artist. She proposes sloppy craft as an Aboriginal and intercultural form of expression, squarely placing it within scholarly and artistic discussions of postdisciplinary craft where boundaries (between art and craft, popular and elite, material and conceptual, among many others) are not simply crossed but rather altered, if they aren't already "outright imploding."

Part three: Sloppy craft in practice and pedagogy: A conversation

The final part of this book veers away from the academic chapter format to create instead a forum for five professional and practicing makers/educators to express their strategies and concerns regarding the application of "sloppy craft." As editors, we believe the addition of the voices of this group of people, deeply involved in the intersections of sloppy craft practice, inter- and postdisciplinarity, pedagogy, and scholarship, adds depth and diversity to the views expressed in the scholarly chapters. These contributors share reflections on their experience as professional makers and teachers dealing with students, post-secondary institutions, current practices, and teaching standards. Taking up Adamson's notion of sloppy craft as the "unkempt" product of a postdisciplinary craft education, this final part uncovers what this education might actually look like and how the dismantling of discrete fields, referred to by Adamson, plays out in post-secondary pedagogical practice.[37]

The contributors did not work from hypothetical situations, but rather from real encounters with students, procedures, and institutional directives. While some are stimulated by the concept of a postdisciplinary and/or an interdisciplinary approach, others are concerned with and challenged by the pedagogical implications of this; while some are quite comfortable with the idea of "sloppy craft," however they understand it, others find it unprofessional within particular contexts. The maker/teacher position has been essential to the emergence of sloppy craft as a critical term and practice. It was first employed by Anne Wilson in her role as teacher when she encountered the textiles of Josh Faught, her student. Validation of this original use of the term rested within the professional context of the teacher—not the student; Wilson's recognition and confirmation of Faught's work as a political/social intervention legitimized his work and the expression sloppy craft. Within her dual functions as teacher and professional maker, Wilson could be aware of Faught's work as part of broader historical moments that might be exploited to make such an intervention.

The two parts of this section complement one another: the question/response chapter acts as a space where these maker/teachers reflect on, respond to, and enlarge upon questions posed to them by the editors; the three short chapters that follow express individual approaches to many of the issues raised around the teaching and practice of sloppy craft. Consensus among the contributors is not the aim here. Rather, the goal of this discussion is to articulate concerns, explore various viewpoints and offer a diversity of solutions.

Contributors to this part bring a wide range of professional and pedagogical experience. Eliza Au, a west-coast Canadian ceramist with an MFA from Alfred University, New York, has taught at several universities from coast to coast across Canada. While Au's work is mainly ceramic-based and centers around the process of slipcasting, her practice has recently expanded to include other materials, including paper, metal, glass, and wax. She lately completed a residency with the Pilchuck Glass School and was a 2011 finalist for the prestigious RBC Emerging Artist People's Choice Award administered by the Gardiner Museum of Ceramics. Ceramic sculptor Jean-Pierre Larocque, MFA Alfred University, is Associate Professor of Ceramics and Head of the Ceramics Department in the Faculty of Fine Arts, Concordia University, Montreal, Canada. He has been a self-supporting artist and has taught throughout the United States and Canada, including Alfred University and California State University. In 2004, he was commissioned to create a large solo exhibition for the reopening of the Gardiner Museum of Ceramics in Toronto. A film of the project was presented at the International Festival of Films on Art later that year. Kelly Thompson, MA Visual Arts, Australian National University, is Associate Professor of Fibres in the Faculty of Fine Arts, Concordia University, Montreal, Canada. She has lived and worked in the United States, Australia, New Zealand, and the United Kingdom, where she was head of the textiles program at Goldsmiths, University of London (England). Her internationally exhibited work addresses a wide variety of themes through the intersections of digital imaging and material engagement with traditional weave and fibers construction, print, dye, and jacquard technologies. Conor Wilson studied ceramics in Bristol and Cardiff, and for 25 years has produced and exhibited in a variety of contexts—public art, performance, sculpture, and ceramics. He was awarded a Jerwood Contemporary Makers Prize in 2010 and has work in several public collections. Wilson has also lectured in the theory and practice of art and design. As an AHRC-funded PhD candidate at the Royal College of Art, London, his attention is now focused on the value of skill and specialized material investigation in his current research into making, writing, and the sites at which they occur. Peter Wilson, PhD Creative Arts, University of Western Sydney, Australia, has taught in Pakistan and extensively in Australia where he is currently Senior Lecturer in Creative Arts at Charles Sturt University, Bathurst. Wilson has taken part in residencies in Italy and the United Kingdom, and as a practicing ceramic artist has received several public commissions. Respecting the craft base of working with clay, he has chosen the vessel as his main means of expression, examples of which are found in national and international collections. These five contributors, all at various stages of their professional careers, bring to this discussion a range of experience as makers in a variety of approaches, materials, and themes, coupled with an accumulation of post-secondary teaching experience throughout the world.

Conclusion—the "sloppy" start to an open-ended conversation ...

The term sloppy craft has gained currency recently within academic and artistic communities. Yet, we believe the interdisciplinarity of sloppy craft remains untapped in all its rich complexity within contemporary scholarship. Given this, we invited scholars, artists, and educators to contribute to this discussion of sloppy craft in areas we felt needed to be expanded or encountered within this discourse, including activist, performance, amateur, queer, and Aboriginal practices as these might engage with a postdisciplinary craft milieu—which itself does not avoid scrutiny in this volume.

Accepting that the crafts are variously appropriated by the everyday world in ways that were perhaps not intended allows for the recognition that, far from being "fixed," meaning is something that is "unstable and endlessly negotiated according to both time and place."[38] With this in mind, this edited volume opens up several new venues of research that add depth and substance to the sloppy craft discourse in unexpected ways.

Sloppy Craft: Postdisciplinarity and the Crafts reflects our ongoing concern for broadening the scope of enquiry into twenty-first-century craft practices. These suggestions for future research are offered up as a means of growing this discourse into a substantial field of study for craft scholars, art theorists, makers, curators, cultural institutions, and collectives, among many others. Viewed through the interdisciplinary lens of "cultural biography," several of the most recent trajectories for craft have been set out in relation to sloppy craft, which is seen here as one among many possibilities for craft. Openings still to develop include: hearing from craftspeople who work with artists to skillfully execute their ideas (including the "fabricators" alluded to in the third part); the "cultural biographies" of sloppy craft objects themselves; the challenge of deskilling in order to be sloppy (a concern perhaps for skilled practitioners); the historic relationship between "sloppiness" as an experimental aesthetic; and the challenges launched against established values by the new generation. These are only a few of the exciting threads waiting to be woven into what we hope will be a continued conversation.

Notes

1   Webb Keane, "Semiotics and the social analysis of material things," *Language and Communication* 23:1 (2003): 409–25.

2   Paul Mathieu, "Towards a Unified Theory of Crafts," in Paula Gustafson (ed.), *Crafts: Perception and Practice 2: A Canadian Perspective* (Vancouver: Ronsdale Press, 2005), p. 201.

3   Lisa Radon, "Craft as a Verb," *American Crafts Magazine* (December/ January 2012), available online at craftcouncil.org/magazine/article/craft-verb (accessed February 20, 2012).

4   Namita Gupta Wiggers, "Craft Performs," in *Hand+Made: The Performative Impulse in Art and Craft*, exhibition catalog (Houston: Contemporary Arts Museum, 2010), pp. 27–33.

5   In "Craft Off," Nicole Burisch discusses *Gestures of Resistance* as it relates to the idea of craft as performance, rather than object, and goes on to suggest ways it might be viewed in a "more antagonistic or competitive form" as a challenge to long held views of craft as collaborative, community-based and "friendly." Burisch, "Craft Off: Performance, Competition, and Anti-Social Crafting," *Cahiers métiers d'art / Craft Journal* 5:2 (2012): 92.
    Craft in performance was also showcased in the exhibition *Hand+Made: The Performative Impulse in Art and Craft* curated by Valerie Cassel Oliver at the Contemporary Arts Museum, Houston, July 2010 and which, not surprisingly, featured prominently Anne Wilson's *Wind-Up: Walking the Warp Houston*. *Wind-Up* was a two-part performance where Wilson partnered with the local dance ensemble, Hope Stone Dance, to restage this conceptual choreographic work based upon weaving. The fiber was all donated surplus from textile mills in the United States, http://www.annewilsonartist.com/windup-houston-credits.html (accessed August 20, 2014).

6   Richard Serra, *Verb List Compilation: Actions to Relate to Oneself, Material, Place and Process* (1967–68), Graphite on paper, 2 sheets, each 10 x 8 in.

Col. The Museum of Modern Art, New York, http://www.moma.org/explore/
inside_out/2011/10/20/to-collect (accessed July 26, 2014).

7   Yuichiro Kojiro, *Forms in Japan* (Honolulu: East-West Center Press, 1965).

8   Judith Leemann and Shannon R. Stratton, *Gestures of Resistance*, held at the
    MoCC, Portland, USA from January 26 to June 26, 2010, http://mocc.pnca.
    edu/exhibitions/1278 (accessed February 14, 2010).

9   David Pye, *The Nature and Workmanship of Craft* (Cambridge: Cambridge
    University Press, 1968) and Peter Dormer, *The Culture of Craft* (Manchester:
    Manchester University Press, 1997).

10 Mike Press, "Handmade Futures: The Emerging Role of Craft Knowledge in
    Our Digital Culture," in *NeoCraft: Modernity and the Crafts*, pp. 250–1.

11 Love Jönsson, "Rethinking Dichotomies: Crafts and the Digital," in
    NeoCraft: Modernity and the Crafts, pp. 240–8.

12 Adrian Bland, "From Sideboard to Showcase," exhibition catalog essay for
    the Crafts Study Center, cited on http://makingaslowrevolution.wordpress.
    com/2008 (accessed July 26, 2014).

13 Christopher Frayling, *On Craftsmanship: Towards a New Bauhaus* (London:
    Oberon Books, 2011), p. 8.

14 Maria Elena Buszek, "Introduction," in *Extra/Ordinary: Craft and
    Contemporary Art* (Durham and London: Duke University Press, 2011), p. 2.

15 Buszek, *Extra/Ordinary*, pp. 5, 13.

16 Ibid., p. 6.

17 Ibid., p. 8, citing Jean Robertson, "Feminism and Fiber: A History of Art
    Criticism," *Surface Design Journal* 8:1 (Fall 2001): 39–46.

18 Glenn Adamson, "Introduction, Section 7: Contemporary Approaches," in
    The Craft Reader (Oxford and New York: Berg, 2010), p. 586.

19 Ibid., p. 587.

20 Glenn Adamson, *Thinking Through Craft* (Oxford and New York: Berg,
    2007), pp. 2, 4.

21 Richard Sennett, "Prologue: Man as His Own Maker," in *The Craftsman*
    (New Haven and London: Yale University Press, 2008), p. 289.

22 Paul Greenhalgh, "The History of Craft," in Peter Dormer (ed.), *The Culture
    of Craft* (Manchester and New York: Manchester University Press, 1997),
    p. 43.

23 Adamson, *Thinking Through Craft*, pp. 168–9.

24 Ibid., p. 91.

25 Ibid., pp. 100–1.

26 Ibid., p. 78.

27 Howard Risatti, *A Theory of Craft: Function and Aesthetic Expression*
    (Chapel Hill: University of North Carolina Press, 2007), footnote 5, p. 52.
    Risatti is referring to R. G. Collingwood, "Art and Craft," in Isabelle
    Frank (ed.), *The Theory of Decorative Art: An Anthology of European &
    American Writings, 1750–1940* (New Haven and London: Yale University

Press for The Bard Graduate Center for Studies in Decorative Arts, 2000), pp. 236–42.

28 Adamson, *Thinking Through Craft*, p. 78.

29 Walter Crane, "The Importance of the Applied Arts and Their Relation to Common Life," in Isabelle Frank (ed.), *Theory of Decorative Art: An Anthology of European & American Writings, 1750–1940* (New Haven and London: Yale University Press for The Bard Graduate Center for Studies in Decorative Arts, 2000), p. 181.

30 Adamson, *The Craft Reader*, p. 2.

31 Liesbeth Den Besten, "Deskilled Craft and Borrowed Skill," and Jorunn Veiteberg, "Stealing Skill," papers from the 2008 *Think Tank: European Initiative for the Applied Arts* conference *SKILL*, available online from thinktank04.eu (accessed June 20, 2012).

32 Adamson, *The Craft Reader*, p. 586.

33 For more on Ukeles, see Helen Molesworth, "House Work and Art Work," *OCTOBER* 92 (Spring 2000): 71–97, 78. Our thanks to Nicole Burisch for bringing this source to our attention.

34 Wiggers, "Craft Performs," in *Hand+Made: The Performative Impulse in Art and Craft*, pp. 27–33.

35 "What is DIY craft?," at ukdiycraft.blogspot.com/2010/02/what-is-diy-craft.html (accessed March 30, 2011).

36 Den Besten discusses deskilling within the context of Dutch educational institutions, focusing on those where "deskilling policies" advocate a "pick and choose" approach to materials and techniques (students may even create their own processes) for makers who begin with an idea they want to realize and work from there (Liesbeth Den Besten, "Deskilled Craft and Borrowed Skill" (2008), thinktank04.eu).

37 Glenn Adamson, "When Craft Gets Sloppy," *Crafts* 211 (March/April 2008): 28.

38 Bland, "From Sideboard to Showcase," http://makingaslowrevolution.wordpress.com/2008 (accessed July 26, 2014).

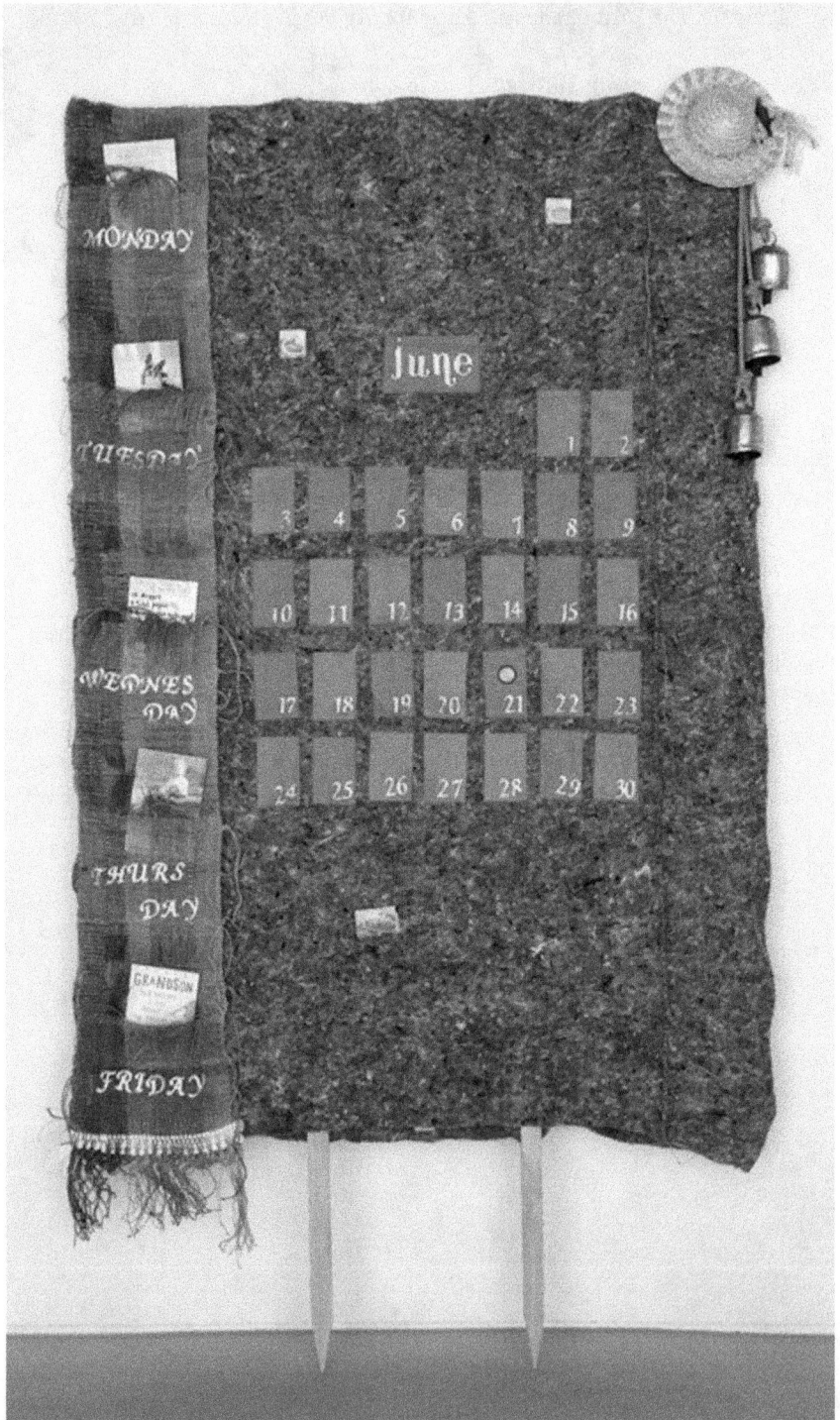

PART ONE

Explorations of postdisciplinarity through sloppy craft

In her Foreword to this volume, artist Anne Wilson suggests that the coupling of "sloppy" with "craft" sets up an enticing "binary of opposites" that demands attention and provokes discussion and may even flip hierarchies of value. The first part in this volume includes chapters that use "sloppy craft" in this original context—to describe a consciously deskilled aesthetic, as elaborated on by Wilson in her Foreword—yet weave into this initial understanding parallels with queer theory, gendered labor, and processes of reskilling.

For Glenn Adamson, the postdisciplinary world that "sloppy craft" inhabits is one in which "no one activity has any more right to be called art than another" and makers are free to call themselves whatever they like, or to not call themselves anything at all.[1] This questioning of identity—self-imposed or culturally constructed—is Irish scholar Joseph McBrinn's point of entry into recent discussions of sloppy craft within a textile or fiber context.

Taking as a starting point the complex relationship between amateurism and sewing from which sloppy craft emerges, McBrinn asks us to consider "sewing amateurishly as a performative and queer act." In his essay "Male trouble," the interconnections between sewing, amateurism, and gender are examined by McBrinn as a means through which to investigate the textile origins of the term "sloppy craft" and bring to light the crucial place that gay, or queer, self-identification plays within the work of artists such as Gavin Fry, Fernando Marques Penteado, and, in particular, Josh Faught, the original "sloppy" crafter.

The *dematerialization* of the craft object that frequently accompanies current considerations of craft, while not new, has been used recently to position craft as a methodology, as a form of knowledge and as performance. Given this turn, it is worth noting how second wave feminist art strategies may be read as informing much contemporary "performative craft" showcased in exhibitions such as *Gestures of Resistance* and *Hand+Made*. As American art historians Elissa Auther and Elyse Speaks explain, several of these are also woven into the "sloppy" work of Josh Faught in a moment of recuperation. Reflecting upon studio craft, feminist and conceptual art, and queer theory to contextualize the sloppy craft aesthetic, their "Sloppy craft as temporal drag in the work of Josh Faught" lays the groundwork for its broader relevance within contemporary culture. Building upon scholarship at the intersection of craft and queer theory, Auther and Speaks advocate here for a "queering of craft" through strategies embodied in sloppy craft.

In his initial forays into postdisciplinarity, most notably in his 2008 contribution to *Crafts* (reprinted here as a postscript to this volume), Adamson acknowledges that craft is challenging given its continued relationship to certain modes of making, many of which, he contends, retain their value in the cultural field precisely because of their difficulty and requisite skills. Indeed, that same year, craft theorists Liesbeth Den Besten and Jorunn Veiteberg proposed deskilling as a methodology for questioning the nature of craft itself, especially when craft is understood as skilled production, which is often the case.[2]

This strategy is explored by Canadian curator Denis Longchamps and coupled with reskilling in the context of Canadian craft practices as these relate to a sloppy craft aesthetic. Longchamps's chapter, "An impression of *déjà vu*: Craft, the visual arts and the need to get sloppy" moves us away from textile and fiber, to present the ceramic work of French-Canadian artist Laurent Craste. Craste's deconstructed porcelain forms are used to reinterpret the recognizable object and its attendant histories, including those of French Sèvres porcelain and sloppy craft within the Quebec artistic milieu. In this close study of Craste's work within a Canadian visual and material context, Longchamps argues that skill remains important, even when artists are "getting sloppy."

Much as conceptual approaches in fine art practices have always depended upon an audience fluent with, or at the least familiar with, painting and sculpture, the effectiveness of these conceptual approaches to craft depends upon an audience educated in the materials, processes, skills, history, and even consumption of studio craft, or what ceramic theorist Jo Dahn rightly refers to as their cultural competence.[3] Indeed, a lack of such competence within scholarship in related disciplines often hinders a more extensive and richer reading of sloppy craft. These chapters, on the other hand, open up for fruitful discussion the convergence within some sloppy craft practices of design, decorative art, craft, and art within postdisciplinarity. Are Faught's interiors sloppy design as well as sloppy craft? Is the work of Craste or Basque sloppy decorative arts, or part of the deskilling and reskilling of interior design and the decorative arts?

Through their contributions to this constellation of meanings for craft, which includes the discourses of skill (viewed as encompassing deskilling and reskilling), process, materials, and materiality alongside concerns for gendered labor, professionalism, global economies, sexuality, and identity, as these relate, or not, to a discrete object, the chapters in this first part explore and explode the notion of "sloppy craft" as it was first introduced by Anne Wilson and Glenn Adamson.

Notes

1   Glenn Adamson, *The Craft Reader* (Oxford: Berg, 2010), p. 586.

2   Liesbeth Den Besten, "Deskilled Craft and Borrowed Skill," and Jorunn Veiteberg, "Stealing Skill," papers from the 2008 *Think Tank: European Initiative for the Applied Arts* conference *SKILL*, thinktank04.eu (accessed September 15, 2012).

3   Jo Dahn, "Elastic/Expanding: Contemporary Conceptual Ceramics," in Maria Elena Buszek (ed.), *Extra/Ordinary* (Durham and London: Duke University Press, 2011), p.169. Dahn is specifically referring to conceptual ceramics, but the principle of her remarks can be extended to craft materials in general.

1

"Male trouble": Sewing, amateurism, and gender

Joseph McBrinn

The American director John Waters's 1974 *Female Trouble* was one of the first in a series of films to establish the campy, outlandish, and monstrous domestic characters and situations that attracted both recognition and notoriety. In *Female Trouble* the everyday suburban life of the lead character, Dawn Davenport (played by the transvestite Divine), is transformed into a life of crime and ultimately violence, carnage, and murder by a rather mundane incident endemic in late twentieth-century consumer-driven society. She doesn't get what she wants for Christmas. But, as Dawn's parents tell her before she explodes into a rage and attacks them, "nice girls don't wear cha-cha heels." Waters's highly distinctive "vulgar, sophomoric, sloppy, [and] subversive" style of cinema has more recently been "adopted, improved and made profitable," in a process of slow co-option by the mainstream movie industry.[1]

Waters's amateurish aesthetic and subversive subtext had, however, already, rather surprisingly, been co-opted by feminism. In 1990, Judith Butler defined "female trouble" as "that historical configuration of a nameless female indisposition, which thinly veiled the notion that being female is a natural indisposition. Serious as the medicalization of women's bodies is, the term is also laughable, and laughter in the face of serious categories is indispensible for feminism."[2] Butler singled out Waters's *Female Trouble* and its creation of a female protagonist (no matter how sloppily the role was played by a transvestite) as directly relevant to contemporary feminism:

Her/his performance destabilizes the very distinctions between the natural and the artificial, depth and surface, inner and outer through which discourse about genders almost always operates. Is drag the imitation of gender, or does it dramatize the signifying gestures through which gender itself is established? Does being female constitute a "natural fact" or a cultural performance, or is "naturalness" constituted through discursively constrained performative acts that produce the body through and within the categories of sex? Divine notwithstanding, gender practices within gay and lesbian cultures often thematize "the natural" in parodic contexts that bring into relief the performative construction of an original and true sex.[3]

Although many women shared Amelia Jones's conviction that "from a feminist point of view, it is worth being wary of the ways in which masculine performance can be too easily recuperated into rather predictable and self-serving clichés of male artistic prowess," Butler's deconstruction of gender's taxonomic instability reflected a wider shift in thinking about gender.[4]

Indeed by 1988, "female trouble" aside, Constance Penley and Sharon Willis had already posited that "the idea of masculinity itself is both theoretically and historically *troubled*."[5] They further suggested that through approaching the study of masculinity "from an explicitly feminist theoretical and historical perspective" it would be possible to deconstruct the oversimplified assumption of "gender polarization, where all women are victims and all men are unimpeded agents of patriarchy."[6] We can update Butler's use of Divine and Waters's *Female Trouble* as a historical moment that exposed the mutability of gender performance by exploring the work and celebrity of British artist Grayson Perry. Although better known as a ceramist, he has also worked in textiles, such as embroidery and quilting and even dressmaking, placing these on a par with his pots, limited edition prints, and performances.

In October 2000, Perry held a "coming out ceremony" for himself at the Laurent Delaye Gallery in London, where he made a short speech to friends and family about "coming out" as a transvestite. For the occasion he made and wore a special "Coming Out Dress" made from silk satin, rayon, and lace and hand-embroidered. It is, Perry said, a "classic little girl dress" using "pretty sugary colours" to embody "frilliness and sissiness—the absolute antithesis of macho."[7] In 2003, when Perry won the prestigious Turner Prize, he attended the ceremony dressed as his transvestite alter-ego Claire in the very same dress. In a subsequent interview in the *Guardian* newspaper, Perry stated that one of the joys of having a dress hand-sewn "is that it is almost a political statement. It's a way of rebelling against capitalism which makes money out of gender identity by supplying you with the consumer goods you need to support that identity."[8]

There is a multitude of other examples of male artists appropriating not just the gender-bending rhetoric of drag but more particularly the rather abject amateurism of needlecrafts to explore this slippage between gender construction and lived reality. Being a man and working with historically feminized craft techniques may be a double bind of acceptance and rejection, but it is undeniable that it has brought some men such as Grayson Perry enhanced visibility at some of the most prestigious international platforms in the art world. For example, consider the case of Italian artist Francesco Vezzoli's film installation and small portraits of female celebrities made of metallic thread stitched onto photographically printed canvas, sometimes shaped into embroidery hoops, shown at the 2001 Venice Biennale;[9] or the British-Nigerian artist Yinka Shonibare's installation *Gallantry and Criminal Conversation* for Documenta 11 in Kassel, Germany, which consisted of a series of headless life-size mannequins dressed in exquisitely stitched clothes, made in an affective homespun manner like Perry's baby-doll dress but using faux-authentic African batik fabric, and arranged in a scene of sexual debauchery to highlight the exploitative colonial tourism of the eighteenth-century Grand Tour. And like those of Perry and Vezzoli, the fabrication of this installation, although arguably reliant on professional outsourced labor, plays in its most basic (fabric) form on the rhetoric of amateurism.

The description of Divine and Waters's cinematic collaborations as "vulgar," "sloppy," and "subversive" uses terms that often circulate around men's engagement with various needlecraft activities, revealing anxiety, even today, in relation to the materialization of gender construction. Although the term "sloppy" was notably used in the late twentieth century by British critic Peter Dormer to describe the complexity in defining craft as a cultural category as handmade objects tended to look amateurish and "untidy" in contradistinction to the industrial perfectionism of manufacturing, the term has a very specific lineage within textile history.[10] "Slopwork" generally refers to the making of cheap clothes, almost exclusively by women, for starvation wages under sweated labor conditions, which was taken up as a cause célèbre by Victorians from Thomas Carlyle to Charles Dickens. Although the term has become something of an anachronism, the practice of slopwork still continues today in the physical and psychological slavery fundamental to the globalized apparel industry and its associated networks such as human trafficking.[11] The making of things by hand in a self-consciously amateur (or sloppy) manner by artists in the contemporary West carries, without doubt, some resonance of this history—what feminists such as Christina Walkley have called "the ghost in the looking glass."[12]

With widespread deindustrialization in the West and the fragmentation of both labor and leisure, it was believed that as men became increasingly deskilled, women were gradually able to work more and more with "men's tools." As Steven Gelber, a historian of modern DIY culture, has argued, by the mid- to late twentieth century as the idea of women's labor gained purchase within the workforce and marketplace, the "situation was inverted for men; they could use woodworking tools but not needle and thread."[13] Men working with historically feminized processes such as amateur needlecrafts remained extremely stigmatized. Although late capitalist society increasingly replaced labor alienation with hyper-consumption and ennobled the concept of the amateur as a nuanced form of consumption in itself, "hedonizing" previously functional domestic activities as new forms of commodified leisure, gender demarcation remained, and remains, rigidly in place for needlecrafts.[14]

Feminist artists have long sought to reclaim and reinvest in feminine subjectivity through exploration of this history of exploitative sloppy amateurism and its degradation of women, women's labor, and women's skills. However, by the 1980s and 1990s many saw the exclusion of men from areas such as needlecrafts as reinforcing a system of essentialism that strengthened polarized positions within patriarchal structures and actively worked to negate political, social, and cultural enfranchisement of women. Indeed, in 1994 American artist Anne Wilson argued that in textiles "this field is losing something for both men and women by not finding ways to include more men. How much is the conservative backlash in contemporary society, which insists on traditional gender roles, affecting this field?"[15] Although artists such as Grayson Perry, Francesco Vezzoli, and Yinka Shonibare work within a wider system of global art production that has slowly been co-opting craft-making skills and cloth as signifiers and transmitters of social meaning, there is a growing engagement with textiles and textile history as a means to explore the construction of masculinity as "the asymmetrical pendant to the more critically investigated femininity" and to extend feminism's critique of "the fixity of all subject positions."[16] By engaging directly with the feminine and amateur associations of needlework, many gay men in particular find a language that can contest masculinity as a normative, fixed category of being and deconstruct its implicit heterosexism and homophobia.

In her novel *Oranges Are Not The Only Fruit* (1985), Jeanette Winterson memorably used the term "sloppy" to describe something badly made, not in terms of aesthetic appearance but rather as a visual register of a young gay person's inner fear and turmoil.[17] This materialization of interiority has been the subject of important textile work, not just by women but also by men. For example, the English artist Gavin Fry's *Orlando*, made especially for the *Men of Cloth* exhibition in Manchester in 2010, encompasses a suite of nine hand-embroidered panels based upon Virginia Woolf's modern masterpiece *Orlando: A Biography* (1928), which upon publication one caustic critic dismissed as "fanciful embroidery, wordy and naught else" (see Plate 1).[18] Like Woolf's novel, Fry's embroideries play with the fiction and fantasy of sex as a fixed category through cross-dressing and gender dissolution. Onto amateur pre-stitched needlepoint kits of innocuous rural scenes, Fry stitched symbols as escape portals to other worlds and times to subvert the kitschy Thomas Kinkade-like vision of the pastoral English past.[19]

Fry used as his base the once hugely popular pre-worked kits and some original Berlin woolwork embroideries, now universally discarded as relics

FIGURE 1.1 *Men of Cloth exhibition, Manchester, 2010, installation view. Courtesy of Stuart Royse.*

of female subjugation through bourgeois fancywork and knickknacks—a reference to textile's amateur past increasingly apparent in contemporary art that prompted American craft critic Elissa Auther, in a different context, to call such sources "the ground zero of craft shame and embarrassment."[20] They also draw attention to the role of needlecrafts such as embroidery and knitting, not just in the life and work of Virginia Woolf, who was a keen needleworker, but in the wider Bloomsbury group, where the key embroidery designer was male artist Duncan Grant. Indeed, aside from Grant's mother, Woolf and her sister, artist Vanessa Bell, would stitch Grant's designs.[21] In some ways Fry redirects our thinking about Bloomsbury back to embroidery, whilst simultaneously using readymade kits sourced in charity shops and on ebay to root us in the present and our increasing alienation from labor (particularly male labor in contemporary Britain) as anything but commodified pleasure.

To take another example, in 2001 Brazilian artist Fernando Marques Penteado's project *Prison Speech*, conducted in the (all-male) HMP Wandsworth prison in London, sought to reimagine the traditional (all-female) sewing-circle: the male prisoners recounted personal stories about their incarceration which were then visualized in embroidered panels. The work was shown as part of the important *Boys Who Sew* exhibition at the UK Crafts Council's gallery in London in 2004.[22] Following this,

Penteado made a series of embroideries in 2002 entitled *Prison Vernacular* that suggested sewing not as some cliché of handwork as redemptive process, but rather as a genuine confrontation with a little-known reality of contemporary masculinity in a brutal environment where the very act of sewing exposed the private, the intimate, and the vulnerable. Penteado was especially keen to show how in a homosocial context men could establish social and even sexual relationships that perhaps they would not have outside prison. Focusing on the creation of new vocabulary to describe this, Penteado took terms such as "flip flop," which is used to convey the change in sexual relations between two specific men over time, or "butched in," to mean the exchange of sexual favors between men on a single, or perhaps multiple, occasion(s) (see Plate 2), creating embroidered imagery that reflected a fluidity of masculine identity. Like Gavin Fry, Penteado used the tropes of amateurism and all its "vulgar, sophomoric, sloppy, [and] subversive" connotations to explore and deconstruct the idea of masculinity/femininity and open up spaces to explore and interrogate queer, that is, non-heteronormative, identities.[23]

For many other artists, such acts as the appropriation of sewing, still unequivocally perceived as a feminized domestic activity, may serve to implicate them in the global economics of art production and other webs of deceit, but for Fry and Penteado, sewing serves as essentially an act of agency. It allows both artists, in different ways, to trouble and destabilize fixed assumptions not just about gender identity but also the sexualization of amateur and craft practices.

FIGURE 1.2 *Fernando Marques Penteado, Prison Speech project, 2003. This panel, Danny Brooker, 2003, dust twill cotton linen.* © *Crafts Council.*

FIGURE 1.3 *Boys Who Sew exhibition entrance, February 5–April 4, 2004, front gallery.* © *Crafts Council.*

Sewing for leisure, pleasure, and pure creative expression, no matter how amateurish, may also be further understood as part of a wider reconsideration of men's relationship to domesticity and home life, a debate that in the past decade or so has resulted in the conceptualization of masculine domesticities, domestic masculinities, and queer domesticities.[24] However, something about the act of men sewing, even if accepted as a post-industrial phenomenon or as a simple paradox with no problematic past, has been and continues to be perceived as troubling. In the popular press, men taking up amateur needlecrafts is often seen as a symptom of the much talked about millennial "crisis in masculinity." Anthony Clare has suggested that although patriarchy is in disarray, as opposed to dead, at the beginning of the twenty-first century, it is "difficult to avoid the conclusion that men are in serious trouble."[25] John Roberts has, however, cautioned that the so-called crisis of masculinity since the 1980s, in which the social construction of masculinity in post-industrial society saw deskilling and emasculation dovetail, was accompanied by "vociferous attacks on gay identity and lifestyle, with the spread of AIDS."[26] And indeed for Roberts, men's new engagement with domesticity has been generated, if anything, by "capitalism's relentless capacity to commodify all social relations."[27] Fintan Walsh has more recently suggested that culturally performative acts such as theater, cinema, dance, and especially performance art have begun to expose the fragmented nature and apparent crisis of contemporary masculinity. Walsh takes the work of Italian artist Franko B as an example of "the performance of so-called masculinity in crisis." Franko B has included various forms of needlework, from medical suturing (where his bleeding body is sewed after being lacerated) to conventional embroidery (large wall-hung figurative canvases), in his work and his use of his own blood or red cotton thread is an attempt to create what Walsh terms "sacrificial offerings."[28]

Over the last 20 years a series of exhibitions such as *Boys Who Sew* or *Men of Cloth* have directly explored masculinity and queer identity in terms of textile crafts, but nearly all of the documenting and theorizing around such practices still seems to suggest that this is an exclusive realm of women.[29] As early as the 1990s, James Lewis detected with some surprise that, in North America at least, historically feminized amateur and domestic acts such as sewing and other textile practices were becoming increasingly conspicuous in the work of male artists such as Meyer Vaisman, Mike Kelley, Robert Gober, Joel Otterson, David Robbins, Jim Isermann, and Michael Jenkins. For Lewis, it was "precisely the estrangement of men from sewing" in everyday life that gives such work something more than novel "esthetic charge."[30] Indeed, as Lewis concluded, "When women try to come to terms with home life through its practices, the argument goes, it's just craftwork. When men appropriate those practices toward the same end, it's Art," but work by men using traditional textile craft practices

> is a little less prone to cliché than some of its apparent models; there are no homespun pities here, no paeans to the Ur-Woman, no truck given to the claim that domesticity is woman's thing, and you wouldn't understand. Instead, as befits and honors the medium, work sewn by men has been everything from consoling to disturbing, and [has] proved—again, from another angle, toward another end—that "women's work" is powerful and expressive enough to serve as the grounds for an esthetic practice equal to any, and that home life acts out its own complex account of the world.[31]

In 1994, *Artforum* commissioned a special issue on the theme of "Man Trouble" where Donald Kuspit singled out the artist Mike Kelley, who had featured in James Lewis's earlier article, as one of a group of male artists currently "acting out" or performing a sense of gender identity through the marked use of materials and processes associated with femininity and, by implication, feminist art.[32] Although Kelley vocalized a desire to deconstruct his own white, blue-collar, masculinist background in late twentieth-century America, it remains significant that he chose various forms of domestic crafts, such as sewing, knitting, crocheting, and macramé, along with a whole array of taboo materials, as symbolic of domestic detritus.[33] Domestic crafts had, however, been subject to a long process of remembrance, reclamation, and reinvestment by feminist artists in the 1970s and 1980s, and Kelley's use of such techniques as "signifiers of the 'pathetic', 'abject', or failed" was seen as reifying "his bad boy masculinity" rather than genuinely destabilizing "gender codes."[34] As Faith Wilding suggested, such work by male artists that amount to "a mere reversal of gender signifiers (while often funny and consciousness-raising) does not seem to be enough to get rid of gender roles and stereotypes."[35] Indeed, Mira Schor suggested that Kelley's much admired *More Love Hours Than Can Ever Be Repaid* (1987) was essentially "derivative of Miriam Schapiro's earlier celebratory collage of lace, samplers, and gaudy textiles, *Wonderland* (1983)."[36]

Another American artist much more taciturn than Kelley about the influence of feminism on his work is Charles LeDray. The intricate garments he sews by hand he suggests owe more to historic yeoman, artisan tailoring skills than feminist art. Like Kelley, he has been critiqued for not acknowledging feminist origins in the "use of gendered materials that deal with sexuality and gender in new ways opening up the normative façade of masculinity."[37] However, he was one of a handful of male artists happy to be represented in the *Division of Labor: "Women's Work" in Contemporary Art* exhibition at the Bronx Museum of Art in New York in 1995.

More recently, Mike Kelley's work has been talked about as part of what Nicolas Bourriaud has termed "postproduction," where "artworks have been created on the basis of preexisting works" and where "more and more artists interpret, reproduce, re-exhibit, or use works made by others or available cultural products."[38] Bourriaud's idea suggests "that artists' intuitive relationship with art history is now going beyond what we call 'the art of appropriation,' which naturally infers an ideology of ownership, and moving toward a culture of the use of forms, a culture of constant activity of signs based on a collective ideal: sharing."[39] Whether Kelley's use of amateur types of craft is understood as a form of postmodernist "sharing" or more problematically as unacknowledged appropriation, his work, like that of many male artists who have taken up such techniques, has attracted critical praise from the major art institutions and media, invitations to show at prestigious international venues such as Documenta and the Venice Biennale, and what could easily be dismissed as all the other trappings of patriarchal privilege which clearly distinguished him from feminist artists. However, recently Cary Levine has suggested that the use of feminist crafts that conflated "canonical modernism and homespun knicknacks" needs to be read in Kelley's work as "in dialogue with" rather than in opposition to feminism.[40] Levine further suggests that in Kelley's textile work "the objective is not to rescue regressive gender identities in jeopardy, but rather to offer a broad deconstruction of the bankrupt categories upon which such identities are founded."[41] Kelley himself did state, retrospectively, that "if America's problem was that it was militaristic, patriarchal, and male, then the antidote would be the embrace of the prototypically feminine" and he continued "if the female is Other, then the homosexual is doubly Other."[42]

Although Kelley's appropriation of feminist craft practices is often picked over, little is made of his interest in what he saw as a developing "queer aesthetic" in other formative influences on his work, such as the films of John Waters and Divine, in which Kelley found "a similar play with gender slippage."[43] Kelley also pointed to the performances of the San Francisco radical drag act of the early 1970s, the Cockettes, as an example of this queer and sloppy aesthetic. Michael Moon and Eve Kosofsky Sedgwick have suggested that the collaborative work of Waters and Divine directly followed the example of the Cockettes by giving space to what was considered "grotesque, obscene, perverted, decadent, and/or déclassé by the mainstream."[44] Sedgwick's argument for gender "as culturally mutable and variable, highly relational (in the sense that each of the binarized genders is defined primarily in relation to the other)" is borne out in the work of the Cockettes, Waters/Divine, and Kelley.[45] Sedgwick, who was taught to crochet and embroider by her grandmother, was a keen textile maker herself, seeing value in "funky craft" as opposed to "finely done craft," and suggested that the "the craft aspect of art making—or, more simply put, of thing making—does seem (doesn't it) to be an exceptionally fruitful place for exploring those middle ranges of agency."[46]

In a recent discussion of the amateur and "sloppy" and its attendant meanings in terms of contemporary craft, Alexandra (Jacopetti) Hart pointed out that the "focus on the political and conceptual agendas [rather] than craftsmanship" in contemporary textile art had affinities to the "transvestite couture" and "cutting-edge counterculture wearable art by craft-cum-performers [such as the Cockettes] more concerned with personal expression than perfect hemlines" that featured in her 1974 book *Native Funk & Flash: An Emerging Folk Art*.[47] Hart pointed to the example of Cockettes performers such as Pristine Condition and Vickisa Firebird, who believed "a grounding in technical skills is nice but not necessary," and who clearly saw parallels between the "loose abandon" and "sloppy aesthetic" of gender bending and hand making.[48] The idea of what Julia Bryan-Wilson has termed the "queer handmade aesthetic" of groups like the Cockettes resonates, Hart suggests, in the work of contemporary textile artists.[49]

The term "sloppy" has recently resurfaced in the UK Crafts Council's magazine *Crafts* to illustrate an article by the American critic Glenn Adamson, chronicling a supposedly new turn in contemporary craft that he defined as work that was "really badly made" and which was soon after discussed as "sloppy craft."[50] The term "sloppy craft" had first been used publicly just a year or two earlier by Anne Wilson, in reference to the work of artist Josh Faught, in conversation with Adamson at the 2007 *Fabrications* symposium at the V&A Museum in London.[51] Since then, Wilson, who perceived the term "sloppy" as similar in its dematerialization to terms such as "plop art" and "blobject" coined in the 1990s, has further suggested that rather than being a reductionist expression, "sloppy craft" could capture the revitalization in the twenty-first century of "a range of ways of making" which were both "born out of high skill" and were in essence "a critical choice."[52] Wilson commented that "technical skills are presented and taught quite rigorously [at the School of the Art Institute of Chicago], but not with an emphasis on fine-tuning high skill as the goal" and in some ways what Faught had succeeded in doing was overturning or destabilizing the hegemonic role of skill within craft and absorbing it into his concept.[53] Adamson further suggested that Faught's approach was a conscious return to the ideas of the feminist textile art of the 1970s as well as a "response to the economics of art-making" where craft, with its obvious imperfect handmade qualities (exaggerated or overperformed in Faught's case), stand "in opposition to the slick and soulless products of systemized industrial" manufacture.[54]

Another American critic, Elissa Auther, in *Fiberarts* magazine, echoed Adamson's argument that Faught, and "sloppy craft" in general, followed a lineage back to 1970s feminism, suggesting that contemporary artists like Faught were attempting an "affront to the standards of high craft" through their use of "dysfunction," "the abject," and more pointedly "the amateur."[55] Auther's article was illustrated not just with the work of Faught but of another American artist, L. J. Roberts; however, what both Adamson and Auther seem to have overlooked is the crucial place that gay or queer self-identification seems to play with the work of these artists. Roberts has, for example, argued that her "use of overperformative, amateur and sloppy craft was a tactic to magnify the negative stigmas that 'craft' carries with it," since, as she says, "by overperforming these stereotypes we are forced not only to face them but to realize that they are constructed to maintain systems of power."[56] She further suggests that those theorizing about craft could learn from the example of queer theory, whose premise rests on the deconstruction of the seemingly stable and coherent categories of gender and sexuality and the framing discourses of binarism and essentialism. Roberts has further stated that the term "queer," like the term "craft," itself embodies the "virtues of non-normative, other and peculiar" which can enable artists to "dismantle and reconfigure" cultural stereotypes and therefore "gain agency."[57]

Josh Faught has equally argued that, rather than generate a queer identity in his work through literal "iconic imagery or declarative content," his use of textiles and especially of needlework techniques is a way of trying "to articulate or visualize queer subjectivity."[58] And indeed, Faught's work not only looks back to a heritage of women working with textiles such as 1970s feminists, as Adamson and Auther have argued, but also less consciously to a history of men working with sewing and stitched textiles and dealing, perhaps more obliquely, with the troubling issue of gender and sexuality. Faught himself has said that he does look back to the work of women artists in North America of the 1970s—what he calls a "purposeful disre-membering," where he appropriates "strategies from the past to bastardize them for queerness"—but he also has stated that the work of Mike Kelley is another important point of reference.[59] If we accept that Faught's work "stands firmly within a lineage of makers who transgress the contested boundary of genre that separates the domestic crafts from fine art," must we understand it only in terms of feminist art?[60] Faught himself says that unproblematically accepting the notion of "sloppy craft" in opposition to the "well made" could be read as a form of essentialism in itself.[61] Indeed, L. J. Roberts's rather uncomplicated equation of queer and craft fails to unpack the inherent ambiguities of these terms as categories in themselves: simply inverting systems of power and privilege serves to reinforce them and fails to take on board the lessons of feminist discourse and even queer theory itself. As Rozsika Parker and Griselda Pollock have argued, "whilst women can justifiably take pride" in needlecrafts such as embroidery "it does not displace the hierarchy of values ... [and] by simply celebrating a separate heritage we risk losing sight" of the base ideology that constructs and maintains systems of difference.[62]

Although largely dismissed as plagiarism and indefensible, men's engagement with needlecrafts, from embroidery to knitting and crocheting to home sewing and dressmaking, remains uncanny, unsettling, and troubling, perhaps even traumatic. Maybe the practice is better read as a process of decontextualization and dehistoricizing of women's skills—or as vampiric or cannibalistic commodification of "the Other," as Deborah Root has argued, reinforcing rather than inverting systems of power within patriarchy.[63] But are all men who engage with such techniques monstrous, parasitical interlopers or outlaws? Many gay men have long been attracted to such practices as a way of seeking some sense of agency as their identities are feminized—in discourses from popular culture to the law and medicine—in a complicit communal conspiracy that pathologizes gay men as womanly, thus devoid of power and worth. Misogyny and homophobia are clearly variations on a theme. Perhaps the initial examples of "dressing up" as gender-bending performance, like that of Divine and Grayson Perry, that opened this discussion are not necessarily reflective of endemic "male trouble" but rather, like the adoption of needlecrafts by male artists, something that has been grossly overestimated as a troubling "phenomenon of our time."[64] Indeed, as Judith Butler has argued, "gay and lesbian cultures often thematize 'the natural' in parodic contexts that bring into relief the performative construction of an original and true sex."[65] If we see the interrelation between sewing, amateurism, and gender as troubling binaries, taxonomies, and hierarchies, we would do well to mind Butler's words that "trouble need not carry such a negative valence."[66] Sewing amateurishly as a performative and queer act has many resonances in contemporary art and I would suggest we think of it not so much as "sloppy" as a process but rather "slippery" as a concept. Maybe saying craft shouldn't look sloppy or men shouldn't sew is about as silly as saying "nice girls don't wear cha-cha heels."

Notes

1   Gary Thompson, "Waters' Bitter 'Demented' Leaves a Sour Taste,"
    August 18, 2000, http://articles.philly.com/2000-08-18/news/25593416_1_
    john-waters-mainstream-movies-early-movies (accessed August 10, 2011).

2   Judith Butler, *Gender Trouble: Feminism and the Subversion of Identity* (New
    York and London: Routledge, 1990), p. viii.

3   Ibid., p. ix.

4   Amelia Jones, "'Clothes Make the Man': The Male Artist as a Performative
    Function," *Oxford Art Journal* 18:2 (1995): 30.

5   Constance Penley and Sharon Willis, "Editorial: Male Trouble," *Camera
    Obscura*, "Male Trouble" Special Issue, 6:2 (May 1988): 4.

6   Constance Penley and Sharon Willis (eds), *Male Trouble* (Minneapolis:
    University of Minnesota Press, 1993), p. xvii.

7   Jacky Klein, *Grayson Perry* (London: Thames & Hudson, 2010), p. 113.

8   Liz Hoggard, "Look, no kaftans ...," *Observer*, February 8, 2004, p. 5.

9   See Sandra Sider, "Fiber Art at the Venice Biennale," *Fiberarts* (January/
    February 2010): 46–9.

10 Peter Dormer (ed.), *The Culture of Craft: Status and future* (Manchester
    and New York: Manchester University Press, 1997), pp. 7, 11. The cover of
    Dormer's book was illustrated with Michael Brennand-Wood's *Charlemagne*
    (1978). Michael Brennand-Wood is one of Britain's key artists to work in
    embroidery and other textile crafts over the past 40 years.

11 For this, see Andrew Ross (ed.), *No Sweat: Fashion Free Trade and The
    Rights of Garment Workers* (New York and London: Verso, 1997); Jane Lou
    Collins, *Threads: Gender, Labor, and Power in the Global Apparel Industry*
    (Chicago: University of Chicago Press, 2003); and Robert J. S. Ross, *Slaves to
    Fashion: Poverty and Abuse in the New Sweatshops* (Ann Arbor: University
    of Michigan Press, 2004).

12 Christina Walkley, *The Ghost in the Looking Glass: The Victorian Seamstress*
    (London: Peter Owen, 1981). And also see Lynn M. Alexander, *Women,
    Work, and Representation: Needlewomen in Victorian Art and Literature*
    (Athens: Ohio University Press, 2003); Beth Harris (ed.), *Famine and
    Fashion: Needlewomen in the Nineteenth Century* (Aldershot: Ashgate,
    2005); Maureen Daly Goggin and Beth Fowkes Tobin (eds), *Women and the
    Material Culture of Needlework & Textiles, 1750–1950* (Aldershot: Ashgate,
    2009).

13 Steven M. Gelber, "Do-It-Yourself: Constructing, Repairing and Maintaining
    Domestic Masculinity," *American Quarterly* 49:1 (March 1997): 70; and
    Steven M. Gelber, *Hobbies: Leisure and the Culture of Work in America*
    (New York: Columbia University Press, 1999).

14 See Andrew Keen, *The Cult of the Amateur: How Today's Internet is
    Killing Our Culture* (Doubelday: New York, 2007); and Rachel P. Moines,
    Hedonizing Technology: Paths to Pleasure in Hobbies and Leisure
    (Baltimore: Johns Hopkins University Press, 2009), pp. 3–4. For an overview

of thinking about the amateur and modern craft, see Stephen Knott, "Editorial Introduction," *Journal of Modern Craft* 5:3 (November 2012): 255–58.

15 Anne Wilson, "A Plea for Broader Dialogue," *Fiberarts* 21:1 (Summer 1994): 52.

16 Maurice Berger, Brian Wallis, and Simon Watson, "Introduction," in Maurice Berger, Brian Wallis, and Simon Watson (eds), *Constructing Masculinity* (New York and London: Routledge, 1995), p. 2.

17 Jeanette Winterson, *Oranges Are Not The Only Fruit* (London: Pandora Press, 1985), p. 146.

18 Arnold Bennett's review of Virginia Woolf's *Orlando: A Biography* in the *Evening Standard*, November 1928, p. 8, reprinted in Robin Majundar and Allen McLaurin (eds), *Virginia Woolf: The Critical Heritage* (London: Routledge and Kegan Paul, 1975), pp. 232–3. The *Men of Cloth* exhibition was held at the Waterside Arts Centre, Sale, in Manchester from July 3 to September 4, 2010; see my review in *Embroidery* 61 (November/December 2010): 56–7.

19 Email from Gavin Fry to author, November 15, 2010.

20 See Nancy Dunlap Bercaw, "Solid Objects/Mutable Meanings: Fancywork and the Construction of Bourgeois Culture, 1840–1880," *Winterthur Portfolio* 26:4 (Winter 1991): 231–47. Elissa Auther used this term to describe the American artist Josh Faught's recent use of Dona Z. Meilach's how-to craft books in his work. See Elissa Auther, "'He is survived by his longtime companion': The Representation of Feeling in the Work of Josh Faught," podcast, November 9, 2012, http://americanart.si.edu/multimedia/webcasts/archive/2012/nationbuilding/frontiers (accessed August 10, 2013). I am very grateful to Elissa Auther for letting me read her two essays on Faught: "'He is survived by his longtime companion': The Representation of Feeling in the Work of Josh Faught," in Nicholas Bell (ed.), *National Building: Craft in Contemporary American Culture* (forthcoming); and "Sloppy Craft as Temporal Drag in the Work of Josh Faught," co-authored with Elyse Speaks, in this book.

21 See Isabelle Anscombe, *Omega and After: Bloomsbury and the Decorative Arts* (London: Thames & Hudson, 1981), p. 110.

22 *Boys Who Sew* ran from February 5 to April 4, 2004 at the Crafts Council gallery in London.

23 My use of the term "queer" draws on David Halperin's statement that "Queer is by definition *whatever* is at odds with the normal, the legitimate, the dominant. *There is nothing in particular to which it necessarily refers. It is an identity without essence.* 'Queer', then, demarcates not a positivity but a positionality *vis-à-vis* the normative," in David M. Halperin, *Saint Foucault: Towards a Gay Hagiography* (Oxford and New York: Oxford University Press, 1995), p. 62; and Eve Kosofsky Segwick's suggestion that "queer" could "refer to" the "open mesh of possibilities, gaps, overlaps, dissonances and resonances, lapses and excesses of meaning when the constituent elements of anyone's gender, of anyone's sexuality aren't made (or *can't be* made) to

signify monolithically," in Eve Kosofsky Sedgwick, *Tendencies* (Durham: Duke University Press, 1993), p. 8. All italics are original.

24 For an overview, see Andrew Gorman-Murray, "Masculinity and the Home: a critical review and conceptual framework," *Australian Geographer* 39:3 (2008): 367–79.

25 Anthony Clare, *On Men: Masculinity in Crisis* (London: Chatto & Windus, 2000), p. 3.

26 John Roberts, "Masculinity, Politics and Art," in idem, *Selected Errors: Writings on Art and Politics, 1981–90* (London: Pluto Press), p. 257.

27 Ibid., p. 256.

28 Fintan Walsh, *Male Trouble: Masculinity and the Performance of Crisis* (London: Palgrave Macmillan, 2010), p. 142.

29 For instance, see Julia Bryan-Wilson, "Knit Dissent," in Alexander Dumbadze and Suzanne Hudson (eds), *Contemporary Art: 1989 to the Present* (Oxford: Wiley-Blackwell, 2013), pp. 245–53.

30 James Lewis, "Home Boys," *Artforum* (October 1991): 105.

31 Ibid.

32 Maurice Berger (ed.), "Man Trouble" Special Issue, *Artforum* (April 1994): 122.

33 For this, see John Waters and Mike Kelley, "The Dirty Boys," *Grand Street* 57 (Summer 1996): 8–22.

34 Faith Wilding, "Monstrous Domesticity," *M/E/A/N/I/N/G* 18 (November 1995): 8, reprinted in Susan Bee and Mira Schor (eds), *M/E/A/N/I/N/G: An Anthology of Artists' Writings, Theory and Criticism* (Durham: Duke University Press, 2000), pp. 87–104. And see Mira Schor's criticism of Kelley in her "Backlash and Appropriation," in *The Power of Feminist Art: The American Movement of the 1970s, History and Impact* (New York and London: Harry N. Abrams and Thames & Hudson, 1994), pp. 248–63.

35 Wilding, ibid.

36 Mira Schor, "Backlash and Appropriation," p. 251.

37 Mira Schor, *A Decade of Negative Thinking: Essays on Art, Politics, and Daily Life* (Durham: Duke University Press, 2010), pp. 58–9.

38 Nicolas Bourriaud, *Postproduction: Culture as Screenplay* (New York: Lukas & Sternberg, 2002), p. 13.

39 Ibid., p. 9.

40 Cary Levine, "Manly Crafts: Mike Kelley's (Oxy)Moronic Gender Bending," *Art Journal* 69:1–2 (Spring–Summer 2010), p. 76; and see idem, *Pay for Your Pleasures: Mike Kelley, Paul McCarthy and Raymond Pettibon* (Chicago and London: University of Chicago Press, 2013), pp. 107–14.

41 Levine, "Manly Crafts," p. 91.

42 Mike Kelley, "Cross-Gender/Cross-Genre," *PAJ: A Journal of Performance Art* 22:1 (January 2000): 2.

43 Ibid., p. 3.

44 Michael Moon and Eve Kosofsky Sedgwick, "Divinity: A Dossier/A Performance Piece/A Little-understood Emotion," in Eve Kosofsky Sedgwick, *Tendencies* (Durham: Duke University Press, 1993), p. 249.

45 Eve Kosofsky Sedgwick, *Epistemology of the Closet* (Berkeley and Los Angeles: University of California Press, 1990), pp. 28, 31.

46 Eve Kosofsky Sedgwick, *The Weather in Proust* (edited by Jonathan Goldberg) (Durham and London: Duke University Press, 2011), pp. 71, 79.

47 Marci Rae McDade, "Funk and Flashback," *Fiberarts* 37:4 (Winter 2010/11): 4.

48 Alexandra (Jacopetti) Hart, "Sloppy Craft Revisited," *Fiberarts* 37:4 (Winter 2010/11): 6.

49 For Julia Bryan-Wilson's discussion of the Cockettes, see her, "Grit and Glitter," *October* 4 (Fall 2008): 19–30; and idem, "Handmade Genders: Queer Costuming in San Francisco circa 1970," in Elissa Auther and Adam Lerner (eds), *West of Center: Art and the Countercultural Experiment in America, 1965–1977* (Minneapolis: University of Minnesota Press, 2011), pp. 77–92.

50 Glenn Adamson, "When Craft Gets Sloppy," *Crafts* 211 (March/April 2008): 36. The cover of this issue of *Crafts* magazine showed the work of another so-called "sloppy" American craft artist, Shinique Smith.

51 *Fabrications: Craft in the 21ˢᵗ Century* symposium, V&A Museum, London, November 23, 2007.

52 See Anne Wilson's "Foreword" to this volume. See also, *Open Conversation: Sloppy Craft (with Josh Faught, Jessica Jackson Hutchins, Namita Gupta Wiggers and Anne Wilson)*, October 10, 2009, audio podcast, http://www. museumofcontemporarycraft.org/exhibitions/programs (accessed July 25, 2011.

53 Adamson, "When Craft Gets Sloppy," p. 36.

54 Ibid., p. 38. These ideas are further explored in Glenn Adamson, "Sloppy Seconds: The Strange Return of Clay," in Ingrid Schaffner and Jenelle Porter, *Dirt on Delight: Impulses That Form Clay* (Philadelphia: Institute of Contemporary Art/University of Pennsylvania, 2009), pp. 73–80.

55 Elissa Auther, "Sloppy Craft: An Introduction," *Fiberarts* 37:3 (November/ December 2010): 38.

56 Lacey Jane Roberts, "Thoughts on Being Sloppy and Amateur," November 5, 2009, http://www.madblog.org/2009/11/thoughts-on-being-sloppy-and-amateur-by-lacey-jane-roberts/ (accessed June 14, 2011).

57 Lacey Jane Roberts, "Put Your Thing Down, Flip It, and Reverse It: Re-imagining Craft Identities Using the Tactics of Queer Theory," http:// viscrit.files.wordpress.com/2010/08/07roberts.pdf (accessed July 20, 2011). Also see Lacey Jane Roberts, "Craft, Queerness, and Guerilla Tactics: An Extended Maker's Statement," in Jessica Hemmings (ed.), *In the Loop: Knitting Now* (London: Black Dog Publishing, 2010), pp. 112–17; and idem, "Put Your Thing Down, Flip It, and Reverse It: Re-imagining Craft Identities Using the Tactics of Queer Theory," in Maria Elena Buszek (ed.),

Extra/Ordinary: Craft and Contemporary Art (Durham and London: Duke University Press), pp. 243–59.

58 *The Way Things Work: Josh Faught in conversation with Kate Mondloch* (2009), http://www.callreponse.museumofcontemporary.org/pairings/faught (accessed October 21, 2011).

59 Ibid. And email interview with Josh Faught, December 9, 2013.

60 Glenn Adamson, "Analogue Practice," in Mary Jane Jacob and Michelle Grabner (eds), *The Studio Reader: On the Space of Artists* (Chicago and London: University of Chicago Press, 2010), p. 254.

61 Email interview with Josh Faught, December 9, 2013.

62 Rozsika Parker and Griselda Pollock, *Old Mistresses: Women, Art and Ideology* (London: Pandora, 1981), p. 58.

63 See Deborah Root, *Cannibal Culture: Art, Appropriation, & the Commodification of Difference* (Boulder, CO: Westview Press, 1998).

64 See Marjorie Garber, *Vested Interests: Cross-Dressing & Culture Anxiety* (New York and London: Routledge, 1992).

65 Judith Butler, *Gender Trouble*, p. ix.

66 Ibid., p. vii.

2

Sloppy craft as temporal drag in the work of Josh Faught

Elissa Auther and Elyse Speaks

> *Recently, I've heard discussions that suggest that the site of queerness in fact, no longer resides in the body. But instead, it exists immaterially or spiritually, like a specter that has the ability to haunt culture.*[1]
>
> JOSH FAUGHT

There are at least two senses in which working in fiber invokes a past. On the one hand, it summons up a very specific temporality—the 1970s, a period in which fiber was introduced into art making as a practice that, among other things, collapsed hierarchies by appealing to the handmade and domestic. It also invokes a past in the sense that it recalls prior familial associations and spaces for most of us today: a grandmother, a house, a scarf, as well as objects that belonged to daily life at some point, if not now.

It is the collapse of these two associations, in part, that seems to motivate fiber's place in contemporary aesthetic practice today, and the reason why, since the 1990s at least, fiber has progressively embodied the terrain of the political. Fiber has come to embody a mode of making that signals an attitude and a climate, one that is increasingly pervasive among a new generation of artists invested in trying to harness a usable past. This chapter considers the work of Josh Faught, whose work over the past decade has used fiber to lay claim to the past in ways that demonstrate its inevitable place in the present. He does not perform a resuscitation so much as a kind of bringing to light, a demonstration, as Elizabeth Freeman has suggested, of the benefits of allowing the past to come back and puncture the present, such that we might acknowledge its utility.[2]

A distinctive aspect of Faught's practice—one that is intimately connected to the way he invokes the past—is his cultivation of a style more often associated with amateur making than fine craft. His contravention of craft skill, which one might think of as a kind of *performative* craft, distinguishes his practice from the studio craft movement in fiber and it was behind the coining of the term "sloppy craft," which was applied to his work in 2007 by the artist Anne Wilson, his graduate advisor at the School of the Art Institute of Chicago at the time.[3] As with artists like Grayson Perry who "do" pottery or ceramics in ways that manifest both its practice and its failure, Faught makes the terms of his practice all the more palpable by engaging with it in ways that suggest it as a performative act: gendered, value-laden, and otherwise conceptually driven.

In considering Faught's particular way of making and its relationship to the past, this chapter expands the critical framework initiated by artists such as L. J. Roberts and others, by examining the phenomenon of sloppy craft in relation to Elizabeth Freeman's concept of temporal drag. Roberts has explicitly argued for the import of viewing fiber and other craft methods as an embrace of the politics of queer theory, whereby craft's central codes are at once activated, performed, or amplified even, and at the same time, scrambled in order to draw out its associations with the decorative, the abject, and other codes of alterity.[4] Her own and others' adoption of craft's central codes function, not simply as a straight appropriation, but more firmly as a "queering of craft" itself.

The works for which Faught is most well known began to appear while he was still a student at the School of the Art Institute of Chicago, where he produced his first large-scale installation, *Nobody Knows I'm a Lesbian* (2006; see Plate 3). With this work, Faught established his unique style of loose, pieced, asymmetrical or irregular weavings with a variety of surface embellishments, including pods and webs, draped fabric, pockets, fringe, frayed knots, sequins, and loose threads. In this and subsequent work, Faught also integrated a variety of found objects, from greeting cards and self-help paperbacks to pin-backed badges with amusing one-liners. Many of these objects share the common tendency to produce standardized versions of private sentiments encapsulated in stock, clichéd form. Together these collections and their fiber containers or supports often form micro-archives, a strategy that culminates on a larger scale in his most recent installation, *Longtime Companion* (2012).[5] As with previous works, Faught fills the installation with a variety of materially embodied forms of text at its most colloquial, ephemeral, and publicaly personal. The compilation of sources is overwhelming; what are actually authentic, individualized sentiments become indiscernibly enmeshed with the reproducible, affected emotions and thoughts most straightforwardly associated with the mass-produced greeting card.

The works comprising *Longtime Companion* are exemplary for their distinctive style of endowing various forms of text with a decorative and

FIGURE 2.1 *Josh Faught, Longtime Companion, 2012, installation view, Lisa Cooley Gallery, New York. Courtesy of the artist and Lisa Cooley Gallery, New York.*

emotive density characterized by unkempt surfaces and edges. The installation consisted of a group of eight wall-mounted fiber works and two large, identical cedar structures resembling chifforobes, freestanding units that combine a closet and shelving. A cochineal dye is the source of the wall-mounted works' color palette, which ranged from blood-red to soft, petal pink. These works extend Faught's previous use of the badges with tongue-in-cheek refrains like "Destined To Be An Old Broad With Plenty To Bitch About" and "Call Me A Romantic, But I Still Give Head." Other works, such as *Calendar* (2012), include personal mementos like greeting cards received from his mother and grandmother, referencing the passing of time and seasonal transitions.

Time is a theme that Faught returns to regularly. In *Calendar*, increments of time act to compartmentalize the personal effects included in the wall hanging. On a disaster blanket used as a support, he labels woven pockets for each day of the week with felt letters, which hang in a vertical format next to an enlarged, felt replica of a calendar page for the month of June. The freehand, homemade look of the calendar interferes with, but does not counteract, its straightforward utility. Here and in other works, particularly *Five O'Clock Shadow* (2009), Faught seems to allude to Elizabeth Freeman's implication of time in shaping normative conceptions of the body and sexuality. She writes that, "Temporality is a mode of implantation through

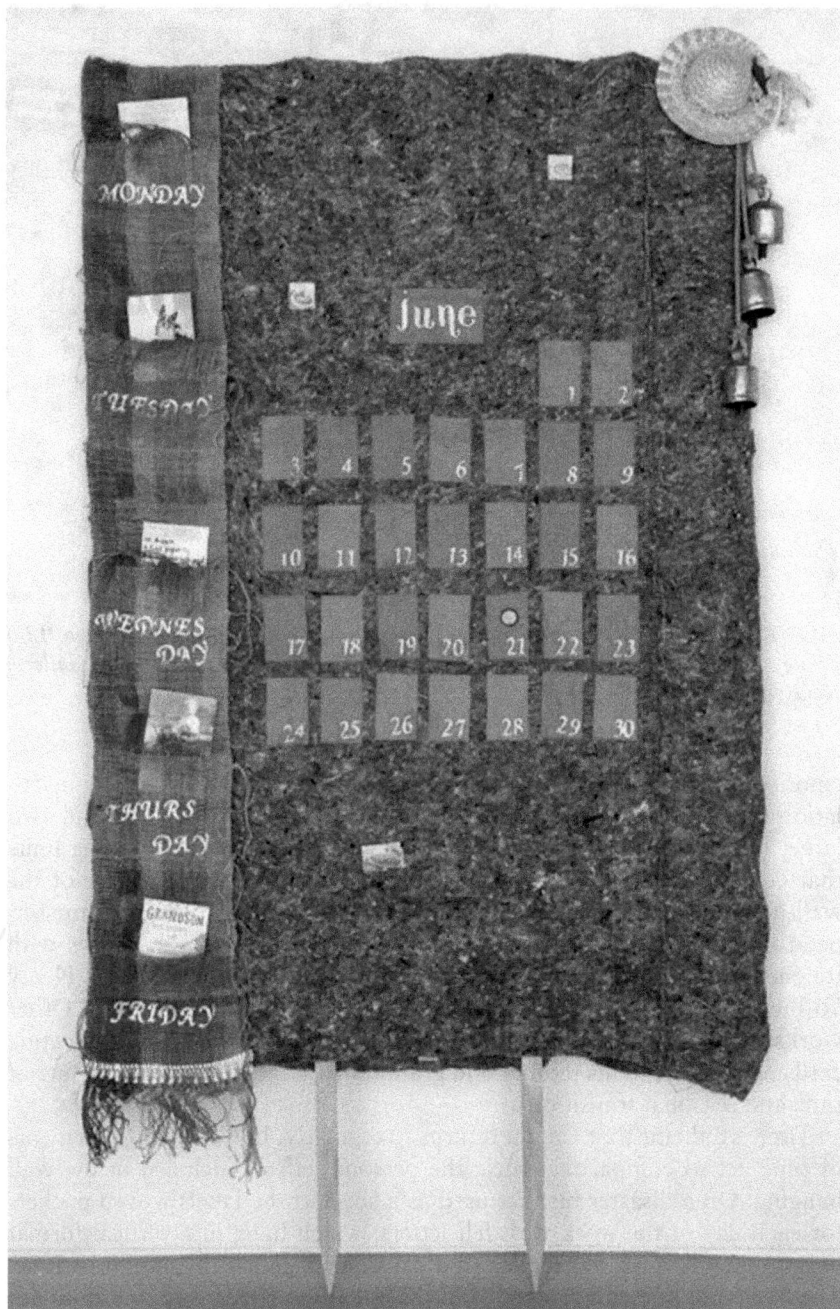

FIGURE 2.2 *Josh Faught, Calendar, 2012, handwoven hemp, TV dinner brooches, cards from Mom and Grandmother, wind chimes, straw hat with lace, scrapbooking letters, felt, disaster blanket and toilet paper on garden trellis, 96 x 48 x 3 in. Courtesy of the artist and Lisa Cooley Gallery, New York.*

which institutional forces come to seem like somatic facts. Schedules, calendars, time zones, and even wristwatches are ways to inculcate what the sociologist Eviatar Zerubavel calls 'hidden rhythms', forms of temporal experience that seem natural to those whom they privilege."[6]

Faught also symbolically references what might be considered natural forms of temporal experience in other works. In *Endless Night* (2008), he produced two near copies of a crocheted window and curtains through which one can look to make out the night sky. In *Longtime Companion*, he uses the Colonial American reversible weaving technique known as Summer and Winter in a series of woven bands; elsewhere in this installation works appear backwards or reappear in reverse. Housed on and within the chifforobes, entitled *Summer (Dona Z. Meilach)* (see Plate 4) and *Winter (Ann Rule)* (2012), are, among other items, sundry *tchotchkes*, giant jacquard replicas of PFLAG (Parents, Families and Friends of Lesbians and Gays) newsletters, and series of books by the how-to author Dona Z. Meilach and Ann Rule, the author of popular true crime novels.

Whereas the type of books and other items contained by the shelving units actively encourage reference to Faught's biography and personal interests (one container is labeled "Josh's lip gloss"), the contents of the closets resist such a direct reading. In *Summer (Dona Z. Meilach)* hang two felt replicas of plaid, long-sleeved shirts; in its pendant, *Winter*, the shirts appear in reverse. Both bring to mind the sentimental gay film *Brokeback Mountain* and the tear-jerking scene where Ennis discovers his lost shirt hung with one belonging to his deceased lover Jack, who had preserved them in the closet of his childhood bedroom.

Faught has long associated his own work with the past in a way that moves readily between personal history and social history. His investment in the former is often manifested when he ties his mode of making to autobiography. In interviews he routinely relates his use of fiber to associations with his maternal grandmother and summer camp. Faught points out that when the source of "making" derives from childhood and personal history there is a motive that alters one's relationship to the object, which ties it up with issues of "identity construction."[7] Making autobiographically, so to speak, at once channels another time (one's own past) while it affirms and materializes a framework of selfhood that is chosen. The process can thereby re-enact and integrate those past actions that are particularly formative in constructions of gender.

Moreover, by working principally in a variety of modes of fiber, such as macramé and DIY instructional pamphlets, Faught prioritizes interests that were fostered independently of his aesthetic training and institutional learning. The final results register more like hobbies, amateur pursuits, or art therapy than they do licensed processes of art making. Faught refers to this as a "queering of labor"—one in which "tentative or inexpert hands" are the visible producers.[8] Faught's eccentric, casual hand making iconographically references just such a lack of expertise and distances his work from the conventional expectations and values of craft including mastery over materials and perfection of technique. The result is that the works are often more cumulative in feeling, even excessive, recalling the way emotive responses can sometimes materialize in their need for expression. They seem to suggest something akin to the sentimental creations made by the fan or teenage enthusiast who collects and collages over time in order to preserve and remember.

Beside those objects and modes of making that are culled from Faught's personal history are elements that refer to a frank, but unofficial, collective "queer" history. Books and sayings are embedded in the wall hangings; nail polish and buttons decorate the fiber constructions. Items that connote specific past events often anchor the more personalized and esoteric histories. Documents are reproduced that reference the fight for gay rights or the invisibility of AIDS and its victims; photographs that summon questions of gender identity and visibility are screen-printed onto fabric surfaces, bookshelves and floors are lined with genre novels that intimate a subcultural obsession.

In the case of *Longtime Companion*, many such elements are integrated into the work physically, so that there is a sense that a series of disparate moments from the past have been materially enmeshed, bound together in ways that juxtapose the disparate associations that craft holds as well as the terms of public histories and private histories and recollections. The show's centerpiece is the monumental *It Takes a Lifetime to Get Exactly Where You Are* (2012; see Plate 5), a 20-ft-long sewn assemblage of woven bands and panels with applied buttons, sequins, hanging bells, adhesive letters and numbers, aromatic cedar blocks, and a woman's straw hat. Two dried gourds and a lifelike ceramic cat sit on the floor in front of the work. *It Takes a Lifetime* terminates on the right with a jacquard woven replica of a segment of the *Names Project-AIDS Memorial Quilt*. The passage highlights some of the quilt's most distinctive features, including the placement of panels devoted to celebrities, in this case, Liberace, next to those of ordinary citizens; the tombstone convention of birth and death dates; and the creative cacophony of the juxtaposition of personalized, handmade panels. But it does so while diluting its material form; the celebratory, colorful appearance of the *AIDS Memorial Quilt* is lost in favor of the look of a uniform, bland *Things Remembered* throw; likewise any sense of the handmade is obviated by its reproduced feel.

The quilt is perhaps the most obvious example of the way that Faught enacts disparate moments of the associations with craft and public and personal histories. The *AIDS Memorial Quilt* operates both as a historical record, one that blends the histories of private individuals with public personas and celebrities, and as an updated version of the historical form of the quilt, here politicized and made to function not as a utilitarian form of support that provides warmth, but one that functions as a vehicle or site for the enactment of public mourning and activism. Yet its presence here as a faded reproduction of a handmade original speaks to what Julia Bryan-Wilson refers to in the context of artist Sharon Hayes's performative re-readings of historical texts as the simultaneous "creation" and "erosion of collective memory."[9]

In *Longtime Companion* the *AIDS Memorial Quilt* remade in woven form embodies less a material artifact than a temporal sensibility and in this way acts as an instance of what Freeman refers to as temporal drag: a way of projecting subjectivity into space, into a site, such that it can produce a means of "haunting" culture, enacting a spectral relationship to the past in order to elicit its residue within the present. It does this, in part, by using the past to puncture the present. Again, in examining the concept in relation to Hayes's re-enactments, Bryan-Wilson writes: "Temporal drag implies a chronological distortion in which time does not progress seamlessly forward but is full of swerves, unevenness and interruptions."[10] Like the hybrid datelines of Felix Gonzalez-Torres, this strategy affects a queer phenomenon through its asynchrony, demonstrating the "pull of the past upon the present" as a way of refusing the linear time of history.[11] As such, they share in the resistance to the official codes of self-evident and naturalized histories, replacing some of the ease of explanatory categories by enacting what Gayatri Spivak has referred to as an "interruption," which "exposes the processes that construct and position subjects."[12]

The effect is to bring craft's history into concert with a more personalized and embodied history in ways that summon up terms that reveal how a prior art form or prior self was constructed, held up and enabled. In discussing one of her own works, *SLA Screeds #13, 16, 20 & 29* (2003), in which she re-speaks Patty Hearst's audio addresses recorded as a captive of the Symbionese Liberation Army, Hayes suggests the process at stake is one at the heart of political subjectivity. Discussing the original speaker, Patty Hearst, whose voice and words Hayes usurps in her video performance, she states:

> One of the running debates in the media at the time, and then very precisely at the trial that followed her arrest in 1975, was whether she had been brainwashed or if she was "speaking for herself". But for me, this question, though parsed over by tape experts and psychologists working for the FBI and the Hearst family, is a question at the heart of political subjectivity itself. Don't we become political people precisely by identifying with certain people, movements, images, speeches, ideas and taking them on as our own?[13]

Projects dedicated to remembering and documenting the early years of AIDS have recently begun to surface in the art world. Examples include New York University's exhibition *Gran Fury: Read My Lips*, the first comprehensive survey documenting the collective's AIDS activist work from 1987 to 1995, and the ICA Boston's *This Will Have Been: Art, Love &*

Politics in the 1980s, a critically rigorous assessment of the art of the 1980s as shaped, in part, in response to the AIDS crisis.[14] Faught's *Longtime Companion* also shares the goal of recovering a particular moment in the history of the gay community that has passed and that many fear is subject to disappearance as the early association of AIDS with gay men wanes and the virus is more and more accepted as a chronic but manageable condition. However, unlike the recent revival of interest in the art and heroic activism of *Gran Fury* or *ACT UP*, Faught's installation focuses on forms of activism hardly recognized as such: for instance, forms of caregiving and grassroots networks of support that are not easily integrated into official histories and often subject to dismissal as merely creative or ameliorative, and thus, non-political. Faught offers a non-narrative combination of nominally historical, yet otherwise unremarkable, ephemera, which he matches with an approach to craft that accentuates fiber's tactile relationship to the body and its myriad cultural associations with the home, family and private life, security, and comfort. Faught's cultivation of an aesthetic that is suggestive of an amateur or hobby style of making enhances fiber's affective, sentimental, and personal valences.

In the recent past, Faught's work has taken the form of fiber-based containers: woven surfaces outfitted with pockets, or hangings that act as domestic backdrops to an assortment of ephemera. These seemingly random compilations of partial and highly subjective collections of things like books and badges form various micro-archives and create moments of textual locatedness—moments in time and place that manifest through language.[15] Sometimes these moments seem to reference a personal history—a period in one's life that was particularly enmeshed in crises and trauma. For example, in *Triage* (2009), beyond the title itself, such an idea is supported by the pairing of greeting cards that say things like "Thinking of you" with a variety of self-help books that look well used. But, as with the quilt or PFLAG newsletters of *Longtime Companion*, archival elements also routinely appear in less distinctly personal forms, as in, for example, the way that Faught integrates various types of fabrics, dyes, and techniques that act to blend the history of craft and textiles with Faught's personal history. Among other examples, in *Longtime Companion* Faught explored the process of dyeing with cochineal, a parasite found on the prickly pear cactus whose crushed carapace produces a blood-red liquid that has been used to create a coveted crimson dye since at least the seventh century. A series of works preceding *Longtime Companion* were suffused in indigo, a plant-based dye that magically reveals its color only after the saturated fabric is exposed to oxygen. Both natural dyes have long and complex histories connected to colonialism, slavery, secretive craft cultures, and pre-industrial textile cultures in which cloth functioned as overt symbols of wealth and power. In Faught's work the range of colors derived from these dyes also communicate contemporary cultural associations of indigo blue with melancholy and a cochineal pink with femininity or childhood innocence.

At times in Faught's works, these histories remain more intact than in others. If the replica of the *AIDS Memorial Quilt* is the most recognizable archival passage in *Longtime Companion*, one of the more obscure and humorous examples is the Dona Z. Meilach library housed within *Summer (Dona Z. Meilach)*. Meilach was the most prominent author of the craft "how-to" genre that has defined craft culture as a lesser artistic form since its inception. Popular titles included *Contemporary Batik and Tie-Dye*, *Soft Sculpture and Other Soft Art Forms*, *Weaving Off-Loom*, *Macramé Accessories*, and *Creative Stitchery*.[16] With this collection, Faught recuperates a moment in craft's history dating from the late 1960s and 1970s marked by studio craft's bid for artistic status, a revival of craft within the counterculture and the related popular spread of hobby-based craft amongst the general public, invoking what Freeman has theorized as a "mode of stubborn identification with a set of social coordinates that exceed [one's] own historical moment."[17] In the 1960s and 1970s, the question of whether the embrace of craft by the counterculture and amateur makers was good or bad for the professional craft-artist was debated with much angst in the pages of *Craft Horizons*, the leading serial for professional artists working in craft media in North America. In interviews and roundtable discussions, crafts professionals struggling to legitimate their work as art in this period regarded the concurrent popular craft boom—encompassing forms as diverse as embroidered clothing, hand-built homes, macramé and ceramic wares of all persuasion—when mentioned at all, as that which gave craft a bad name. From this perspective, Meilach's how-to books might be said to represent the ground zero of professional craft shame and embarrassment. As tremendous as it was, the popular surge of interest in craft in this period has never been comfortably part of the canonical history of craft.

Faught's own history as an artist is implicated here. The artist has variously explained the way his encounters with craft—at summer camp; as a student at the industry-oriented Fashion Institute of Technology; subsequently as a graduate student in the theoretically open context of "material studies" at the School of the Art Institute of Chicago; and in the established, medium-specific world of fiber art where he has been received as something of a gadfly—contributed to his irreverent, *bricoleur* approach to craft. His amalgam of attention to technique and, simultaneously, the look of improvisational free play in loose ends and visible joins, the elevation of low forms like crochet and the juxtaposition of all manner of inharmonious materials illustrates Faught's own complicated relationship to aesthetic normativity. His work, to borrow from Lauren Berlant on the affect of shame, "is a declaration of the freedom to give up getting legitimacy in normal terms." It is shameless.[18]

In *Longtime Companion* another archive appears in the series of woven bands with phrases like "Police at the Door," "Unwanted Marks," and "Difficulty Breathing," incorporated into *It Takes a Lifetime*. These are the chapter titles of the how-to guide *Dungeon Emergencies and Supplies* picked up by Faught in a store catering to the leather subculture.[19] The woven bands, produced in the reversible Summer and Winter weaving technique, are a visual translation of the potential reversal of pleasure into disaster in the sex dungeon. Accompanying works like *Laugh All You Want But Someday We'll Be In Charge*, among others, made of pieced and sutured felt blankets—actual disaster blankets—further the theme of the reversal of fortune in the installation. The author of *Dungeon Emergencies and Supplies*, Jay Wiseman, is something of a Dona Z. Meilach of the BDSM community with eleven books, three videos, a popular workshop program and a website full of additional resources for the lifestyle to his credit. On his website he also records the history of the San Francisco BDSM community's vexed relationship to the sexual mainstream (both gay and straight) in the late 1960s and 1970s as a shameful perversion, a story that in its general contours mirrors that of the craft world's disavowal of popular and DIY practices.[20]

The juxtaposition of the shameless embrace of fiber in all of its manifestations and the moments of perversion and reversal that are woven into the total experience of *Longtime Companion* suggest the ways in which Faught's work uses the past as a way to produce an embodiment of a self in the present. In this, his work once again shares something of the spirit of Sharon Hayes's contemporary practice of re-enacting particular dialogs and situations from history. Bringing a series of actors/enactors into the same situation and asking them to reproduce a text or a behavior materializes the way in which circumstance and history factor into our own embodiments of self. But, by choosing particular texts to inhabit, Hayes demonstrates how choice, how the act of self-materialization, occurs when we inhabit or occupy a certain historical station. The texts act as placeholders, almost as shells, ready to find inhabitation through a new voice. The act of inhabitation proves fruitless to an extent, as the tendency is for the appropriation to tear holes in the fabric of the original. Faught has written of the potential for "threads" to "ventriloquize a political urgency" and part of that urgency derives from those holes that erupt throughout the textual/textural fabric of the sensibility.[21] The use of the term "ventriloquize" is apt; the ventriloquist, like the drag queen, stages a mediated performance that conveys something of the voice of its author. The voice of another inhabits a dummy body in order to parrot a personality that derives from, but is not equal to, the original speaker. It is an exaggerated, often ridiculous, amplified or excessive perversion of an original.

The scale of Faught's works, and the way that the works' loose ends nearly always seem to breach their proper limits, translates this excess into material form. There is another fruitful comparison to be made to the contemporaneous practices of Hayes, particularly her performance *Everything else has failed! Don't you think it's time for love?* (2007). In this work Hayes occupied a noisy public space for a week, delivering public addresses filled with sentiment and urgency to an anonymous lover. To do so, she relied on a somewhat poor means of amplification, consisting of a microphone and portable P.A. system, to be heard. When Hayes performed she inhabited other voices and other texts, as if she were literally amplifying the original, albeit insufficiently, hooking the past up to a technological device that produced an exaggerated version of what one can imagine the original to have been. They feel like shoddy re-enactments. In Faught's case, there is not always an actual machine at play, but the scale and scope of the fiber composites like *It Takes a Lifetime* suggest that there might be; these handmade products no longer share the scale of the human body. Rather, they feel as though they have surpassed the scale and scope of their original utility, and their amplification appears analogously exaggerated, but also similarly underequipped and slipshod. It is as if they too are rather inefficiently attempting to benefit a larger public that might collectively take shelter in their warmth.

Faught and Hayes both blend personal sentiment with language and elements that clearly derive from public discourse. Politics gets in the way and yields a bizarre mix of the world and the individual—a kind of absurdist picture of how politics might inspire or detain us. Their mutual tendency to throw the voice, moreover, raises the question of who is speaking and to whom—and the potential "danger" that might be associated with the uncertainty that surrounds the identity of the speaker(s). Juxtapositions in scale do some of the work of obfuscation in the case of Faught. For instance, the numerous statements of address that pepper Faught's works are nearly illegible unless the viewer gets right up to the surface of the works. The primary examples here are the pin-backed badges, which are miniscule in comparison to the often massive and varied fields of fiber that they inhabit, but other examples include text that he applies directly to the woven surfaces with nail polish, glitter, embroidery, and transfer processes.

Often these texts function as a form of address that establishes an "I" speaking to a "you," though the identity of that voice changes rapidly and randomly. Their contents vary, but they might be fruitfully considered as a kind of support network for the socially marginal. In some cases, their passive-aggressive humor is the stock-in-trade of the beleaguered administrative assistant—as in the popular "Your Deadline Is Not My Emergency"-type declaration—that barely keeps a lid on the anger over power relations in the workplace. Other sayings capture politically incorrect feelings and desires or compensate for personal disappointment and frustration at not fitting in as in "I Don't Drink, I Don't Dance, I Hate Astrology, and I Have No Phone." Yet together they act to imbue the techniques of crochet, weaving, and sewing—techniques historically associated with non-art—with a pathos even more alien to the contemporary art world in their speaking subject's demand for recognition and connection.

The attachment of the buttons to the surface of the works also embodies another connection between craft and social support networks organizing

Longtime Companion. For Faught, "there's something about the process of crochet and weaving that lends itself to accumulation and collection. I really do see a lot of those works as a kind of handspun pegboard like the kind that people hang in their garages ...[with] all the tools you need for survival or just to get through the day." He goes on to say that "Craft on all levels (particularly those crafts taught in Dona Meilach's books) also function as a kind of support system in that way."[22]

Faught's text, like the decision to take up a particular form of crafting—often what looks to the untrained eye as haphazard and imperfect—sets forward manifest proclamations of belief and self-identity, often serving a compensatory role and producing readymade beliefs for the taking. Folksy phrases like "Bless this mess" or "This place is for the birds" sometimes produce visual time warps: sensibilities and belief systems that suggest the stubborn refusal to engage with the present. These become almost interchangeable with other sayings that reference contemporary life and anxieties, loaded warnings such as "Photographing and videotaping are not permitted" or, in the case of *Longtime Companion*, titles of works like *It Takes a Lifetime to Get Exactly Where You Are*, or *Laugh All You Want, But Someday We'll Be In Charge*. Disembodied though they are, such phrases act to fill in when necessary and prop up or uphold an ad hoc identity when disappointment or an inability to cope requires outside help. Idiomatic and euphemistic expressions here tend to stand in for something that is missing or absent—a history as much as a body, lover, friend—in part because it is unsayable and irretrievable.

The constant juxtaposition and variety of both the textual elements and their methods of delivery, moreover, seem to confirm their supplemental role; they act to constantly call into question the locus of anything like sincerity or authenticity. Faught appears to be considering the degree to which language can contain types of history, personal and social, often in euphemistic, loaded ways. Such throwaway forms of sentiment, he seems to suggest, act to interpret experience just as official documents and histories might. At times it can provide a vivid, poignant, and evocative account and at others, a washed-out and somewhat vapid one. What is so compelling is how Faught uses fiber and form to equalize, confuse, and alter these histories. Alongside his collections of objects and ephemera where the homemade or amateur is both a style and an ethos, his work at once raises *and* questions the palpability and durability of more widely-known popular histories like those conveyed through the *AIDS Memorial Quilt*. But it also bestows a new vividness and visibility on such documents as the PFLAG newsletters and other materially insubstantial records. In *Longtime Companion*, the *AIDS Memorial Quilt* becomes a public history and a domesticated afghan. By contrast, the monumentalized PFLAG documents, which are full of redactions, are newly amplified and materialized and become the quasi-classified document that seems to hold the key to the archives housed within the chifforobes they cover.

Taken together, the various types of documents, sayings, clichés, and idioms that are compiled and contrasted in Faught's works reaffirm the fragility and ephemerality of the histories, values, and systems they embody. In this sense, Faught's work points to the potential flimsiness of sentiment when it is severed from its speaker and context. But it also seems to affirm the urgent need to locate or recuperate a position and a voice. Such readymade positions may produce an incomplete copy of the past, but producing that record is essential to psychic survival nonetheless. That incompleteness and inauthenticity may help to explain the lingering sense one has when looking at Faught's work that he infects what are sometimes already embarrassing pasts with a degraded form—producing what may have already been "bad" objects in worse ways—with flaws that are so hyperbolized that they can no longer be read as flaws.

Part of what we argue here is that Faught's work deals with the problem of visualizing nonlinear time primarily through re-enactments, and he does so by producing what one might read as material anachronisms and fissures. Remaking such objects in ways that call attention to their departure from the original frameworks of value—in the case of craft's history associated with skill and perfect workmanship—enables them to exhibit asynchrony, as well as a kind of emotive wear and tear, materially. These fissures appear in the documents and material artifacts as well, which are always partial traces of lifestyles that sit uncomfortably within the historical record. Through his unconventional hand manipulation of fiber that flouts traditional craft skill, Faught invests these remnants with a renewed affective character, while at the same time preserving the sense of their incompleteness. One feels that Faught is aware of the sense in which inheritance tends to obfuscate the history it translates. Photocopies and missing information become the poor substitutes for an absent body (the missing longtime companion) as well as a missing past.

This repetitive theme of support, from the emotive support provided by social networks and family sentiments to the structural supports that frame or hold up the works—the trellis, frame, or containers—brings to light the ways in which a self might have been not only supported, but made "whole" again by the past. Moreover, it suggests that these past systems have a claim on what constitutes that self today. Freeman argues that if we allow the past to come back and puncture the present—if we are able to concede that there's a pull, a hold over us that is there—that this concession can ultimately be fruitful and progressive, in part by allowing us to properly mourn, but also by allowing us to see that the past has something real to offer, that we do indeed "build" on it, that it has contributed to where we are. Such awareness itself can be "transformative."[23] A new form of subjectivity may emerge from such knowledge, one that is built on a reconciliation of an inherited past that may not have been freely chosen with a present in all of its iterations and alterations.

There is a long history of artists affecting casual, amateur-looking ways of making that defy the standards of craft. Faught shares this terrain with a diverse group of elders and peers, including Al Loving, Lynda Benglis, Mike Kelley, William O'Brien, Allyson Mitchell, and Thomas Hirschhorn, a list that cuts across the art–craft divide. These artists have investigated, and currently investigate, the issue of craft skill for a variety of intellectual, critical, and aesthetic purposes. This approach to materials was once—for Loving and Benglis, for instance—a way to negotiate the high art world's dismissal of skill as a source of value and thus, the subordination of craft as a lesser form of art. Nowadays the use of common materials and/or craft media, low techniques, and ways of making that look like deskilling constitute a new visual and material vocabulary for the exploration of historical, personal, and mundane realities.

Notes

1   Josh Faught, as quoted in Steven Frost, "Fiber Art: The Queer Kid On the Bus," http://blog.art21.org/2010/08/05/fiber-art-the-queer-kid-on-the-bus (accessed June 5, 2010).

2   Elizabeth Freeman, "Packing History, Count(er)ing Generations," *New Literary History* 31:4 (Autumn 2000): 727–44. See also Freeman, *Time Binds: Queer Temporalities, Queer Histories* (Durham, NC: Duke University Press, 2010), especially Chapter 2, "Deep Lez; Temporal Drag and the Specters of Feminism."

3   Of course, skill isn't absent in Faught's work at all, and Wilson was remarking upon the artist's cultivation of a consciously deskilled aesthetic. On the contrary, as an artist Faught is highly skilled in all manner of textile and fiber techniques (from weaving to dyeing to non-loom methods), and an informed viewer will recognize this in his work.

4   Lacy Jane Roberts, "Put Your Thing Down, Flip It, and Reverse It: Reimagining Craft Identities Using Tactics of Queer Theory," in Maria Elena Buszek (ed.), *Extra/Ordinary: Craft and Contemporary Art* (Durham, NC: Duke University Press, 2011), pp. 243–59.

5   Josh Faught, *Longtime Companion*, solo exhibition at Lisa Cooley Gallery, New York (June 21–August 24, 2012).

6   Elizabeth Freeman, "Queer time: Introduction," *GLQ: A Journal of Lesbian and Gay Studies* 13:2–3 (2007): 160.

7   Kate Mondloch and Josh Faught, "The Way Things Work: Josh Faught in Conversation with Kate Mondloch," in *Call and Response*, http://callresponse.museumofcontemporarycraft.org/pairings/faught.html (accessed July 26, 2012).

8   Ibid.

9   Julia Bryan-Wilson, "Sharon Hayes," *Artforum* 44:9 (May 2006): 278. Sharon Hayes has produced a number of performances and video works

over the last ten years that address the intersections of official histories, represented through the quotation of political speeches, journalism, and media events, and personal histories, represented through letters, signs, and other forms of personal testimony. Nearly all of her works use text in the written or spoken form to illuminate "the present not as a moment without historical foundation but as one that is always allegorical, a moment that reaches simultaneously backwards and forwards." See http://www.shaze. info/# (accessed November 7, 2013).

10 Ibid., p. 279.

11 Felix Gonzalez-Torres' *Datelines*, which began in 1987, consist of lists of events and dates randomly arranged in a linear structure, spanning personal and collective histories related to both world events and personal memories. They are usually printed in a black font and applied around the perimeter of a gallery or other site inconspicuously above eye level.

12 Joan Scott, "The Evidence of Experience," in Henry Abelove et al. (eds), *The Lesbian and Gay Studies Reader* (New York and London: Routledge, 1993), p. 408.

13 Chris Mansour, "Citing History: Interview with Sharon Hayes," http:// chrismansour.com (accessed June 14, 2012).

14 *Gran Fury: Read My Lips*, NYU 80WSE Galleries, January 31–March 7, 2012, curated by Gran Fury and Michael Cohen. *This Will Have Been: Art, Love & Politics In the 1980s*, Museum of Contemporary Art Chicago, February 11–June 3, 2012; ICA Boston, June 30–September 30, 2012; Walker Art Center, October 26–January 27, 2013, curated by Helen Molesworth.

15 On the topic of the archive in contemporary artistic practice as it is understood here, see in particular Ann Cvetkovich, *An Archive of Feelings: Trauma, Sexuality, and Lesbian Public Cultures* (Durham, NC: Duke University Press, 2003); see also Hal Foster, "An Archival Impulse," *October* 110 (Autumn 2004): 3–22.

16 Faught includes the complete library of Meilach's publications, which extended beyond the world of fiber craft to wood and iron working, papier mâché, computers, exercise, and Bible interpretation.

17 Freeman, "Packing History," p. 728.

18 Sina Najafi, David Serlin, and Lauren Berlant, "The Broken Circuit: An Interview with Lauren Berlant," *Cabinet Magazine* 31 (Fall 2008), http:// cabinetmagazine.org/issues/31/najafi_serlin.php (accessed January 10, 2012).

19 Jay Wiseman, *Dungeon Emergencies and Supplies* (San Francisco: Greenery Press Toybag Guides, 2004).

20 Here we merely make a general comparison, not one that equates these two different histories.

21 Josh Faught, Faculty Biography, California College of the Arts, http://www. cca.edu/academics/faculty/hfaught (accessed June 10, 2012).

22 Josh Faught, email correspondence with the authors, September 27, 2012.

23 Freeman, "Packing History," p. 743.

3

An impression of *déjà vu*: Craft, the visual arts, and the need to get sloppy

Denis Longchamps

In his new series of works, Canadian artist Laurent Craste pushes the boundaries of the ceramic world, on the one hand, being technically close to perfection and, on the other, redefining what have been the tenets of the discipline for thousands of years. Discussions abound on avant-garde strategies in the craft world, with ideas about sloppy craft and postdisciplinarity at the forefront of these recent considerations. While Craste's work arguably fits within postdisciplinarity, the term "sloppy craft" raises a few questions. Are we not presented with an oxymoron when we bring together such contradictory ideas as those of craft and sloppiness? And, if so, is the work still considered craft or is it something else? While the term may have been coined in the new millennium, could the idea of sloppy craft, and associated movements such as craftivism, shed new light on the work of avant-garde craft makers of previous eras? For instance, in Québec (Canada) the works of François Houdé (1950–93) in glass and those of ceramist Loraine Basque during the 1980s beg for re-examination and new considerations within this sloppy craft context.

My aim is to examine these historical precedents in order to demonstrate how the "sloppy road" in craft was paved several decades ago by artists, like Houdé and Basque, who pushed boundaries in order to cross over to the visual arts. Furthermore, I will demonstrate how the work of Laurent Craste exemplifies a form of postdisciplinarity that remains true to its discipline without getting "sloppy." Examined within craft practices, in Québec in particular, Craste's work is avant-garde as it brings something new to the fore and blurs the disciplinary boundaries of both the crafts and the visual arts. Loaded with layers of meaning, the work also stays true to the more traditional expectations of the craft world in terms of its mastery of techniques.

In *Les frontaliers: design et métiers d'art*, curator Paul Bourassa writes that in Québec "maybe the crafts are too confined to the idea of the well-done, and they might need to explore, like contemporary art, avenues of imperfection in order to resurface in a better light."[1] It is true that the idea of "la belle ouvrage" (a work well done) has been at the heart of craft education in Québec from the start. Jean-Marie Gauvreau, director of the École du meuble from 1935 to 1958 and then of the Institut des arts appliqués until 1968,[2] made this clear in his book *Artisans du Québec*, published in 1940, when he claimed that his goal was "to endow work, that is perfected and in good taste, with a noble status while also restoring a French tradition: the cult of work well done."[3] In Québec during the 1940s, the Catholic Church still had a strong hold on the population and its education. Gauvreau chose his words carefully for their political meaning then, and now, for some Québecois: the significance of "restoring a French tradition" still resonates and lends a nationalist interpretation to the concept of "work well done." Thus Bourassa's suggestion to revisit "avenues of imperfection" in craft might carry a certain social significance for artists working in Québec. Yet I contend this tactic was already underway as early as the 1980s in the work of glass blower François Houdé, with his *Broken Vases* series, and in Loraine Basque's ceramic pieces which examine the world of fine art and that of Canadian hockey. Both artists produced works that transgressed the paradigm of technical mastery in their respective crafts. Arguably, Laurent Craste's work follows in this vein but in a very different way.

Craste's recent works do have one thing in common with the 1980s production of Houdé and Basque: like them, he is technically skilled in his medium and he chooses to subvert his discipline by attacking its technical tradition. His practice raises the question: how do we distinguish the intention of such conceptual work from that of an amateur trying to be "good"? There is uneasiness with the concept of sloppy craft. In his essay, "When Craft Gets Sloppy," Glenn Adamson claims "a cynically-minded person, however, could view [fiber artist Josh] Faught's work as a transparent bid for success in the contemporary art world, which has long made a point of embracing my-kid-can-do-that aesthetics."[4] Adamson further contends that it is "not only OK but necessary for a contemporary artist to be amateurish." More importantly, he points out that the same is found when "avant-garde designers approach craft"[5] to create utilitarian objects in a sloppy aesthetic. Among the examples given are Marteen Baas's clay furniture and the studio work of the Droog collective. In both cases, it could be argued that the designers are attempting to turn the individual pieces of furniture into art works and, in so doing, move away from the craft world.

The idea of intentional sloppiness has been, and still is, present in the contemporary art world and in many cases is employed successfully. The problem lies not with art practices, but in the need to question the relevance of sloppiness within the craft world. I do think that a different approach is *de rigueur* but that of interdisciplinarity alone doesn't fulfill this requirement. As Julia and Yolande Krueger write in their essay on François Houdé, "one of the principal notions of craft is the mastery and fetishistic dedication to one's chosen medium or discipline. To claim inter-disciplinarity runs the risk of being a jack-of-all-trades and a master of none."[6]

In a recent issue of *Studio,* craft historian Sandra Alfoldy explained that, contrary to popular belief, craft is in fact included in the collection of the National Gallery of Canada (NGC). "The difference," she writes, "was that neither the didactic panels and exhibition catalog nor the curators and artists employed the term craft. Instead, these objects were silently separated from craft by the absence of the term, and of course, their placement in Canada's pre-eminent gallery."[7] Alfoldy opens her "Comment" by relating the anecdote of a Nova Scotia College of Art and Design student asking Marc Mayer, then director of the NGC, why they were not collecting craft. His answer was that it is the mandate of the Canadian Museum of Civilization to do so, not that of the NGC. This begs the question: does the subversion of technique automatically erase the origin of the work within a craft discipline and transform it into a work of contemporary visual art? Furthermore, does the use of craft material by visual artists eradicate the craft side of the work?

In order to formulate an answer to these questions, one might ask: how can craft stay true to itself, keep its identity, while at the same time push its boundaries of both technical and conceptual exploration? Or better yet, can these works still be understood within the discipline of craft? What language needs to be used to have a discourse that is current and progressive without being repressive?

Bourassa mentions the artist Robert Filliou who, in the 1970s, established a "principle of equivalence: well done = poorly done = not done," where what is important is not the object created but "the desire to create." Central to this discussion is the notion that the "*mal fait*—poorly done" underlines "an error, a transgression."[8] So instead of considering sloppiness, let's look at the concept of transgression of the rules of technically perfect craft. Transgression implies the disrespect of rules, a breach in discipline. The Kruegers discuss this idea, citing art historian J. W. T. Mitchell's claim that "discipline is a way of insuring the continuity of a set of collective practices (technical, social, professional, etc.), 'indiscipline' is a moment of breakage or rupture, when the continuity is broken and the practice comes into question."[9] One approach to this break in continuity is discussed by Garth Clark in his "The Death of Craft," where he presents craft as an "art with an inferiority complex," highlighting the perception within the field of its status as "less than the fine arts." Clark goes on to claim that matters became increasingly acrimonious in the twentieth century as art moved away from craft-based values, closer to conceptualism and the dematerialization of the art object.[10] He argues that the death of craft happened somewhere around 1995 and blames it on the "toxicity of art envy."[11]

If craft is so steeped in the mastery of technical skills, the idea of transgression might be explored usefully within the concepts of deskilling and reskilling as discussed by John Roberts in *The Intangibilities of Form*[12] or Benjamin Buchloh et al. in their discussion on conceptual art and Duchamp's Readymade.[13] After all, notions of deskilling and reskilling are underpinned by the presence of skills, so important to craft—they may be transgressed (deskilling) and new skills of a different kind can be brought in (reskilling).

According to Roberts, "reskilling is emergent from deskilling precisely because as non-heteronymous labour the deskilling of art is open to autonomous forms of transformation, and these forms of transformation will of necessity find their expression in other skills than craft-based skills: namely, immaterial skills." He concludes that "reskilling ... invariably means non-productive forms of dexterity."[14] For Roberts, reskilling is nonetheless "a rupture that dislocates and delegitimizes established competencies."[15] Thus, I would suggest that from a craft perspective, deskilling occurs when makers distance themselves from technical mastery of their craft medium and engage in a form of reskilling by expressing their artistic concept.

This is exactly what François Houdé aimed to do with many of his works, most prominently in his series *Bols Brisés – Broken Vessels*, presented in 1982 at the Elena Lee Gallery in Montreal. Here, the artist defied the established norms of his craft by "transforming broken glass and scratches, traditionally [perceived as] signs of ineptitude, into the starting point of his creative process."[16] With this series, Houdé evoked "literally and metaphorically a 'break' with tradition and [defied] the hierarchical borders between fine arts and craft."[17]

Each vessel was first blown to perfection before being broken voluntarily into pieces—the deskilling process. The reskilling took place when the artist reassembled each one with hot glue, wire, wood, or screws in a "startling and violent manner," leaving "razor-sharp edges exposed making it impossible for one to handle and use the vessel."[18] Houdé explained his process: "In a way I was destroying my own preconceptions about art glass ... I tried to make the 'unacceptable' acceptable."[19] Scratches, breakages, and chips were always signs of weaknesses, technical difficulties or ineptitude, in short a lack of technical mastery. By breaking the glass, Houdé brought to the fore what others tried to hide: the fragility of the material. By breaking the glass, Houdé "had broken the barriers that usually separate art from craft."[20]

Houdé had mastered blown glass techniques, and it is exactly this knowledge that allowed him to express his concept with such eloquence. This mastery of the technique, of deskilling and reskilling, is also evident in his *Pygmalion* series of 1983 where he "explored divitrification and

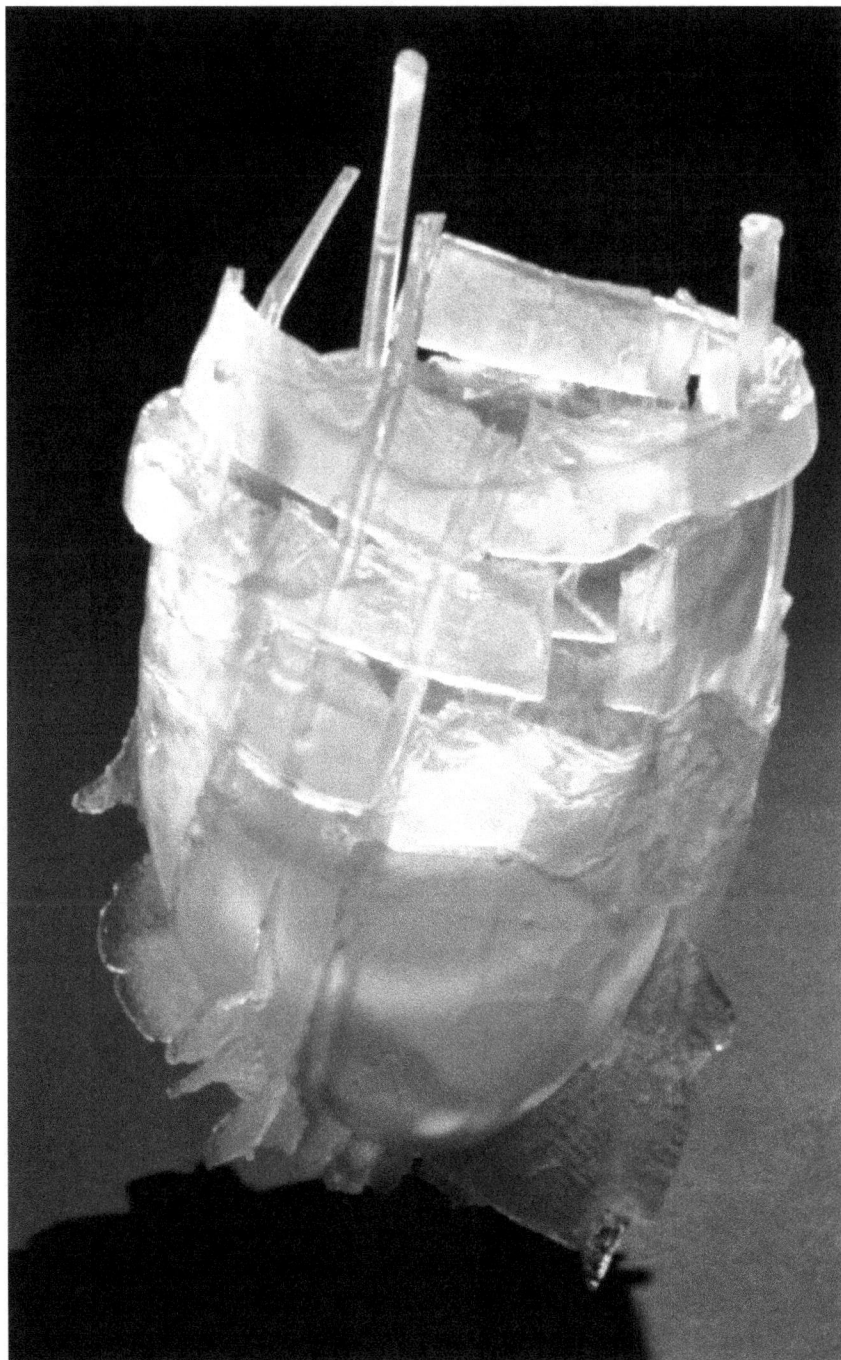

FIGURE 3.1 *François Houdé, Bol Brisé, 1982, blown and cast glass. Courtesy of the Houdé family.*

slumping" using "flat panes of manufactured glass."[21] The material of industrial quality is not the finest and was rarely, if at all, used to create art works, yet in the hands of Houdé it became magnificent sculptures. In Greek mythology, Pygmalion, believed to despise women in general, was an artist who created a sculpture of the ideal woman; he then fell in love with his work. Answering his prayers, Aphrodite gave life to the statue. The title of the work highlights how manufactured glass panes, though loathed by artists, in the right hands might become a beloved object of beauty layered with meaning. Moreover, "like the story of Pygmalion, the warm glass worker 'prays to the kiln gods' to bring the work to life."[22]

In his last series, *Ming*, Houdé forces the viewer to reconsider the fragment and the artifact in cultural, historical, and metaphorical context while exploring the equestrian motif.[23] Created from fragments of old windows and frames as archaeological reminders, these horse sculptures are thesis and anti-thesis of tradition. Here again the material is used in unusual ways and the work is layered with meaning. The frame has long been used to contain or to emphasize, while the window can be viewed as an entry point or an opportunity. Of this series, Rosalyn Morrison writes: "Houdé explores the portal structure of the window frame as a means of gaining access to other periods of civilization."[24] In an archaeological sense the fragments, of course, refer to the construction of history. The horse is a recurrent figure in the history of art from cave paintings to today. The title evokes the celebrated Chinese dynasty; however, the inspiration for Houdé was in fact the ceramic horses of the Tang Dynasty (618–907) and one emperor in particular, Ming Huang (712–56), who reputedly had 40,000 of these horses. The horse is also a recurring subject in art history, from the Lascaux caves to the Trojans to Picasso to Susan Rothenberg. The use of glass here acts as a reminder that histories can be found and pieced together or can be shattered and lost forever.

In 1987, François Houdé presented one of his *Ming* sculptures in the exhibition *Beyond the Object*, presented by the Saskatchewan Craft Council. The curator, Brian Gladwell, writes of Houdé's work that "he makes deliberate reference to his craft's traditions, he eliminates decorativeness and what he calls 'the facile tricks' in the course of an articulate inquiry into the nature of the material and its possibilities."[25] In the main catalog essay, the author claims that of the craft pieces in the show, "the work which struck me with the greatest resonance and interest falls within a third group. This work shows a particularly thoughtful approach to the meaning of the object, and refers to a content which goes beyond the object itself. In addition to offering us an object of beauty and contemplation on a sensual level, this work invites discussion of a verbal dimension."[26] There is no doubt that Houdé's work is part of this third group.

From a series that was intentionally broken and reassembled to his last series made of fragments, Houdé deals with history and traditions, craft mastery and appropriation. The artist pushed the boundaries of glass and craft through processes of deskilling and reskilling. At first glance these works appear to be sloppy, but closer inspection reveals Houdé's mastery and understanding of the technique and its tradition.

During this same period of Québec craft history, ceramist Loraine Basque presented her series of 14 sculptures on the theme of hockey (see Plate 6). In the later part of the 1970s, the Montréal Canadiens hockey team won four consecutive Stanley Cup trophies, starting with the 1975–76 season. Hockey, and the Montréal team, was in a period of resurgence. Since the 1950s in Québec, with the likes of Maurice Richard, his brother Henri, and Jean Béliveau, hockey attained a kind of religious status. Fans all over the province sat in their living rooms every Wednesday and Saturday nights to watch their *glorieux* play. Influenced by the naïve work of Edouard Jasmin (1905–87),[27] whom she interviewed for a college research paper, and encouraged by her teacher Leopold Foulem,[28] Basque explored her subject in a series of sculptures, two of which had religious overtones. Nothing more was needed for critics of the time to mistakenly assume that she meant to refer to the 14 Stations of the Cross.[29] Rather, her work draws from her interest in theater decor and props, and her affinity with painting. While highly skilled in ceramics, Basque chose to rebel against its technical tradition in order to express her concerns. These are outlined by Canadian ceramist, scholar, and teacher Mireille Perron as a "complex stratification: Stations of the Cross, theatrical scene, arena, paintings, that reveal as much a social satire as a questioning on the art milieu or of her formal choices to achieve her goals."[30]

In fact, Basque's research was formalist in approach. The setting of her pieces allowed her to play with slabs of clay, where the pictorial and the sculptural merged with one another, as in *Glace II*. In this work, a lone three-dimensional hockey player faces three two-dimensional opponents quickly drawn in the clay and painted. Her expressive uses of glazes, paint, pigments, and oxides are inspired by the history of painting. In an earlier series, Basque visited so-called masterpieces of the history of art. The idea for this series comes from a deep love of painting and art history, and a fascination with Jacques Louis David's oeuvre. Basque created scenes by bringing to life works by David and Édouard Manet, among others, staging David's *The Death of Marat* and Manet's *Olympia* in three-dimensional settings. For Perron, "the citation is used as a presentation structure"[31] where the figures, with their featureless faces, have, in the words of another critic, "lost their 'historical' seriousness."[32]

Interestingly in February 1986, Alan Elder, then the new curator of the Gallery of the Ontario Craft Council (now Curator of Craft and Design at the Canadian Museum of Civilization),[33] brought together Loraine Basque and Édouard Jasmin in an exhibition tilted *Tableaux*. In her review of the exhibition for *Ontario Craft* magazine, Diana Reitberger wrote of the hockey series that "Loraine Basque, in her direct manipulation of the clay and its surface, reinforces her theme that culture is manipulated

FIGURE 3.2 *Lorraine Basque, 1982, La mort de Marat, d'après David, porcelain, glazes, oxides, paint, 30 x 18 cm. Photo: Michel Legeais. Courtesy of the artist.*

by the media."[34] On the style chosen to render her subject, the reviewer commented that Basque's "biting satire on the impact of television, the consequences of hero worship on society, and its promulgation through the media is fully realized by her expressionistic approach to clay," and concluded that "what gives the image power is the rawness of the clay modeling." [35] The formal choices Basque made indeed support her ideas and her critique of society, professional sports, and the media.

This exploration of Houdé and Basque highlights how the strategies of deskilling and reskilling are not new in craft and contemporary art. On the international scene, other artists working in this vein include Peter Voulkos and Grayson Perry.[36] Have the avant-garde works of Houdé and Basque, along with their underpinnings, simply been forgotten? If forgetting is a form of extinction, is craft becoming the new endangered species, as Garth Clarke so eloquently points out? Looking back still further, was it not similar ideas that gave birth to Raku? Chojiro (b. 1516), a Japanese ceramist master, modeled tea bowls by hand for the tea master Sen no Rikyu (1522–91). The tea bowls were to embody *wabi sabi* ideals, an aesthetic centered on transience and imperfection. Designer Leonard Koren writes that "Wabi sabi is a beauty of things imperfect, impermanent, and incomplete."[37] Thus more than four centuries ago, imperfections were already celebrated and respected.

Similar strategies are now used by Laurent Craste, yet the results are anything but "sloppy." On the contrary, each piece is carefully planned, executed, and finished. Like Houdé and Basque, Craste possesses a mastery of the techniques of his medium. He oversees and executes each and every creative step of his works from kneading the clay to turning to painting and decorating. However, this dutiful application of the techniques is paired with an iconographical hijacking in which his decorative art object slips into the self-referential world of contemporary art. The mastery of his craft through the knowledge of its techniques, their deskilling, and the subsequent reskilling by Craste is the means by which he attains his conceptual dimension.

Craste's recent series is inspired by the porcelain of Sèvres manufacture and the sumptuous decors of Pierre Dagoty (1771–1840), but they are not copies of the originals. He physically and metaphorically alters the piece by bending or disregarding technical rules. The pieces are deformed, violently attacked but never destroyed, by a baseball bat, a wrench, or an ax— stereotypical tools of the working-class trades and blue-collar men. Each piece highlights the know-how and the know-how-to-undo of the artist. The historical models are deconstructed, technically and conceptually, to be reconstructed. The resulting sculptures form a political and economic critique of both their historical and contemporary meanings in relation to the art market then and now. Craste cites, hijacks, and subverts, all the while remaining true to his craft.

Sèvres, founded in 1740 at Vincennes, France, came under royal patronage and moved near Paris in 1759. The discovery of kaolin in

Limousin in 1768 allowed for the creation of real porcelain.[38] Soon, the
richly decorated Sèvres porcelain was sought after for its luxury and found
on most of the royal tables of Europe; it became an international icon of
wealth, culture, and elegance.[39] A service for King Louis XVI contained 400
pieces, with the delivery and cost spread over a period of ten years starting
in 1783.[40] Such orders were considered to support the local economy,
and were often viewed in patriotic terms. They underlined the good taste
and wealth of the Royal Family but also testified to its power. Indeed, the
objects used by the king were seen as extensions of his body and the act
of decorating them became a means of royal veneration."[41] Ultimately, of
course, an economic crisis brought on the Revolution and, with it, the end of
the monarchy. In this context, *Vase 14 juillet* (2011), *Princesse de Lamballe*
(2011), or *La fin d'une potiche I* (2012; see Plate 7) take on obviously rebellious meanings: the first, referring to the taking of the Bastille on that date
in 1789; the second, to a close princess friend of Marie-Antoinette who was
beheaded; the last, to the many hangings witnessed on both sides during
the Revolution. Craste carefully plans his attacks, with working-class tools,
on the vases he has turned so meticulously. It is the moment of impact,
in all its violence, which is frozen in time. The porcelain paste is ripped,
deformed, and cracked but does not shatter to pieces as one might expect.
The whiteness of the piece adds a touch of innocence to the "victim."
Other works highlight the rejection of ornament such as *Ornements et
crimes* (2011) and *Adolf Loos' Wet Dream III* (2013; see Plate 8 and cover
image). These two pieces refer to Adolf Loos (1870–1933), the Austrian
architect who wrote *Ornament and Crime* at the beginning of the twentieth
century, in which he claimed the "evolution of culture needs to move away
from ornaments ... we have surpassed ornamentation."[42] Craste's attack is
a crime against ornament, but here ornament is not a victim but a crime in
itself. The opposite could also be true and thus becomes "a critique of all
successful attempts to systematically eradicate ornament that occurred in
the twentieth century."[43]

In today's market, the Sèvres pieces are still sought after and prized
possessions for collectors, reserved for a select few of the privileged
classes. Paradoxically, Craste critiques the collectors' market which actually
supports him by collecting his work. History repeats itself—Craste's
deskilling and reskilling strategy highlights his personal, intense but
ambiguous relationship to the object.[44] In his article, Adamson writes that
"the lack of evident skills somehow implies the presence of concept."[45]
While this illusion may seem true for the work of Houdé and Basque, it
is also true that they are both skilled in their respective mediums. They
chose a process of deskilling to support their artistic ideas. Their works
highlight that sloppiness as a strategy has been around for a number of
decades already. Craste takes this strategy to another level through the
reskilling process, where his technical skills are and remain evident, where
the sculpture begs to be looked at above and beyond its anthropomorphic

form. Craste's work pushes the boundaries of his craft without rejecting it; his sculptures, with their layered meanings, concepts, and technical mastery, are evidence of a highly skilled artist and ceramist. His pieces exemplify craft as visual art, in much the same way as those of Houdé and Basque.

Most dictionaries define "sloppy" as "something being done in a careless and lazy way" and offer as synonyms "botchy, careless and messy."[46] All of these could result in unintentional and unplanned results. Craft artists, however, are not sloppy. Their pieces may present an aesthetic that looks messy at first but which, upon closer inspection, in fact highlights technical knowledge and mastery as well as an understanding of the material necessary to deconstruct it. The results are carefully planned, with just the right dose of randomness. Skills are highly important, even when getting "sloppy." In this exciting postdisciplinary environment, these artists are expanding the discourse of craft by embracing sloppiness and imperfection and creating a craft aesthetic richly layered with conceptual meaning.

Notes

1   Author's translation of "Les métiers d'art ont peut-être jusqu'à maintenant été trop confinés au "bien fait" et ils devront peut-être visiter, comme l'art contemporain, les cloaques de l'imperfection pour resurgir dans la pleine lumière." Paul Bourassa, "Les frontaliers: design et métiers d'art," *Itinéraire: Rendez-vous en métiers d'art – Actes du colloque* (Montréal: *Cahiers métiers d'art / Craft Journal*, 2010), p. 55.

2   The École du meuble became the Institut des arts appliqués in 1958 and from 1966 until 1968, the institute was part of the Cégep du Vieux Montréal. The Parent report (published in five volumes, 1963–4) on Québec education brought some major changes across the board, starting with the secularization of the school system and the creation of a provincial ministry. It also brought a decline in craft training in public institutions for almost 20 years. In 1989, studio-schools were formed and joined the Cégep system, in Cégep du Vieux Montréal and Cégep Ste. Foy in Limoilou, to provide education and training of various crafts in a three-year program.

3   Author's translation of "Rendre au travail fait avec goût et perfection ses titres de noblesse, c'est accomplir une tâche bien-faisante et c'est restaurer une tradition bien française: le culte de *la belle ouvrage*." Jean-Marie Gauvreau, *Artisans du Québec* (Trois-Rivières: Les Éditions du Bien-Public, 1940), p. 66.

4   Glenn Adamson, "When Craft Gets Sloppy," *Crafts* 211 (March–April 2008): 38. Josh Faught is an American artist working in textiles and teaching at the California College of the Arts.

5   Ibid.

6   Julia and Yolande Krueger, "François Houdé," *Contemporary Canadian Glass/Verre Contemporain Canadien* 5:4 (Winter 2007): 13.

7   Sandra Alfoldy, "Comment," *Studio* (Fall–Winter 2011–12): 3.

8   Laurent Thierry, "Robert Filliou, génie sans talent," *Chroniques: Les archives*, www.visuelimage.com/ch/filliou/index.htm (accessed October 5, 2012); and Bourassa, p. 55.

9   Krueger, p. 15.

10   Garth Clark, "The Death of Craft," *Crafts* (January–February 2009): 48.

11   Clark, p. 50.

12   John Roberts, *The Intangibilities of Form: Skill and Deskilling in Art after the Readymade* (London: Verso, 2007).

13   Benjamin Buchloh, Rosalind Krauss, Alexander Alberro, Thierry de Duve, Martha Buskirk, and Yve-Alain Bois, "Conceptual Art and the Reception of Duchamp," *October* 70 (Autumn 1990): 126–46.

14   Roberts, pp. 87–8.

15   Comments of John Miller in discussion with George Baker, Rosalind Krauss, Benjamin Buchloh, Andrea Fraser, David Joselit, James Meyer, Robert Storr, Hal Foster, and Helen Molesworth. "Round Table: The Present Conditions of Art Criticism," *October* 100 (Spring 2002): 208.

16   Denis Longchamps, *Looks on the Future: A Retrospective of the François Houdé Awards* (fold-out publication accompanying the touring exhibition of the same title produced by the Conseil des métiers d'art du Québec in collaboration with the Musée des maîtres et artisans du Québec, with the support of the Conseil des arts de Montréal, 2004).

17   Ibid.

18   Krueger, p.19.

19   Ibid, pp. 15–19.

20   Ann Duncan, "Artist's Glassworks Broke Grounds; Québec City's François Houdé Dies at 43," *The Gazette*, August 28, 1993, p. 4.

21   Krueger, p. 19.

22   Ibid, p. 27.

23   A catalog was published when the series was presented at Gallery Elena Lee: *François Houdé: Mémoires Illusoires* (Montreal: Galerie Elena Lee Verre d'Art, 1991).

24   As cited in Krueger, p. 27.

25   Brian Gladwell, *Beyond the Object* (Saskatoon: Saskatchewan Craft Council, 1987).

26   Ibid.

27   Edouard Jasmin (1905–87). Self-taught ceramist known for his naïve style, he started working with clay when one neighbor found some red earthenware while digging up a basement. He had his first solo exhibition in 1975.

28   Léopold Foulem (b. 1945). Ceramist, professor, and author, he received his MFA from Indiana University. He received many awards and distinctions including the Jean A. Chalmers National Craft Award in 1999 and the

Saidye Bronfman Award in 2001. He has exhibited worldwide including in Denmark, France, Italy, Japan, and United States.

29　Station of the Cross: 14 paintings or sculptures depicting the Passion and death of Christ; used in the Catholic Church for devotions and prayers.

30　Mireille Perron, "Sculpture-céramique. Pourquoi pas?," *Vie des Arts* 122 (March 1986): 64.

31　Ibid.

32　Marie Delagrave, "De l'ironie, douce ou mordante," *Le Soleil*, February 22, 1986, p. D12.

33　Renamed in October 2012 as the Canadian Museum of History.

34　Diane Reitberger, "Edouard Jasmin & Loraine Basque," *Ontario Craft* (Summer 1986): 28.

35　Ibid, p. 29.

36　Peter Voulkos (1924–2002). An American artist known for his abstract expressionist ceramic sculptures. Grayson Perry (b. 1960) is a British artist mostly known for his ceramic vases. He won the Turner Prize in 2003.

37　Leonard Koren, *Wabi-Sabi: For Artists, Designers, Poets & Philosophers* (Point Reyes, CA: Stonebridge Press, 1994), p. 7.

38　Anthony du Boulay, Tamara Préaud, and Lars Tharp, "Early Continental Porcelain," in David Battie (ed.), *Sotheby's Concise Encyclopedia of Porcelain* (London: Chancellor Press, 1998), p. 109.

39　Howard Coutts, *The Art of Ceramics: European Ceramic Design, 1500–1830* (New Haven and London: Yale University Press for the Bard Graduate Center for Studies in the Decorative Arts, New York, 2001), p. 118.

40　Steven Adams, "Sèvres Porcelain and the Articulation of Imperial Identity in Napoleonic France," *Journal of Design History* 20:3 (2007): 184.

41　Ibid, pp. 183–4.

42　Adolf Loos, "Ornement et Crime," in *Malgré tout (1900–1930)* (Paris: Éditions Champ Libre, 1994), p. 199.

43　Laurent Craste, in email exchange with the author, August 25, 2011.

44　Laurent Craste, *Démarche artistique* (2011).

45　Adamson, p. 38.

46　Merriam Webster Collegiate Thesaurus (Springfield, MA: Merriam Webster, 1976).

PART TWO

The implications of sloppy craft

The second part of this book presents four chapters that offer alternative approaches to this so-called new aesthetic within the craft and art worlds. They challenge the notion of sloppy craft as a casual approach to making based on an antagonistic relationship to the history of fine craft's privileging of skill, precision, and physical finish. Linking several recent strands of enquiry within the crafts—those of performance and dematerialization as well as knowledge and interdisciplinarity—American curator Namita Gupta Wiggers claims that the performance of craft is a transaction between the viewer and the producer in which the former gains knowledge of how an object is made.[1] But what of the finished object as embodying the knowledge of the making process? This is where the amorphous, grassroots Do-It-Yourself (DIY) understandings of craft might offer meaningful contributions to curatorial, academic, and professional discourses for craft. To be noted here is how objects outside the gallery system explored in the first part also rely upon particular audiences to appropriately contextualize them. In the case of MacDonald, this audience comprises members of local communities who participated in craft projects; for Alfoldy, it entails family; Hickey cites social and environmental activist communities; while Kalbfleisch refers specifically to cross-cultural references between the Native and non-Native communities, both historically and presently.

In contrast to the first part, these four chapters draw together different aspects of craft falling within a sloppy craft paradigm. Amateur and professional craft, DIY and traditional studio craft, or traditional craft and fine art practices are not seen as functioning at opposite poles; rather, these chapters explore their points of convergence within a variety of case studies drawn from a range of social and cultural contexts wherein the finished objects could be, and even were, disparaged as sloppiness in craft. In each case, professionalism plays an important role.

In her chapter "Doomed to failure," leading Canadian craft scholar Sandra Alfoldy unravels the many implications of the unintentional resemblance between the work of amateur Do-It-Yourselfers and the sloppy craft of professional artists, as these relate to the economic interests of the DIY craft market and those of the professional artistic community. In her cautionary chapter, Alfoldy warns us that this recent constituency of craft, that of sloppy craft, will result in professional studio craft being marginalized. Skilled studio craft practice with its emphasis on the finished object can appear as too traditional, not cutting-edge or conceptual enough for the spaces of the gallery. On the other hand, accidentally sloppy hobby crafters remain marginalized within the crafts in spite of visual parallels to a sloppy craft aesthetic.

Furthering the discussion of the amateur maker initiated by Alfoldy, Scottish design historian Juliette MacDonald frames craft practice as part of a broader social endeavor, rather than individual pursuit. Using social anthropologist Tim Ingold's approach to thinking about creativity as a generative and iterative process, MacDonald assesses the value of sloppy craft in relation to community in Glasgow, Scotland. In "The value of 'sloppy craft': Creativity and community," she mounts a convincing argument for the ways in which contemporary collaborative craft practices—whether domestic (though performed in public), amateur, or professional—demonstrate a potential for complex webs of meaning and connection to community and locale. MacDonald links sloppiness to processes of sharing and renewal.

In "Why is sloppy and postdisciplinary craft significant and what are its historical precedents?" Canadian curator Gloria Hickey suggests that sloppy craft might embrace many social currents, such as think global/act local, feminism, gender politics, social justice, and ecological concerns. She examines its historical precedents to contextualize current postdisciplinary craft practices. By focusing her attention on craft communities already living a postdisciplinary practice, thinking of the effects rather than results of sloppy craft, and exploring how institutions may adapt to a postdisciplinary environment for the crafts, Hickey draws her historical lineage into a current, twenty-first-century context.

Finally, Canadian scholar Elizabeth Kalbfleisch's "From Maria Martinez to Kent Monkman: Performing sloppy craft in Native America" interrogates the stakes of the postdisciplinary and performative aspects of sloppy craft. Through a discussion of craft objects within the space of North American Aboriginal performance art and performance within the space of Aboriginal craft, Kalbfleisch presents the possibilities for sloppy craft outside the dominant culture. To date unexplored, this topic is essential to this book dedicated to a broad examination of sloppy craft discourse. This chapter focuses on the relationship between postdisciplinary craft and performance in the work of "current art world star" Swampy Cree multimedia artist Kent Monkman (b. 1965). As with Hickey, a concern for contextualizing this relationship by looking to a history of Aboriginal craft demonstrators (Pueblo potter Maria Martinez and Abenaki basket weaver Anna Panadis) underpins Kalbfleisch's effort to test the limits, and the potential, of the discourse emerging around sloppy craft.

Indeed, a pitfall of some current strands of craft discourse is the characterization of studio craft as traditional and even moribund in opposition to emerging craft practices positioned as avant-garde, including sloppy craft, as well as sloppiness in crafting that involves DIY and craftivism. Tracing a history of craft from the nineteenth-century Arts and Crafts Movement, through its mid-twentieth-century revival within the Back to the Land Movement, reveals rather its oppositional stance to rampant capitalism, unchecked industrialization, and sloppily made industrial goods. Perhaps, rather than framing sloppy craft as creative innovation in the face of traditional craft, it could be understood as improvisational.

The distinction between innovation and improvisation is suggested by Tim Ingold, who locates sources of creativity in the performance of activities, rather than in completed images and objects.[2] He argues that innovation has been privileged by modernism, situated within the "novelty of outcomes and then traced to its antecedent conditions in the forms of unprecedented ideas in the minds of individual agents."[3] Ingold advocates for a reframing of creativity as improvisation where the repetitive movement associated with the acquisition of skill might allow for the extension and modification of skill, or the creative gesture. While sloppy craft *is* creative, so too is craft encountered through traditional practices or fine craft. Ingold and cultural historian Elizabeth Hallam propose a reframing of creativity. This is especially important for craft and art theoreticians and historians who have privileged the avant-garde as a site for creativity.

> Because [creativity] is generative, it is not conditional upon judgments of the novelty or otherwise of the forms it yields. Because it is relational, it does not pit the individual against either nature or society. Because it is temporal, it adheres in the outward propulsion of life rather than being broken off, as a new present form a past that is already over. And because it is the way we work, the creativity of our imaginative reflections is inseparable from our performative engagements with the materials that surround us.[4]

Traditional craft practices are then not moribund, but rather part of improvisational processes, where creative decisions are taken at every level of the interactions among the maker, the material, and the tools. In a sense, the sloppy craft objects and practices explored in the following four chapters highlight these improvisational processes, where unexpected decisions arise from moments of startling awareness. Archaeologist Bjørner Olsen suggests there might be a more fruitful way of understanding these processes as a continuum, a "coming-to-mind," rather than two poles.[5] This approach opens up a more subtle way of addressing the levels of skill involved in manipulating tools and applying and modifying numerous craft techniques. Through these approaches, sloppy craft and traditional craft practices can be understood to exist in a symbiotic relationship.

At the 2008 European *Think Tank* conference *SKILL*, Liesbeth Den Besten remarked that "young craftspeople" are tending to neglect skill, "to purposely abuse proper craftsmanship, like finishing, durability or use,"[6] which begs the question, left unanswered by Den Besten, is it possible to produce craft without being skilled at it? If so, would this outcome be sloppy and how might this interact with the sloppy craft proposed by Wilson and Adamson? The chapters in the second part of this book tackle these questions through a series of nuanced reflections on the differences between a lack of skill and a strategy of deskilling. Their broad scope explores the intersections of performance, interdisciplinarity, grassroots communities, and activism as a platform from which to unpack the term sloppy craft within the wider contexts of Scottish urban renewal, the DIY market, studio craft communities, and intercultural craft practices.

Notes

1   Namita Gupta Wiggers, "Craft Performs," in *Hand+Made: The Performative Impulse in Art and Craft* exhibition catalog (Houston: Contemporary Arts Museum, 2010), pp. 27–33.

2   Tim Ingold and Elizabeth Hallam, "Creativity and Cultural Improvisation: An Introduction," in Tim Ingold and Elizabeth Hallam (eds), *Creativity and Cultural Improvisation* (Oxford and New York: Berg, 2000), p. 2.

3   Tim Ingold, "Creativity Lecture 3—Abduction or Improvisation?" Oxford University Open Education Podcasts, podcasts.ox.ac.uk/creativity-lecture-3-creativity-abduction-or-improvisation (accessed November 26, 2014).

4   Ingold and Hallam, p. 3.

5   Bjørner Olsen, *In Defense of Things: Archaeology and the Ontology of Objects* (Lantham, MD: Altamira Press, 2010), p. 153.

6   Den Besten, "Deskilled Craft and Borrowed Skill," thinktank04.eu (accessed September 15, 2012).

4

Doomed to failure

Sandra Alfoldy

Sloppy craft suggests a purposeful approach to failure. Employing a purposeful approach indicates expertise or professionalism, or the ability to differentiate between good and bad technical skills, which reinforces the idea that the craft artist chooses to work in this way. But what if sloppy craft is completely accidental? What if it is genuinely sloppy, without aesthetic affectation or purpose? "Doomed to failure" focuses on amateur or hobby craft and the idea of technical perfection and skill with materials as portrayed by seemingly endless do-it-yourself craft publications, blogs, YouTube videos and television shows which belie the lived reality of the accidental sloppy crafter, whose results rarely reach the perfectionism advocated through glossy images in attractive, deceptively "easy," step-by-step how-to guides. This chapter will argue that these projects are doomed to failure on purpose and thereby sustain the multi-billion-dollar North American market for hobby craft. In the United States alone, $20 billion was spent on craft supplies by hobby enthusiasts in 2010.[1] If these hobby crafts did not fail, the public would no longer have to rely on popular culture icons like lifestyle brand leader Martha Stewart, nor would they spend money on her line of perfectly finished and mass-produced products at Walmart and Michael's. And this would spell the end for semi-professional and hobby craft fairs, where the good crafters, the ones who can actually follow the step-by-step instructions successfully, sell their triumphant objects. It is the intention of this chapter to demonstrate that, in opposition to accidental sloppy craft, fine art sloppy craft is an elitist fallacy that belongs to the inner circle of the fine arts world, far removed from popular culture's sad leftovers—the real hobby constituencies of sloppiness. The one shared trait between the accidental and purposeful sloppy crafter is their reaction to the perfectionism that defined both studio and hobby craft in the twentieth century. In our post (post?) modern world, craft standards are breaking down, to the glee of art students and harried housewives alike. However, a closer reading of this rejection of studio craft standards is necessary as it may be misinterpreted as falsely suggesting that studio craft has achieved equality with fine art.

When Glenn Adamson published his views on sloppy craft in the March/ April 2008 issue of *Crafts* magazine, it gave rise to a catchy sound-bite that supported his assertion that the crafts have entered a postdisciplinary world where a maker's technique with certain materials need not be perfect. In fact, it could be argued, the lack of technical perfection indicates conceptual prowess.[2] Not only did this replicate the age-old argument over manual skill versus conceptual art, but opened up questions around professional craft's strong judgment of material and technical perfection. Before deconstructing these craft tenets it is important to remember why they developed. In the nineteenth century, Augustus Pugin, John Ruskin, and William Morris lamented the degradation of craft skills as a result of industrialization, and a key component of the Arts and Crafts Movement was re-educating people in basic craft techniques. The movement "codified and publicized its practices through various societies and organizations"[3] and achieved a renewal of interest in the control of the individual craftsperson over his or her labor. When Bernard Leach published *A Potter's Book* in 1940, known widely as the bible for studio ceramics, he was still fighting against industry and the division of craft labor. His introductory chapter, "Towards a Standard," argued that the world lacked guidance for individuals wishing to pursue a career in studio ceramics: "even more unfortunate is the position of the average potter, who without some standard of fitness and beauty derived from tradition cannot be expected to produce, not necessarily masterpieces, but even intrinsically sound work."[4]

Whether one agrees with Leach's standard or not, the salient point is that in 1940 studio craft was still in a nascent stage and, in order to professionalize the field of craft, technical skill and material expertise were highly valued. This was not done by creating uniform approaches to making. Instead, leaders in all materials emphasized the importance of artistry, like the weaver Anni Albers, who wrote in 1944: "We come to know in art work that we do not clearly know where we will arrive in our work, although we set the compass, our vision ... We have plans and blueprints, a shorthand of material and its treatment, but the finished work is still a surprise."[5] As sloppy craft develops in the early twenty-first century, it is entirely too easy to forget the reasons why studio craft established a respect for individualized technical skill and to pigeonhole it as a set of cookie-cutter approaches emphasizing standardized perfection.

Textile artist Anne Wilson argues that sloppy craft is too much of a fun sound-bite, and that we should use terms like "raw, informal or casual" to describe what she calls "artists [who] now seem to 'take on' crafting only when they need it."[6] The fact is that many sloppy craft artists are not professional craftspeople finding sudden liberation through lazy technique, but art students just proficient enough in a craft material to have fun playing with it, or sculptors enjoying the opportunity to riff off craft materials. This has been happening for decades. Take for example Robin Peck, a member of the Halifax Sculpture movement which was rooted in the conceptualism and minimalism of the Nova Scotia College of Art and Design in the 1970s. Peck's work is "solidly grounded in conceptualism and in ideas about seriality and repetition as sculptural tools"[7] and it is incredibly and unapologetically sloppy. His hastily produced sculptures that consist of cardboard boxes wrapped in burlap soaked in plaster—so many of them that they completely fill the gallery—appear opposed to the materials and processes of craft, but Peck emphasizes his "truth-to-materials ethos" which echoes the writings of John Ruskin and William Morris. So does Peck's sloppy approach to plaster and burlap and the found material of cardboard pay homage to the craft amateur? Of course not. What today's use of craft materials within contemporary sculpture and sloppy craft suggests is that craft continues to be misunderstood as merely skillful making; that Anni Albers's call to remember that "the conception of a work gives only its temper, not its consistency. Things take shape in material and in the process of working it, and no imagination is great enough to know before they are done what they will be like"[8] is being overlooked in favor of the view of the studio craftsperson as mindless perfectionist. Or as Louise Valentine says, "this common misperception fails to address the maker's capacity to retain the integrative nature of thought."[9]

In their research project on past, present, and future craft practice, Louise Valentine and her team argued that "the practice of craft is a journey through the mind, reliance on building an individual vision through tacit knowledge";[10] the borrowing of craft materials by contemporary sculpture or its placement within gallery spaces as sloppy craft reduces the idea of craft to simply materials while preventing the craftsperson from exhibiting his or her own conceptual skills unless he or she enters the arena as a sculptor. So craft is again marginalized as merely the skilled manipulation of materials, making it an easy target for appropriation as the mindfulness or conceptual nature behind its materiality has never been fully recognized.

What is left out of this equation is the power of learning a skill. This may be a traditional argument, but studio craft relies on the acquisition of technical skills in order to enable the professional crafter to avoid being doomed to failure in the treacherous arena of public taste. Skillful making was a political act of resistance to industry in the late nineteenth and early twentieth centuries, and it became the marker of professional fine studio craft. In 1959, Harold Burnham, head of the Textile Department at the Royal Ontario Museum, published the article "What is a Professional Craftsman?" in *Canadian Art* magazine. Burnham noted that Canada had a very small number of professional studio craftspeople (he estimated only a dozen in the province of Ontario), but in order to grow the field he made two things clear: first, for studio craft to succeed it needed to differentiate between the hobbyist and the professional; second, the only way to do this was to stress the importance of the professional who designed and skillfully executed his or her own work.[11] For craft to be taken seriously it had to be so well done it would be beyond critique.

Much has changed during the more than 50 years since Burnham's article, notably the resistance of many studio craftspeople to the idea of technical perfection even though their work combines conceptual prowess with skilled making. It could be argued that the American ceramist Peter Voulkos was the original sloppy crafter, with his purposeful slashing and slumping of his cylindrical vessels, a practice he was establishing at the same moment Burnham was advocating for skillful precision. And as Voulkos's success in the fine arts world attested, the embracing of this approach by curators in art galleries happened early on. So while sloppy craft continues to enjoy a successful home in art galleries, and while professional studio craft continues to find successful public homes, what is really doomed to failure is hobby craft that happens at home.

Sloppy hobby crafts are doomed on two counts: first, in the face of the perfectionism of the hobby craft industry, and second, in relation to the conceptually elite realm of gallery-worthy sloppy craft. While there are many examples of perfectionism in hobby craft, this chapter will focus on the most famous North American example, Martha Stewart. As Michael J. Golec describes in his 2006 article, "*Martha Stewart Living* and the Marketing of Emersonian Perfectionism," "since its inception in 1990, *Martha Stewart Living* has endeavored to introduce its readers to Stewart's point of view. The magazine's graphic design and art direction in photography have made visible a view of the world 'through sparkling windows'."[12] In this place, "private self-cultivation is projected outward into the public spheres" through predetermined craft projects that feed into our age-old need for competition and judgment of contemporary craft skills and domestic spaces. Therefore, successfully completed hobby crafts can be read as reinforcements of the marketing philosophies behind them and the continued ideal of the home as site of perfectionism.[13] The mission statement of Martha Stewart Omnimedia continues to spin the domestic leanings of women but with a self-empowerment tone: "We elevate the familiar elements of daily life, infusing them with the pleasure and confidence that comes from the growing sense of mastery and discovery we foster in our customers and ourselves."[14] But what if there is no mastery of the crafts? As cultural studies scholar Nancy Shaw argues, Martha Stewart's "investment in perfection" is shared by her audiences.[15] This is communicated not only through the glossy images that whisk readers and viewers away to their ideal environments. It is supposedly achieved through the how-to advice contained in all of Martha Stewart's enterprises: "In each case, the step-by-step instructions are supplemented with images of key steps in the outlined process. The samples are for comparison; they lay side-by-side with the reader's step-by-step project in progress."[16] This immediate comparison can have frustrating results for the hobby crafter.

I would like to use a specific example of accidental sloppy craft to highlight how a project can be doomed to failure. Despite the old adage "those who can do; those who can't teach," I like to think that I have attained a certain level of craftiness in my life. In order to test my hypothesis that the majority of how-to hobby craft instructions are doomed to failure, I purchased the October 2011 edition of *Martha Stewart Halloween* and asked my enthusiastic five-year-old son Nicholas to select the craft he wanted to make with me. I must confess that when he selected "This Old Haunt," which urged, "personalize your home with custom signs featuring familiar warnings. And while you're at it, spin some cobwebs out of thick cord, 'board' up the windows, and make a shoebox coffin for handing out treats,"[17] I redirected him to something more simple, and he chose "Classic Creatures with Paper Features," specifically the "Fanned-Out Faces." At first it went well. Nicholas and I read and re-read and re-read the instructions, and we began to "accordion-fold three 8 ½ 11 inch sheets of coloured paper vertically into ½ or ¾ inch fold" (see Plate 9). Next we bent "each folded sheet in half to make a fan (each fan will be one third of the circle)." Then we attached the fans with a glue stick. After that we "glue[ed] 1 edge of the folded paper to the next until you form a circle."[18]

FIGURE 4.1 *Nicholas Alfoldy choosing a Martha Stewart craft project. Photo courtesy of Sandra Alfoldy.*

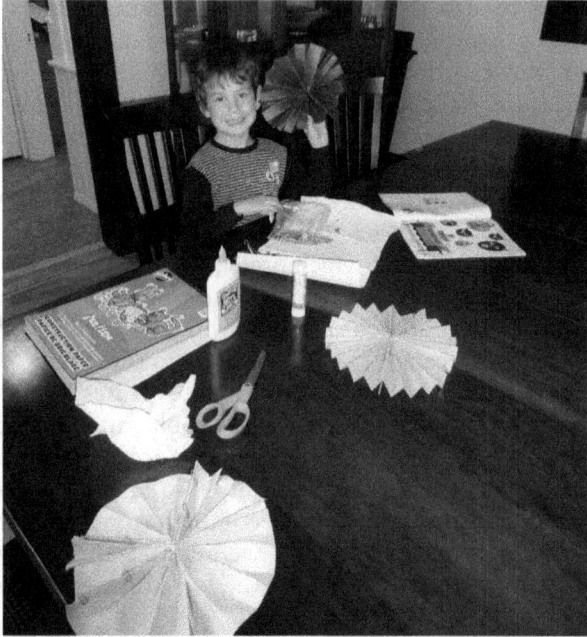

FIGURE 4.2 *Beginning "Fanned-Out Faces." Martha Stewart craft project by Nicholas Alfoldy. Photo courtesy of Sandra Alfoldy.*

FIGURE 4.3 *Gluing. Martha Stewart craft project by Nicholas Alfoldy. Photo courtesy of Sandra Alfoldy.*

It was here that the wheels started to fall off. Our glue stick ran out and we had to substitute white glue, which poor Nicholas and his mom couldn't control. After successfully downloading the features for our "Fanned-Out pumpkin, cat and owl" templates, we ran out of colored paper to trace them on. We improvised with oil pastels, but Nicholas soon tired of the coloring. We did manage to successfully cut out the features and white-glue them on, thus completing the craft. Although our two were far from perfect, they were not completely doomed to failure. Well, almost. What the experience did reinforce was the fact that even the "easiest" craft in *Martha Stewart Living* requires a certain amount of skilled experience, denies easy innovation, and is restricted to those who can afford the time and expense of materials to create the perfect upper-middle-class home. I can't even imagine what the expenses behind "This Old Haunt" would total, never mind the cost in time. Nicholas and I were satisfied with the final product, but he did complain that he felt "stupid" because it wasn't as "good or pretty" as the pictures in the magazine (see Plate 10). When I asked him if he wanted to try another paper craft in the magazine, his reply was telling: "No mom, can't we just go and buy one?"

There is nothing unusual in Nicholas's response. When the hobby craftsperson is unable to achieve the final object as depicted in the magazine or needs help with specific materials to complete the project, the solution is simply a matter of increased consumption—you can buy your way to

FIGURE 4.4 *Oil pastels. Martha Stewart craft project by Nicholas Alfoldy. Photo courtesy of Sandra Alfoldy.*

perfection. This has been called "interpretive consumption," and as Kevin
Melchionne argues in his article "Of Bookworms and Busybees: Cultural
Theory in the Age of Do-it-Yourselfing," interpretive consumption is "a
complex process of interpretation in which consumers often remake the
meanings of products."[19] Melchionne explains that "Do-it-yourselfing
is mass culture insofar as its products are mass-produced ... yet do-it-
yourselfing is not finished at the point of sale. The product takes on
meaning and value in the context of the project."[20] Returning to Martha
Stewart Omnimedia, this is why the craft projects must be doomed to
failure to a greater or lesser degree: the company produces both unfinished
products at the point of sale, like the colored papers and paper cutters
required for "Fanned Out Faces," and finished craft products for those who
have completely given up on their craft talents. As Melchionne argues, the
booming do-it-yourself craft market knows that while it requires a certain
level of imperfection in its products, it must also consistently offer enough
success to keep makers purchasing their products: "The do-it-yourselfer's
aesthetic sensibility is engaged with latitudes established by the manufac-
turer, who seeks to limit the risk of botching the job while promoting
diverse applications."[21] Melchionne makes a further material distinction
between successful hobby crafts and successful professional crafts:

> For the most part, the [professional] crafter distinguishes the hand-
> crafted object from the industrially-produced one by emphasizing the
> qualities achievable only through traditional handwork, such as diversity
> (the subtle divagations in form achieved only by hand), uniqueness,
> and off-the-beaten-track design. In contrast, the do-it-yourselfer largely
> seeks to make the work look as if it were bought in a store or a profes-
> sional contractor had done the job. The do-it-yourselfer's benchmark is
> commercial, professional, industrial.[22]

And here is the greatest irony of the doomed to failure hobby sloppy craft—
the dream, the desire of the maker is the absolute perfection shown in
Martha Stewart Living or on Home and Garden Television (HGTV). They
will never be satisfied with anything less.

Some recent publications, however, suggest that hobby crafters are
growing tired of the perfectionism espoused by Martha Stewart's empire.
In 2010, Amy Sedaris published her hilarious book, *Simple Times: Crafts
for Poor People*, which pokes fun at the earnestness of domestic crafts and
demonstrates awareness of the impossible nature of some craft instructions:
"Yes, it is healthy to want to make things, but that desire without guidance
can lead to foreclosure, incest, and forest fires. Too often instruction for
crafting is gutter-learned. Convoluted half-baked lessons picked up from
street corners, back alleys, and scouting. *Simple Times* will provide crafters
with the proper guidance, like a parole officer."[23] What make this book so
funny are the instructions Sedaris includes. For example, the "Tea Cozy

Kitten" instructions read "Self-explanatory,"[24] or in the chapter titled "Teenagers Have a Lot of Pain," the "Felt Eyeballs" only have the following instructions: "These eyes will punch up your skullcap or add character to your jean jacket."[25] Sedaris was a guest on the Martha Stewart show in March 2010 when she took "Martha's Homekeeping Test," resulting in an awkward exchange where Stewart attempted some jokes and Sedaris questioned the reasons behind exercises such as the towel folding test ("You are going to use it, why fold it?") and the whipping egg whites in a copper bowl test ("No one does it like this, they have mixers now").[26]

Lisa Quinn, Home and Garden Television (HGTV) host, published her book *Life's Too Short to Fold Fitted Sheets: Your Ultimate Guide to Domestic Liberation* in 2010 as a form of self-confession, writing in her introduction, "Hello, my name is Lisa Quinn, and I am a recovering Martha Stewart junkie. During my decade-long quest to be exactly like her, I built a career as a Home and Garden Television host, author, and columnist. Housekeeping, decorating, crafting, entertaining, and gardening—I had it covered ... But I had a dirty little secret: I was living a lie. Ironically, while I strived to be the perfect picture of domestic bliss at work, I could never quite pull it off in my own home."[27] Quinn's book is written as a self-help guide for female domestic hobby crafters, whom she encourages to get "rid of your inner control freak ... set the bar a little lower, we'll move on to the half-assed homemaking basics ... Perfection is overrated. Live a little."[28]

Amy Sedaris's book is a parody, while Quinn attempts to take a more political position, arguing that women today have "too many choices: stay at home or go to work, paint or wallpaper, private or public, red or white, organic or poisonous? Who really knows? Overwhelmed and resentful is no way to go through life. We are intelligent, educated women. How did we end up here?"[29] She is very willing to be critical of the "if you don't stack up, well, then, you don't get to play" perfectionism expected of hobby craft, but nowhere in *Life's Too Short to Fold Fitted Sheets* does she take a feminist approach to the larger context behind why women feel compelled to "rac[e] around, hot gluing and glittering like drunk monkeys."[30] Like sloppy craft's avoidance of the discussion of its relationship to studio craft, the disconnection between hobby craft failure and societal expectations for women seems disingenuous.

I believe there is a parallel between this gap and Angela McRobbie's theory of postfeminism in relation to popular culture. McRobbie posits that popular culture portrayals of young women who appear to have it all—sexual liberation, careers, an abundance of lifestyle choices—still rely on the trope of finding that one special man to make it all worthwhile. She cites *Bridget Jones's Diary* and *Sex in the City* as media examples. This reading can be applied onto the hobby craft world, where Quinn laments the excess of choices available to "intelligent, educated women," all of which conspire to make women feel like failures while simultaneously encouraging them to beautify their homes, albeit on a less frenzied scale.

What is the end goal of hobby crafts? A perfect home designed to please your husband or to fulfill societal expectations of domestic bliss? McRobbie believes that our postfeminist world relies on popular culture because it is "perniciously effective in regard to the undoing of feminism" by suggesting that feminist goals have been achieved, which results in the ambivalence of young women, "who must in more public venues stake a distance from it, for the sake of social and sexual recognition."[31] You will be hard pressed to find overtly feminist popular texts on Martha Stewart or hobby craft for exactly the same reasons. Even *Bust* magazine, the most overtly feminist publication featuring a regular craft column, "She's Crafty," feeds into the message of female power through craft, by "Bringing back these 'housey-girly' things [that] just felt so good, so right ... DIY is not just about making things—it's also about making a life. Aside from learning how to knit a scarf, we wanted our readers to learn how to create a life on their own terms."[32]

But what if this life is overwhelmed with pressure to create perfect crafts, and for what purpose? And what of the labor involved in these women's efforts? The greatest trick the hobby craft industry plays on North American culture is getting women to spend countless unpaid hours working to produce objects that could be cheaply and quickly produced overseas. Furthermore, audiences for hobby craft pay billions of dollars to support their free labor habits. As referenced earlier, the Craft Organization Development Association of the United States' 2011 report on *Craft Artists, Income and the US Economy* states that 50 million Americans made artisan crafts, spending $20 billion on supplies. Of this, 30,000 to 50,000 Americans sold artisan crafts (studio crafts) as their main income, spending $500–$900 million on supplies, real estate, and employees.[33] These numbers do not include the cost of labor time invested by the hobby crafter (and the professional crafter), nor do they include the secondary spending on completed craft objects manufactured by companies like Martha Stewart. Read cynically, William Morris's desire to overcome capitalism's oppression of labor through a return to the dignity of hand-crafting has led to a twenty-first-century hobby craft industry composed of free female labor, the women Quinn identifies as "racing around, hot gluing and glittering like drunk monkeys."

As an increasing number of women stop to question their pursuit of flawless crafts, both hobbyists and artists can relate to the power of sloppy craft within the spaces of art galleries. Being situated in this space allows sloppy craft to attempt a reversal of this perfectionism, but sadly, its elite role only further serves to alienate the *accidental* sloppy crafter. Sloppy craft seeks neither the "commercial, professional, industrial" perfection of do-it-yourselfers, nor the carefully cultivated materials and techniques of professional studio craft. Sloppy craft, like sculpture, pushes against this desire for control by producing ostensibly uncontrolled, sloppy, raw objects. However, a very careful control underscores this aesthetic. In the hands of the sloppy crafter even, or especially, manipulated mass-produced objects give rise to a form of aesthetic conceptualism that can infiltrate the elitist spaces of high art. By operating wholly outside either of these two traditional categories of craft—hobby and professional—sloppy craft appropriates the cultural consumption of hobby craft, where crafters remake the meanings of craft, while defying cultural expectations and creating conceptually challenging material statements. However, the result is that professional studio craft becomes further marginalized as traditional in its approach to craft, not cutting-edge or conceptual enough for the spaces of the gallery, and the accidentally sloppy hobby crafter gets marginalized as well. Objects classified as sloppy craft, or even new sculpture, are often recognized thematically for their relationship to everyday consumer objects and materials. This is easy to relate to hobby crafts, but these become rooted in the idea of domestic perfection while sloppy craft finds itself in the conceptual realm, moving further and further away from accessible ideas of craft.

McRobbie's theory of postfeminism offers a different perspective on what binds sloppy craft, hobby craft, and studio craft. If postfeminism "draws on and invokes feminism as that which can be taken into account in order to suggest that equality is achieved, in order to install a whole repertoire of meanings which emphasize that it is no longer needed, a spent force,"[34] then can't the same thing be said of sloppy craft? This artistic movement would not have much impact if it was simply called "sloppy." It needs the word craft, with all its negative and positive connotations, to succeed. Its materials are limited to the repertoire associated with studio craft, and its producers are trained enough to recognize when it is right to make a conscious decision to get sloppy. If the creators of sloppy craft did not have the expertise and technical skills within craft's material categories to make these determinations then they would be simply sculptors. This is the power that is missing from the world of the doomed hobby crafter. After all, as Anni Albers pointed out decades ago, it is the "struggle with rugged material [that] teaches us best a constructive discipline,"[35] and only once you have won that struggle can you move forward. The hobby crafter has neither the time nor the training to win that battle.

Utilizing the postfeminist model for the postcraft world, it appears that the gaps between hobby craft, professional studio craft, and fine art sloppy craft continue to widen. But I do see some possibility of alleviating the painful reality of consistently dooming the hobbyist to failure. First, there is humor. So much of sloppy craft contains a humorless edge, as do the sculptures that borrow craft materials and techniques for elevated conceptual messaging. Martha Stewart is equally earnest. As Nancy Shaw argues, while Martha Stewart's "performance of impeccable domestic comportment"[36] makes her an easy target, it also leads to much-appreciated levity for the accidental sloppy crafter. There is something viscerally satisfying in seeing an icon like Martha Stewart fail. That is why over half a million people have watched the various "Martha Stewart" bloopers posted on YouTube. However, when Martha Stewart makes heartfelt attempts to be funny, she often fails. Viewers, readers, and consumers still desire her perfectionism and her perfect, if unattainable, craft ideals. But best of all are comedians like Amy Sedaris who makes the very same point as sloppy craft: it is okay to let loose with the perfectionism. Despite this, there is still a long way to go before the separations between these realms are erased. When Sedaris first appeared on Martha Stewart's daytime show on October 31, 2006, Martha Stewart said to her: "Where I try to make everything look like it should, you just try to make it look like it does."[37] What an opening for sloppy craft.

A postfeminist interpretation of this humor suggests that it is a popular culture tool for undermining feminist advances. While this is true, it is also high time that all types of crafters poked fun at their situation. But no matter how far apart the worlds of sloppy craft, studio craft, and hobby craft might appear, it is remarkable how they can agree on which objects created within these worlds attain perfection: whether it is the perfectly imperfect edges of a sloppy craft wall hanging, a breathtakingly executed clay cylinder, or a room full of lovingly hand-crafted "Classic Creatures with Paper Features," there is a visceral reaction to skilled making. As Anni Albers summarizes: "Still, there is one right opinion, as to quality of a work of art, spontaneous and indisputable—one of our absolutes! There is final agreement upon it, of those initiated, no matter how much personal taste or trends of the time influence the judgment."[38]

Notes

1   Craft Organization Development Association (CODA) "Craft Artists, Income and the U.S. Economy" (2011), http://craftemergency.org/ professional_resources/single/the_coda_review_2011_craft_artists_income_ and_the_u.s._economy (accessed October 2, 2011).

2   Glenn Adamson, "When Craft Gets Sloppy," *Crafts* 211 (March/April 2008): 38.

3   Jeffrey Petts, "Good Work and Aesthetic Education: William Morris, the Arts and Crafts Movement, and Beyond," *Journal of Aesthetic Education* 42:1 (Spring 2008): 31.

4   Bernard Leach, "Chapter One: Towards a Standard," *A Potter's Book* (London: Transatlantic Arts Inc, 1973), p. 1.

5   Anni Albers, "One Aspect of Work" (1944), in Vicki Halper and Diane Douglas, *Choosing Craft: The Artist's Viewpoint* (Chapel Hill: University of North Carolina Press, 2009), p. 6.

6   June Underwood, "Sloppy Craft: It's Getting Interesting," *Art and Perception* blog, http://artandperception.com/2009/10/sloppy-craft-its-getting-interesting. html (accessed September 25, 2011).

7   Ray Cronin, "Robin Peck" (2007), essay for the Canadian Cultural Property Export Review Board while Senior Curator of Contemporary Art at the Art Gallery of Nova Scotia.

8   Albers, "One Aspect of Work," p. 6.

9   Georgina Follett and Louise Valentine, *Future Craft Research Exposition*, September 12–24, 2011, Anna Leonowens Gallery, Halifax, Nova Scotia.

10 Ibid.

11 Harold B. Burnham, "What is a Professional Craftsman?" *Canadian Art* 16:4 (1959), pp. 248–9.

12 Michael J. Golec, "*Martha Stewart Living* and the Marketing of Emersonian Perfectionism," *Home Cultures* 3:1 (2006): 6.

13 Ibid.

14 Ibid.

15 Ibid., p. 11.

16 Ibid., p. 14.

17 "This Old Haunt," in *Martha Stewart Halloween*, October 2011, p. 17.

18 "Fanned-Out Faces," in *Martha Stewart Halloween*, October 2011, p. 36.

19 Kevin Melchionne, "Of Bookworms and Busybees: Cultural Theory in the Age of Do-It-Yourselfing," *Journal of Aesthetics and Art Criticism* 57:2 (Spring 1999): 247.

20 Ibid., p. 249.

21 Ibid., p. 251.

22 Ibid., p. 250.

23 Amy Sedaris, *Simple Times: Crafts for Poor People* (New York and London: Grand Central Publishing, 2010), p. 13.

24 Ibid., p. 37.

25 Ibid., p. 232.

26 "Amy Sedaris Takes Martha's Homekeeping Test," March 19, 2010, http://www.youtube.com/watch?v=kqdHtboWhi8 (accessed September 2, 2012).

27 Lisa Quinn, *Life's Too Short to Fold Fitted Sheets: Your Ultimate Guide to Domestic Liberation* (San Francisco: Chronicle Books, 2010), p. 10.

28 Ibid., p. 11.

29 Ibid., p. 12.

30 Ibid., p. 13.

31 Angela McRobbie, "Notes on Postfeminism and Popular Culture: Bridget Jones and the New Gender Regime," in Anita Harris (ed.), *All About the Girl: Culture, Power, Identity* (Oxford: Psychology Press, 2004), p. 3.

32 Debbie Stoller, "Introduction," in Laurie Henzel and Debbie Stoller, *The Bust DIY Guide to Life: Making Your Way Through Every Day* (New York: Abrams, 2011), p. 10.

33 CODA, "Craft Artists, Income and the U.S. Economy," p. 2.

34   McRobbie, "Notes on Postfeminism and Popular Culture," p. 4.

35   Albers, "One Aspect of Work," p. 6.

36   Golec, "*Martha Stewart Living*," p. 11.

37   See the video clip at http://www.youtube.com/watch?v=te-MKE6kPzo (accessed September 2, 2012).

38   Albers, "One Aspect of Work," p. 6.

5

The value of "sloppy craft": Creativity and community

Juliette MacDonald

*Craft is a starting place, a set of possibilities. It avoids
absolutes, certainties, over-robust definitions, solace.
It offers places, interstices, where objects and people meet.
It is unstable, contingent. It is about experience. It is about desire.
It can be beautiful.*[1]

EDMUND DE WAAL

De Waal's observation of craft as an unstable set of possibilities or experiences provides a starting point for this discussion of urban-based creativity and community. The description does not work well as a definition, because it does not provide a clear picture, giving instead a somewhat sloppy outline of the possibilities brought about by craft. The beauty of the words, however, lies in their ability to sum up the potential of craft, especially suggesting the synergies to be found through active participation in creativity. Glenn Adamson echoes de Waal's point in an article on sloppy craft for *Crafts* magazine when he comments that "knitting and homespun craft activities are restless phenomena"[2] because they can be viewed from a range of perspectives: from formal and conceptual to political and social. This chapter will focus on some of the synergies produced when craft is used as a "restless" connector to foster a sense of place.

Nineteenth-century critics, designers, and architects such as John Ruskin, William Morris, and William Richard Lethaby were well aware that craft had an important function in society and were strong advocates of craft as a crucial determinant in reducing the growing sense of alienation and passive consumption evident in British society by the mid-1800s. For example, Lethaby noted the importance of seeing art (for Lethaby the term "art" served as a representative of making and production) as an active and participatory activity with far-reaching effects on individuals and community:

> Art is many things—service, record, and stimulus ... Writers on aesthetics have not sufficiently recognised that Art is service before it is delight; it is labour as well as emotion; it is substance as well as expression. What they say here and there is true enough, but it is a way that leads to destruction; it is concerned with appearances rather than conduct.[3]

More recent academic work shows that there is a renewed interest in the psychological and social phenomena associated with craft. The social anthropologist Tim Ingold, for example, has much to say about creativity, agency, and materiality. In an essay on materiality he states that his intention is "to shift the focus on to processes of formation rather than on final products, and to flows and transformations of materials as against states of matter."[4] Psychologist Mihaly Csikszentmihalyi's work on "flow" centers on happiness and creativity and emphasizes the value of activities which completely absorb an individual and temporarily remove them from the pressures of everyday life. Craft clearly conforms to this description.

> To overcome the anxieties and depressions of contemporary life, individuals must become independent of the social environment to the degree that they no longer respond exclusively in terms of its rewards and punishments. To achieve such autonomy, a person has to learn to provide rewards to herself. She has to develop the ability to find enjoyment and purpose regardless of external circumstances.[5]

Sociologist David Gauntlett's text *Making is Connecting* has also provoked a greater academic focus on the importance of community and creativity. Moreover his approach is in keeping with that of Ruskin and Morris as he argues that, because creativity is socially relevant, it has a political aspect too. For Gauntlett it is of little matter whether the artifacts created are "silly" or essential; the important point is that time and effort have been put into the making itself:

> You may note that my examples just above are not the absolute essentials of life—people can survive without silly entertainment, flowers, gloves, or songs, if they have to. But it is the fact that people have made a choice—to make something themselves rather than just consume what's given by the big suppliers—that is significant. Amplified slightly, it leads to a whole new way of looking at things, and potentially to a real political shift in how we deal with the world.[6]

The connections between craft, creativity, and community can generate strong emotional ties, with the landscape itself or with our individual histories, often producing a merging of the private and public. Ingold points this out when he argues that:

> A place owes its character to the experiences it affords to those who spend time there—to the sights, sounds and indeed smells that constitute its specific ambience. And these in turn depend on the kinds of activities in which its inhabitants engage.[7]

These approaches have undoubtedly renewed awareness of, and interest in, the value of "making" within communities, of being engaged in a project from start to finish and sharing it with others. Such new perspectives have been paralleled by a rising interest in DIY, community craft projects, and craft blogs as well as a flourishing of the "indie craft" movement. This shift of emphasis and arguments for thinking about creativity as a generative and iterative process also presents an opportunity for evaluating sloppy craft in relation to creativity and community. Finding a way to connect people to each other and to the area within which they reside is as essential now as it was in the nineteenth century. Craft, then, is not just about the wealthy few commissioning or purchasing exquisite status pieces; it can be a power tool for the disenfranchised too.

In light of the rise of academic and popular interest in craft, community, and creativity, this chapter intends to explore some of the socio-political possibilities arising from the shifting of focus from a perfect end-product to an emphasis on process. It will argue that craft as a shared phenomenon has an important role in encouraging creativity, particularly for those who would not necessarily consider themselves "artistic" or profess to have any interest in making or producing work, goods, or produce of their own. The discussion will focus chiefly on two community projects in Glasgow, Scotland. Both projects cultivate craft practice as a social endeavor and highlight the relevance of craft as a political tool. They use craft's ability to foster an investment of time and energy; to encourage other ways of looking at the world; and to develop an individual's relationship to a locale.

These examples are selected from a range of Glasgow-based projects and events which fall into de Waal's criteria of "places and interstices, where objects and people meet." The first draws upon a historic building, Maryhill Burgh Halls, and demonstrates nineteenth- and twentieth-century civic aspirations associated with the use of craft. Maryhill Burgh Halls in the north-west of the city has recently been renovated with a strong emphasis on engaging local inhabitants from the design and planning phase through to the execution of work. The second example focuses on community work in a group of multi-story buildings known as Red Road, an area in the north of Glasgow. A program to demolish all of these buildings by 2017 is in progress but part of the estate is currently home to refugees, asylum

seekers, and first-time home occupants who have previously been living in
hostels or on the streets.

Glasgow context

In the late nineteenth century, Glasgow witnessed a period of rapid growth
and industrialization with the city becoming renowned for its shipbuilding,
engineering, and metalworks. This rapid industrialization was equaled by a
surge in population which by the early twentieth century had reached over
a million, but as the number of residents increased, so living conditions
deteriorated drastically and poor housing became a serious issue. Glasgow
was not alone in experiencing such phenomena. Sociologist and town
planner Patrick Geddes noted of Scotland in general that "no population
in the world is now so predominantly urban, and, as sanitary reformers
know, none so ill-housed at that."[8] However, despite Glasgow's many social
problems it was known for its unrivalled feats of engineering and many of
the citizens were keen to establish the city as contemporary and forward-
thinking. Art historian Juliet Kinchin has argued that this attachment to
technological progress and industrial skills was

> expressed metaphorically in the aggressively modern, sleek and stylised
> forms of much Glasgow Style furniture. Certain detailing evoked the
> formal language of engineering, and pleasure in the manipulation of
> metal upon which Glasgow's industrial wealth was founded.[9]

Whilst the "Glasgow Style" of the late nineteenth century made reference
to nature and landscape, Kinchin argues that an awareness of, and pride
in, the city informed the creativity associated with this style, as its forms
were filtered through an urban sensibility, expressing a psychological
identification with the city and its industrial, urban culture.

Maryhill Burgh Halls

This case study of Maryhill Burgh Halls provides an account of craft and
creativity being used to rejuvenate a building and the area associated with
it. It is a story of community/craft being an integral part of a regeneration
process to build a stronger network of belonging and of encouraging participants to develop a strong sense of ownership and local character.

Maryhill Burgh Halls were designed by Duncan McNaughton in 1876
and opened in 1878. Situated in the north-west of Glasgow, they contained
a public hall large enough to hold 1,000 people, a court room, and suffi-
cient accommodation to provide for an increased level of policing for

the area as part of an attempt to reduce some of the anti-social behavior associated with the rapidly rising population. The Halls were used for local events and functions until the 1980s; over the following decade the Halls fell into disrepair and were eventually closed. In 2004 the Maryhill Burgh Halls Trust (a collaborative community initiative involving local residents, Cube Housing Association, Maryhill Housing Association, and Glasgow City Council) was set up with the aim of redeveloping and refurbishing the buildings to be an integral element in the planned housing and leisure developments for the surrounding area and once again to function as an important focal point for community activity.

Twenty stained-glass panels provided one of the most striking decorative elements in the original public hall. Created by the Glaswegian stained-glass studio Adam and Small, and designed by Stephen Adams, each window depicted a local trade or industry including images of calico workers at Kelvindale Mills on the River Kelvin, a glassblower representing two large glassworks in nearby streets, iron moulders, linen bleachers, and paper-makers. The realism of the portrayal of the industries and trades in the Maryhill Burgh Halls's windows is in marked contrast to Adams's other stained-glass treatments of similar subjects where workmen are portrayed in classical, late-medieval, or Renaissance clothing and static poses. Many of the landscapes incorporated into the designs are similarly realist, portraying the nearby canal or distant steeples.

The windows were removed from the Halls in the 1990s to protect them from vandalism and were stored in the Glasgow Museums collection. As part of the refurbishment it was agreed that ten of the originals should be reinstated into the Halls and that ten new panels should be commissioned. Stained-glass designer Alec Galloway and community artist Margo Winning were commissioned to create the new designs. At this point in the commissioning process the local community was invited to suggest contemporary trades as subjects for the designs, and workshops were run to engage the Maryhill residents with the nineteenth-century crafts used in the building and subsequent repair of the Halls.

The brief for the new series of windows stipulated that the designs should continue the themes of trades and industries of Maryhill, whilst depicting an up-to-date picture of contemporary business, life, and leisure in the area. The Trust was convinced that the success of the project lay in the hands of the local community in order to ensure that the new windows became as much a legacy of the Halls as the original nineteenth-century glass. The project *Windows of Today* was launched, with a vision of creating "some new stained glass windows to record what is important in the area today, and to give the restoration project a lasting legacy."[10] A call to invite people to contribute ideas, memories, and stories; participate in glass-making workshops; and attend artist's talks and visits was at the center of this aim to enable the local community to have an insight into the process of making as well as designing.

FIGURE 5.1 *Maryhill Burgh Halls, Windows of Today Workshop. Courtesy of Maryhill Burgh Halls Trust.*

A variety of individuals and groups responded, including primary school children, local businesses, and residents, assisting the artists to discover and explore local civic history. Winning commented on the enthusiasm of the community input:

> It quickly emerged that the multiple layers of communities that make up Maryhill were very keen to express their thoughts and ideas in a range of ways; including writing, drawings, glass making and in endless interesting discussion and chat. It provided an enormously valuable introduction and connection to the area and community, letting me learn more about the place and people in a few weeks than I otherwise could have in years. It has been a delightful project to be involved in.[11]

The themes for the ten new windows were eventually agreed to be: education; culture; social heritage; heavy trades; workers; space age; youth; sport and leisure; regeneration; and diversity. Although these titles are generic, the designs themselves incorporate well-known artists and sportspeople who were born in the area, local companies who provide components for satellites, and long-established families associated with local shops and cafes.

Gordon Barr, Heritage Development Officer for the Trust, commented on the importance of the community's interest in the project:

> We're really excited to finally see the results of all the hours of workshops and talks, and the effort put into this ... from the literally hundreds of local people who got involved in various ways to have their say, try out some of the techniques involved in making stained glass, and in some cases, have their images actually featured in the glass itself.[12]

The windows are now complete, but the long-term success of this project will depend very much on this early involvement of the local community, who will recall and recount their contribution. The hope is that the new windows will become as much a part of the permanent legacy of the Burgh Halls as the original glass from 1878.

It was not just the stained glass that provided opportunities for locals to be involved with the crafts relating to the building. Joinery and stone-masonry workshops for adults and school children were run alongside pointing and roofing sessions, providing opportunities to learn about traditional crafts, the intricacies of the building, and, most importantly, to participate in the rebuilding process. The connections made by participating in this process facilitated unconscious connections with the place and the location.

FIGURE 5.2 *Maryhill Burgh Halls, School Children Workshop. Courtesy of Maryhill Burgh Halls Trust.*

Over recent years, architectural and urban planners have often revived, reinterpreted, and recreated historical events, folklore, and myths relating to an area in order to redefine the sense of what the place was and is and provide an added dimension to people's appreciation of a location. However, this attempt often misses the mark because it is added on rather than integral to the development. As Geddes rightly noted:

> "Local character" is thus no mere accidental old-world quaintness, as its mimics think and say. It is attained only in [the] course of adequate grasp and treatment of the whole environment, and in active sympathy with the essential and characteristic life of the place concerned.[13]

The workshops and events organized at Maryhill Burgh Halls together represent an involvement at the "craft face" of the building and were an essential element in inspiring the many constituencies in Maryhill to be involved with the Halls and in encouraging a strong sense of the new building as very much a part of the community itself rather than an added component.

Red Road

This second case study focuses on multi-story apartment blocks in an area to the north of Glasgow known as Red Road and provides an opportunity to reflect on the role of craft in sustaining a sense of community during a program of demolition and relocation. The numerous art and craft projects produced for Red Road have been designed to empower the inhabitants of the apartments as they faced the uncertainty of losing their current homes.

Designed in 1962 by Sam Bunton and Associates for the Glasgow Corporation and erected between 1964 and 1969, the Red Road flats comprised a cluster of eight high-rise buildings, some of which contained as many as 31 stories. Given the combination of Glasgow's interest in design, technology, and engineering and the city's long-term social issues of overcrowding and poor housing, it is unsurprising that the New York-inspired high-rise architecture appeared to provide an exciting solution to the city's housing problems. Since the 1920s, New York City's skyline functioned as a sign of modernity, inspiring hopes for a utopian future and providing a blueprint for countless architects and planners across Britain. At the time of their completion, Red Road's skyscraper skyline formed the highest steel-framed social housing structures in Europe and contained over 1,300 dwellings. Bunton was obviously aware of the severity of his design but he emphasized the Modernist tenets of form and function with the practical and rational taking precedent: "Housing today isn't domestic architecture—it's a public building. You mustn't expect airs and graces and things like different-sized windows and ornamental features."[14]

Without doubt the Red Road buildings can be seen as the result of Bunton's own interests in efficiency, function, and experimentation as well as municipal and public desire to deal with social problems of overcrowded and unhealthy tenements. They should, however, also be understood as part of Glasgow's pride in its industrial and technological achievements and identity as a forward-looking, contemporary city.

Although visually distinctive and functional, by the 1970s the social and political climate had changed and there was generally less enthusiasm for such large-scale modernist architectural solutions. More importantly it became apparent that:

> Such peripheral housing schemes were thus a kind of parody of the traditional tenement life of Glasgow: they consisted of tenements indeed but they were far removed from the urban context in which that mode of life had developed, and incapable of generating their own community life. In spite of the literature of planning, already vast, and containing so many hard earned lessons, these new units were not only devoid of facilities themselves, but were miles from the traditional centre of Glasgow life.[15]

FIGURE 5.3 *View of Red Road. Courtesy of Philip Mason.*

Red Road's occupants began to report problems of vandalism and the flats quickly fell into a poor state. In the 1980s some of the flats were transferred for use by the YMCA and also as student accommodation and when, between 1999 and 2001, the city of Glasgow became home to 18,000 people seeking asylum, Red Road became one of the key areas for relocation. Community projects grew in parallel with this development, offering opportunities for integration and support. Red Road's future is now that of rehousing, relocation, and demolition: in July 2012 the first demolition took place and the remaining blocks will be demolished in a rolling program up until 2017. Despite its impoverished and declining state, some occupants remain firmly committed to living in the flats. In an attempt to deal with the occupants' future of uncertainty and upheaval as plans for the demolition unfolded, Glasgow Housing Authority (GHA) has funded and implemented many art projects to attempt to support the individuals and families who were long-term residents as well as those newly arrived seeking asylum in the UK. A number of craft-based and visual art groups became involved with the residents in order to help settle new people into their short-term environment.

Fab Pad was created in 1998 by community arts group Impact Arts in order to support vulnerable young people in their first tenancy. GHA allowed Impact Arts to develop four community flats in the Red Road complex to demonstrate the possibilities for personalizing the home through making simple home textiles and furnishings on a very limited budget. Participants received travel expenses and a budget of £100 to spend on their home and were able to attend local weekly workshops with professional interior designers to develop their ideas, and to plan, design, and create their space. Activities included personal design consultation, shopping and inspiration trips, whilst also having the opportunity to meet other young people in the same situation as themselves. The project also contributed towards better chances of being employed by encouraging those on the scheme to take positive steps to secure training and education. The intention was that by providing basic craft skills such as sewing to turn unwanted textiles into cushions, wall hanging, or covers, a sense of pride in achievement, a deeper attachment to the place, and a sense of home might start to develop. Program manager Alison Sommerville said:

> Some people have had a difficult time or a difficult background, and some have been in care or lost their job. All they want is to make their place nice and homely ... This project makes people realise that they can achieve a lot on a limited budget. They see the end product and that they have a nice house and their self-esteem goes up. Then they can think of the next step; getting a job or going back to college.[16]

Multi-story was another community-based agency at the core of the Red Road creative program. It provided "opportunities for people to take part in creative activity alongside makers and artists and aim[ed] to support dialogues across communities."[17] Their projects drew upon traditional and contemporary practices to explore issues of concern amongst the residents from relocation and regeneration to new communities. Many of Multi-story's projects were concerned with photography, film, and animation, but some activities were craft-based. Mothers of Purl is a good example: here women from the site came together to learn to knit, improve their skills, share stories, or just to knit and to enjoy each other's company. The women who gathered together were drawn from across the community with long-term Scottish residents, asylum seekers, and refugees from many countries participating. As I discovered whilst participating in a Mothers of Purl workshop, one of the interesting outcomes of their sharing of stories, skills, and experience is that knitting techniques and patterns indigenous to a specific country have been shared with and taught to others with the result that new and innovative stitches have been created, morphed, and subsequently passed on. This synthesis of knowledge and skill shared over a cup of tea in Glasgow in many ways embodies the sharing of knowledge without concern for ontological or geographic boundaries that is becoming an important theme in the professional world of art and craft practice (see Plate 11).

Precious Metal: 16 Days of Action at the Red Road Centre was a project run in 2010 by North Glasgow Integration Network and Community Studio artists Iseult Timmermans and Ruth Hollywood that provided an opportunity for a group of women from the Red Road area to explore the theme of peace through jewelry making. Over four afternoon workshops the women learnt some basic jewelry-making skills in order to create unique "personal narrative" jewelry that reflected their responses to the global campaign "16 Days of Action to Eliminate Violence Against Women." The work produced in the sessions was fed into a community-wide event: once the work was complete, photographs of the group modeling some of their hand-made jewelry were taken, printed, and shown at the Red Road Community Studio alongside photographic posters made by the Red Road Family Centre Photography Group, and new creative writing and poetry readings group (see Plate 12).

By introducing the women to a basic making process, they were provided with an opportunity to reflect on this international theme and comment at a local level on what for some was a deeply personal topic rather than an abstract issue. Using inexpensive materials, the pieces included necklaces incorporating toy weapons and emblems of love and peace. Mastering a skill and creating an expensive commodity was not the goal; the most important element was that the outcome was experienced as part of a communal creativity, and as such it provided an opportunity for self-reflection which ultimately functioned as an "interstice"—that small place where the various objects and people could meet. As Ruskin comments in *The Seven Lamps of Architecture*, "It is not the material, but the absence of the human labour which makes the thing worthless; and a piece of terra cotta, or of plaster of Paris, which has been wrought by the human hand, is worth all the stone in Carrara, cut by machinery."[18]

The craft processes that have been learnt as a result of the many and diverse projects held at Red Road over recent years similarly embody an approach where value lies not in the end product but within the potential for the freedom of thought and the creativity which lie beneath the surface of the artifact, no matter how ugly or sloppy one might consider that artifact to be. Ruskin again comments: "Examine once more those ugly goblins, and formless monsters, and stern statues, anatomiless and rigid; but do not mock at them for they are signs of the life and liberty of every workman who struck the stone, a freedom of thought."[19]

Discussion

Knitting introduces people to team work, they have gained enthusiasm and confidence, and then they started knitting flowers to make a statement. Through this process we are hoping to achieve something that personally benefits them and contributes on a broader platform to racial attitudes. They are starting to knit random objects now and drop them around the estate with a simple message "Found me?" and the website for the project. Through that we are hoping to encourage more people to get involved.

Iseult Timmermans, Project Coordinator, Mothers of Purl

As noted in the introduction, a strong sense of alienation has played an important role in urban and industrial culture and provides another thread for this examination of creativity and community and the value of sloppy craft in that context. The artist Sabrina Gschwandtner argues in the essay "The Politics of Craft" that "alienation is one of the things drawing people to craft as a hobby ... And part of the pleasure of the knitting or sewing circle is that it doesn't happen in isolation."[20] As city dwellers continue to attempt to address the homogenized and mass-produced phenomenon of the contemporary city, craft as a communal experience functions as a form of resistance to that sense of alienation. Sociologist Frank Furedi argues that today's world is "characterised by the loss of the web of meaning through which people make sense about who they are and where they stand in relation to others."[21] In both the case studies presented here it is clear to see that the involvement of contemporary collaborative craft practices, domestic (albeit performed in a public context), amateur, and professional, has facilitated social interaction. The resulting objects from such projects may be sloppy and not of professional perfection but, rather than providing a superficial sense of belonging, the participatory experiences discussed here demonstrate the potential for the creation of far more complex webs of meaning (social, psychological, political, and cultural), providing a depth of connection achieved through the sharing of process and experience.

Red Road and Maryhill Burgh Halls projects are examples of a more structured approach to involving the community in a local project so that they too feel a part of the history, culture, and ongoing life of the area, and craft as process has played an important role in reinforcing social connections. Both projects demonstrate how the learning of craft skills, even if very basic, can encourage more positive responses to city living, by finding alternative solutions to mass-produced creativity and combating the sense of alienation so frequently experienced in post-industrial cities. Creativity, agency, and material are at the heart of the projects, demonstrating the social connections to be made through engaging with and sharing creative craft processes. Their main thrust has been to find ways of involving people and helping them feel that they belong despite being in impoverished or undifferentiated areas of a city.

As noted in the introduction, Gauntlett in *Making is Connecting* (2011) has analyzed the role of connectivity in contemporary lives. He points out that through making things and sharing we become more engaged in the world and embedded in our surroundings. Gauntlett suggests that although, when questioned, most people would say that more money would make them happier, sociological research finds that contributing to the world, rather than simply consuming it, promotes a greater sense of happiness, or pleasure and achievement.[22]

The Psychological Research Unit at the University of Central Lancaster undertook a study which questioned the efficacy of socially engaged arts and the changes such projects can bring about in individuals and communities.[23] Their research included the Centre for Contemporary Arts, Glasgow, as one of its main case studies because of its commitment to open source programing and its outreach projects which include sales of home-made craft work in the foyer of the gallery and gardening projects in the East End of the city. The team's research highlighted that psychological barriers are most likely to preclude individuals from participating in a project because of a belief that engaging in an art or craft practice is "not for people like us." Despite such reticence, the researchers argue that the chief value of socially engaged art

> lies in the way artists try to provide such experiences through the opportunities they offer for taking part, and the way in which the work they commission and produce enables the discovery of new forms for feelings which connect selves and communities. When aesthetic form is found to contain otherwise inchoate or inexpressible feeling, it can become a "force" that "moves" individuals or becomes a driver of social change.[24]

The philosopher Elizabeth Grosz reiterates this in an essay on "The Thing":

> Things are our way of dealing with a world in which we are enmeshed rather than over which we have dominion ... We make objects in order to live in the world. Or, in another, Nietzschean sense, we must live in the world artistically, not as *homo sapiens* but as *homo faber*.[25]

Engagement rather than a perfect end-product is the key to promoting social capital and the result is that participants become knitted into the fabric of the community.

Acknowledgments

My thanks to the following for their kind assistance and input: Dr Phil Mason, Urban Studies, University of Glasgow; Iseult Timmermans, Education and Development Officer, Street Level Photoworks, Glasgow; and Dr Gordon Barr, Heritage Development Officer, Maryhill Burgh Halls Trust, Glasgow.

Notes

1   From the V&A Museum's webpage "What is Craft," http://www.vam.ac.uk/content/articles/w/what-is-craft/ (accessed October 10, 2011).

2   Glenn Adamson, "When Craft Gets Sloppy," *Crafts* 211 (March/April 2008): 40.

3   W. R. Lethaby, "What Shall we Call Beautiful? A Practical View of Aesthetics," *Hibbert Journal* 1918; reprinted in Lethaby, *Form in Civilisation* (Oxford: Oxford University Press, 1922), pp, 156–7.

4   Tim Ingold, *Bringing Things Back to Life: Creative Entanglements in a World of Materials*, Material Worlds Symposium, Brown University, April 18, 2008, p. 3.

5   Mihaly Csikszentmihalyi, *Flow: The Psychology of Happiness: The Classic Work on How to Achieve Happiness* (London: Rider, 2002), p. 16.

6   David Gauntlett, *Making is Connecting: The Social Meaning of Creativity, from DIY and Knitting to YouTube and Web 2.0.* (Cambridge: Polity Press, 2011), p. 19.

7   Ingold, *Bringing Things Back to Life*, p. 155.

8   Patrick Geddes, *Cities in Evolution* (London: Williams & Norgate, 1915).

9   Juliet Kinchin, "'Dear Green Place' or 'murky simmering Tophet'? Reconciling nature, industry and modernity in Glasgow Style decoration" (2006), http://www.artnouveau-net.eu/ (accessed April 2, 2009).

10 Maryhill Burgh Halls: Modern Stained Glass and Contemporary Artworks, *Mary Hill Burgh Halls* (2011), p. 4.

11 From Maryhill Burgh Halls webpage "Modern Stained Glass," http://www.maryhillburghhalls.org.uk/glass/ (accessed May 9, 2012).

12 Ibid.

13 Geddes, *Cities in Evolution*, p. 397.

14 Bunton quoted by M. Glendinning, *Rebuilding Scotland: The Post-war Vision 1945–1975* (Edinburgh: Tuckwell Press, 1997), p. 107.

15 F. Crawford, S. Beck, and P. Hanlon, *Will Glasgow Flourish? Regeneration and Health in Glasgow: Learning from the Past, Analysing the Present and Planning for the Future* (Glasgow: Glasgow Centre for Population Health, 2007), p. 51.

16 See web article and podcast "Fab Pad: Decorate your home on a budget," and link to Impact Art website on Scottish Television (STV), http://programmes.stv.tv/the-hour/homes-gardens/home-improvements/228821-fab-pad-decorate-your-home-on-a-budget/ (accessed October 10, 2011).

17 See Multi-story's website, http://www.multi-story.org/ (accessed March 5, 2010).

18 John Ruskin, *The Seven Lamps of Architecture* (Oxford: Wiley, 1865) (Harvard University Digitised, 2006), p. 45.

19 Ibid., pp. 198–9.

20 Sabrina Gschwandtner, interviewed by Julia Bryan-Wilson in "The Politics of Craft," *Modern Painters* (February 2008): 82.

21 Frank Furedi, *Therapy Culture: Cultivating Vulnerability in an Uncertain Age* (London: Routledge, 2003), p. 162.

22 Gauntlett, *Making is Connecting*.

23 L. Froggett, R. Little, A. Roy, and L. Whitaker, *New Model Visual Arts Organisations* (Preston: University of Central Lancashire, 2011).

24 Ibid., p. 91.

25 Grosz quoted by S. Attiwill in "A World in Making: Cities Craft Design," *craft + design enquiry* 5 (2013): 1.

6

Why is sloppy and postdisciplinary craft significant and what are its historical precedents?

Gloria Hickey

In 2007, noted craft theorist Paul Greenhalgh challenged the assembled delegates at the NeoCraft conference in Halifax, Nova Scotia, to devise new ways of thinking about craft. Since then the scholarly community in Canada has acknowledged the need for more contemporary and socially relevant understandings of current craft practice and objects. Clearly, in order for theoretical understandings of craft to advance, earlier models of contextualizing craft would have to be replaced, as these relied heavily on either the Arts and Crafts Movement, as popularized by William Morris (1834–96), or the Back to the Land Movement that had influenced studio craft in the 1960s and 1970s. Greenhalgh's keynote speech could be roughly summarized in one sentence: Morris has been dead for about 100 years; it's time to come up with something new.[1] This was do or die time for craft theory. As far as makers were concerned, there was no more exciting time for craft. It was time for the craft theorists to catch up and figure out why.

Traditionally, materiality has dominated the making of craft as well as the thinking and writing about craft in European scholarship since the Renaissance. For centuries, craftspeople defined themselves as potters or weavers, or other titles that were predicated on the material and process of their chosen profession. In the twenty-first century, it is still common for a craftsperson to talk about their chosen medium by rhapsodizing about their first encounter with it in vivid sensory details.

In North America, materiality also characterized the infrastructure of the wider craft community. Art and design colleges organized their curriculum accordingly and academic degrees were granted with majors that concentrated on a specific medium such as clay or textiles. Commercial galleries and public institutions were similarly defined by material or medium. For example, during the 1980s there was a noticeable upsurge of medium-specific galleries and institutions in Toronto. The Gardiner Museum of Ceramic Art opened its doors on Queen's Park in 1984 and the Textile Museum of Canada opened its current 55 Centre Street facility in 1989.[2]

Special interest craft publications were also organized by medium, including *Ceramics Monthly* in the United States, *Ceramic Arts & Perception* in Australia, and *Ceramics Review* in the UK. In Canada, there was *Contact* magazine and *Fusion* covering ceramic art and pottery. Eventually, materiality was recognized in theoretical studies on craft—for example, in 1998 *The Encyclopedia of Aesthetics* included a four-page entry on craft, by philosopher Larry Shiner, which highlighted the importance of materiality.[3]

Gareth Williams suggests in his article "Tales of the Unexpected" for the UK publication *Crafts* that the craft world's emphasis on materiality is in part due to the impact of the art world's emphasis on concept over construct:

> Broadly speaking, this left 20th-century craft practice to focus on the materiality of the object, its substance and techniques, usually in the sphere of the unique and handmade or the limited edition. Forced into a corner by the voracity of the notion of art-as-individualism-as-concept, brow beaten craft fetishised the process of making, the creative act least considered (though not entirely neglected) by art. If nothing else, craftspeople could claim to create their own individualized works, even if constrained by conventions and dogmas of their own making.[4]

Materiality became part of the dogma of craft in both the studio and classroom.

However, the advent of postdisciplinary craft has created a profound gap between the contemporary practice of craft and how scholars understand it. The practice of postdisciplinary craft is not elucidated by either the Arts and Crafts Movement, the Back to the Land Movement or a post-1960s understanding of materiality. Emerging generations of craftspeople no longer worship at the altar of the past. They do not learn in traditional apprenticeships with masters, and a growing number have abandoned classrooms and academic settings in arts and design colleges and universities. Some affiliate themselves with the Do-It-Yourself community or DIY makers. These younger makers are not slaves to specific techniques or materials, nor do they observe the tribal affiliations of clay, glass, textiles, and metal that defined earlier generations of craftspeople. Postdisciplinary craft is a radical shift away from the past. It is time for academics and craft theorists to wake up and notice. Paul Greenhalgh was right to sound the alarm, and that is the reason why this book was necessary.

Perhaps in response to the changing priorities of craftspeople, some art and design colleges and universities began to offer an interdisciplinary degree in addition to medium-specific major degrees. For example, Nova Scotia College of Art and Design's (NSCAD) undergraduate academic programs

> involve four years of study, leading to professional degrees and a foundation of skills and knowledge in a specific field … All programs start with a foundation year that fosters broad exploration of media and concepts. A second year of interdisciplinary studies encourages students to delve more deeply into specific disciplines at the introductory level. By third year, students can declare a major and proceed to advanced level classes in their field or fields of study, though they can also choose to remain on an interdisciplinary path.[5]

According to Professor of Craft History, Sandra Alfoldy, who teaches at NSCAD University in its Division of Historical and Critical Studies, registration in the craft program in 2012 was about 50 percent medium-specific and 50 percent interdisciplinary. She estimates that the interdisciplinary Bachelor of Fine Arts (BFA) is the university's "most popular BFA." It has been offered since 1997.[6]

Interestingly, Paul Greenhalgh left his post at London's Victoria and Albert Museum in 2001 to become NSCAD's 17th president; he resigned from NSCAD in 2006.[7] But it was Greenhalgh's successor at the Victoria and Albert Museum, Glenn Adamson, whose name is most commonly associated with the term "postdisciplinary craft," on which he has lectured extensively. Formerly deputy head of research and head of graduate studies at the Victoria and Albert Museum and tutor at the Royal College of Art, and currently director of the Museum of Arts and Design in New York, Adamson is co-editor of the triannual *Journal of Modern Craft* and author of numerous publications on craft history and theory, design and applied arts. In *Thinking Through Craft* (2007), Adamson explores the concept and practice of materiality in relation to contemporary craft and, more specifically, to contemporary art, concluding that we are in "an apparently post-disciplinary era."[8] Given his role at the V&A, the *Journal of Modern Craft*, and his international career as a lecturer and author, Adamson's promotion of this association between postdisciplinarity and craft carries considerable scholarly weight.

However, if as the saying goes, necessity is the mother of invention, I suggest that in fact small craft communities are the mother of postdisciplinary craft. While academics and craft theoreticians regard the term "postdisciplinary" as the newest diagnostic tool in the toolbox, it has been in practice for decades in smaller communities. For instance, veteran artist Gerry Squires, best known for his authoritative landscape painting, supported himself as an editorial artist for the *Toronto Telegram* before moving back home to Newfoundland in 1969 with his wife Gail, a potter, and settling into an abandoned lighthouse in Ferryland. In an attempt to make a living as an artist and raise a family of two daughters, Squires has carried out commissions in stained glass, ceramics, and bronze as well as painting portraits.

Although Newfoundland and Labrador has always had a vibrant population of professional artists and craftspeople in both its city centres and rural communities, there has never been the luxury of a large pool of resources and the opportunity to associate solely within one's discipline. So, while both the Gardiner Museum of Ceramic Art and the Textile Museum of Canada were opening their doors in the 1980s in Toronto, potters in Newfoundland and Labrador were commiserating with jewelers, problem-solving with textile artists, and conspiring with wood carvers. Some craftspeople hold dual or "multiple citizenship" in a variety of camps that cross visual arts, performing and decorative arts borders.

Active smaller communities are hot beds of cross-fertilization which produce wonderful hybrid makers and practices that are unpredictable yet efficient. The consequences are seen not just in their products and techniques—like those of Ray Cox, who, inspired by ceramics, developed air-cast pewter vessels—but in community attitudes, local educational institutions with a grassroots focus, and a younger generation of postdis-ciplinary practitioners. The Anna Templeton Centre for Craft Arts and Design, for example, is home to the Textile Studies Program of the College of the North Atlantic but it also serves as a hub of creative activity for musicians, actors, and visual artists. In order to survive, it has capitalized on its downtown location and historic British Bank of North America building in St John's, Newfoundland, by forming strategic alliances with the downtown business and heritage communities.

Jason Holley is an energetic, 30-something, restless craftsperson who is both a ceramic artist and a jeweler, practices he links through chainmaille production (see Plate 13). He describes the silver and non-precious jewelry as his production line, which subsidizes his exhibition work in raku-fired clay. After three years of frustration at university—he tried physics, computer science, and women's studies—Holley made a hemp necklace for a girlfriend and found his niche. "All her friends wanted one. That summer I set up on Water Street and made nearly $10,000," Holley recounts of his debut as a craftsperson in downtown St John's. Eager to develop a new product, Holley wanted training but didn't want to go back to university: "I found chainmaille on the Internet while I was looking for a way of making unique jewellery that didn't take much specialized tools or skills." In addition, he took a patchwork of classes at the Craft Council's Clay Studio and drawing at the Anna Templeton Centre. "Pretty soon, I practically started living at the Clay Studio. For $70 a month I got a key and 24-hour access. Can you believe it? I got to do workshops in the day to learn the skills and then spend my nights making stuff up," Holley enthuses.

Now, in his own rural studio, Jason Holley's self-directed and results-oriented approach suggests a youth-fuelled trend. It is different from the traditional approach to craftsmanship, which historically focused on the slow, incremental building of skills under the careful watch of a master. It is also different from the focus in craft and design colleges on acquiring medium-specific skills, techniques, and knowledge of the discipline's history. Holley will readily put in weeks upon weeks of 16-hour days working on a large sculpture or installation but would not be content to work for someone else. As he says, "I pretty much have to be my own boss." The emphasis on self-direction is not extraordinary in a province that has a substantial majority of professional craftspeople who identify themselves as "self-taught."[9]

It is difficult to assess exactly how postdisciplinary craft is related to the current digital age but they do appear to be linked. Academic institutions like NSCAD University seem to be trying to accommodate the phenomenon of postdisciplinary craft with its interdisciplinary degrees, yet a growing number of young makers are deciding to forgo formal education altogether in favor of learning from their peers and the digital community of the internet. The internet is proving to be the great leveler of the playing field in craft. It has helped break down the hierarchy within craft: master and apprentice, teacher and student. Unlike students who emulated their professors, what this generation of digital crafters makes does not look like a teacher's work, which was typically informed by historical precedent and specialized skills. Instead of investing years learning a specialized skill set, these crafters trade skills and work collaboratively. Their skills acquisition is different and so are the resulting craft objects.

The trend toward collaboration was identified in a 2008 essay by Liesbeth den Besten entitled "Deskilled Craft and Borrowed Skill" and presented to the gathering of the European initiative Think Tank.[10] She observes that contemporary makers start out with an end result in mind and then select the materials, techniques, and technologies to achieve that end. I have come to believe that there are roughly two types of craftspeople: one group is based in materiality, and the characteristics of their chosen medium largely determine what they make; the other group is concept-driven and will use whatever medium or technique is at hand that will help them express or realize their conceptual goals. This latter group would be the postdisciplinary makers while the first is more traditional in approach.

In her 2010 report for the Ontario Arts Council, *Tracing Emerging Modes of Practice: Craft Sector Review*, Jen Anisef devotes an entire part to creative collaboration and identifies it as an important trend in Canada and abroad. Writing about the trend toward collaboration, Anisef comments about craftspeople in Ontario: "If they don't possess the skills required, they learn new skills or cooperate with specialists and borrow a skill without the intentions of becoming a master in the field. Skill in contemporary practice frequently involves cooperating with fellow crafts-people and with technical companies that specialize in audiovisual, digital, new technology and other techniques." Anisef cites Eric Nay as expressing a similar viewpoint when claiming that "as things are dematerialized with the proliferation of digital technology, craft is no longer about objects and is instead about relationship and communication."[11]

One of the most vivid examples of the impact of the digital world on craft is the vast proliferation of knitting groups online. It is a sprawling digital community that numbers in the millions. In fact, Ravelry was created out of one active blogger's frustration with wading through the digital jungle of knit groups as she was researching yarns and patterns.[12] An American husband–wife team, Casey and Jessica Forbes founded Ravelry in May 2007 in order to create a digital presence for fiber artists. The site enables knitters, crocheters, designers, spinners, and dyers to keep track of their yarn and tools and to look to others for ideas and inspiration.[13]

More than an organizational and research tool, Ravelry is a social network site for users to discuss their crafts. It also facilitates micro-business, allowing crafters to sell their patterns or yarns.[14] Both large- and small-scale businesses are able to advertise their wares on Ravelry, which has also been used by some for market research. It is a combination of digital club, marketplace, and publication, with over 2 million members worldwide as of February 29, 2012. To quote Gillian Reagan in the *New York Observer*, "Ravelry has become the Internet tool to help the typical needle-wielder navigate through the woolly wild."[15]

The embrace of digital technologies on the part of contemporary crafts-people signals the erosion of the long-held wariness of technology by older generations of craftspeople. It is no longer unusual to see laser-cut furniture combining traditional furniture design with twenty-first-century technology. In fact, curator and furniture maker Fo Wilson explored just this topic in the 2010 exhibition *The New Materiality: Digital Dialogues at the Boundaries of Contemporary Craft* at the Fuller Craft Museum in Brockton, Massachusetts. Some of the pieces included in the exhibition integrated technologies such as computers, video monitors, and motion detectors. The 2009 exhibition *Telling Tales, Fantasy and Fear in Contemporary Design* at the Victoria and Albert Museum also featured stunning laser-cut furniture inspired by the spirit of storytelling.[16] Much of the furniture, lighting, and ceramics featured were by a new generation of international designers, notably from the Netherlands, many of whom were under the age of 40.

It looks as if the digital age could be to craft what the sexual revolution was to feminism. The fossilized definition of craft as a survival skill or something one's ancestors did is finally changing. The digital age has given craft new tools and new cachet. Craft has become re-energized and much more a part of mainstream society than it had been previously, thanks, in part, to a new generation of tech-savvy makers who are also comfortable talking and communicating about their work, be it in an artist statement, interview, or a blog.

With the radical change in the craft landscape, the word "craft" is increasingly linked with terms that might at first seem like oxymorons: sloppy craft, cool craft, extreme craft. The event *Craft Punk* brought together designer makers in Milan "to use discarded materials from the Fendi production line to create something fresh."[17] An attentive public watched the makers at work for four hours each day. The event was complete with a DJ and a free Campari bar. But the UK magazine *Crafts* claimed that the public was not there for the open bar, and concluded, "it proved beyond any reasonable doubt that visitors are fascinated by making and process. And that craft can be ever-so-lightly hip."

Anne Wilson at the School of the Art Institute of Chicago is credited with coining the term "sloppy craft." In 2009, craft theorist Glenn Adamson described sloppy craft as the "unkempt" product of a postdisciplinary craft education.[18] What, exactly, does sloppy craft look like? Craft made from repurposed materials like François Houdé's exquisite Ming Series composed of glass windows, Jennifer Angus's decorative Victorian "wallpaper" installations composed of insects, or Rachel Ryan's glitzy kitsch Nativity manger?[19] It is perhaps noteworthy that these three examples are all made of recycled materials and that none are traditional craft media. These three dramatically different examples also share a common trait in that they are all non-functional. However, each of these three artist-craftspeople received their training at art and design colleges and, in the case of Angus and Houdé, were influential teachers. Currently, Angus is a professor at the Design Studies department at the University of Wisconsin in Madison.

While there is much diversity in what sloppy craft looks like, perhaps it is more fruitful to ask: how does sloppy craft behave? If you think of Adamson's definition of sloppy craft as the "unkempt" product of a postdisciplinary craft education, it is tempting to think of sloppy craft as an unruly child. The child may or may not be disheveled but surely it is disobedient and doesn't follow the craft canons of its parents or predecessors. It is craft that acts out of turn or is rebellious. To me, sloppy craft is craft that demonstrates a willful disregard for the accepted etiquette of craft that preaches straight stitches and propriety. It is craft that is messy because life is messy and, as is the case in Ryan's *Modern Day Nativity*, that is what it sometimes expresses.

Originally from Newfoundland and now a resident of Nova Scotia, Rachel Ryan is a textile artist noted for her superb design sense and finely controlled technique. Ryan's life prior to the making of her Nativity manger had been a roller-coaster ride of events and emotions: among other things, these involved her mother finally passing away after a battle with cancer and the end of her marriage after several years. With this piece she was giving herself permission to "colour outside of the lines."

The exhibition *Waking Dreams* (2011) at the Craft Council Gallery in St John's, in which I first encountered Rachel Ryan's Nativity tableaux (see Plate 14), is arguably where Ryan exploded out of her cocoon. She created a body of drawings, wall hangings, and mixed media installations that bristle with bold energy and powerful emotions. Gone were the contemplative textile landscapes, the icebergs that on closer inspection contained women, or the birch tress that housed stately spirits. They had been replaced with equally soulful work, but the 2011 show was extroverted rather than inward looking. *Waking Dreams* is a centrifugal storm, an outpouring of complex colors, spiraling stitches, and layers upon layers of quilted swatches of fabric and paper. In this exhibition, Ryan's work was about *The Wreckage of Change*—as one piece was titled—not just her personal life but also the social backdrop of tsunamis, financial crisis, and war which had extra meaning for Rachel, as she had been part of a military family, a boat in tow through a succession of postings. [20]

The exuberant expressiveness of some sloppy craft reminds me of abstract expressionism, where sloppiness is equated with authenticity. It is raw, pure, unmitigated and uncensored. It deals with unbridled emotions and feelings rather than cool thinking or the intellect. It has an undeniable physicality and is embedded in the gesture of the craftsperson. It brings to my mind the equivalence of the testosterone-charged pots of an early Peter Voulkos with the wild and unleashed paintings of Jackson Pollock. Is this the triumph of gesture over concept? Is that what art's gift to craft will be?[21]

Pollock's paintings signaled a real revolution in the art world because it was his process that trumped any single idea or message. It was art that you felt first and then thought about secondly. Pollock's paintings made your senses tingle and immersed you as a viewer. For so long, the conceptual had ruled the art roost, and craft didn't fare well in the conceptual art world. Craft, then, was about tradition, materials, technique, and process. It didn't appear to be about ideas. As it turned out, the art world was looking for those very ideas in the wrong places. While contemporary art's ideas were embedded in conceptualism and formalism, contemporary craft's ideas were about evolution rather than revolution. Or, as Bruce Metcalf puts it, craft is an advocate rather than an adversary.[22] With postdisciplinary and sloppy craft, perhaps revolution has finally come to the craft world.

American scholar and jeweler Bruce Metcalf attributes the similarity between abstract expressionist art and some works of craft to art envy. He says that in order to achieve the status of art—its prestige, higher price tags, and spot on the gallery walls or pedestal—craft must mimic art. "The common strategy to achieve art's prestige has been to adopt the style of any recently certified art movement, from Abstract Expressionism to performance art. Yet, to perceive art as a parade of visual styles is an error, for modern art is principally an ongoing debate about the value and purpose of visual experience. Where modern art is defined by theory, postwar craft has avoided it."[23]

I think it is significant that, in art historical terms, sloppy craft seems to be decidedly anti-modern. It is rarely sleek or simplified. Works like the examples of sloppy craft mentioned earlier are awash in detail. It is well-documented that, starting with Adolf Loos (1870–1933) and his *Ornament and Crime*, modernists were suspicious of the decorative detail. Without mercy, they pruned detail away from furniture, buildings, and the domestic environment. For centuries, craft had been about the well-wrought detail, which gave the human eye a resting place and allowed us to imbue our surroundings with personal meaning. Contemporary craft theorists generally agree that contemporary craft is about investing the everyday with personal meaning and that the general public seems to understand this intuitively.

The public aligns its felt uniqueness as individuals with the uniqueness of the handmade and I have previously argued that this is why craft plays such a strong role in the gift trade.[24] In short, some of us as unique individuals crave the unique in our environment and seek it out. In order to express that family and friends are special to us, we offer them handmade gifts. These gifts may be handmade by us or other craftspeople. The gift object is a highly charged extension of the gift giver. The professionalism of the maker is irrelevant to the gift recipient.[25]

Sloppy craft may or may not be part of the DIY movement. Both professional craftspeople and amateur crafters can make sloppy craft. One of the distinguishing markers of the DIY movement is its largely amateur community of crafters. That's the whole point of the DIY movement: it is craft you make yourself—vernacular craft, if you will, or craft made by the people for the people. It is craft without "experts." Jen Anisef dedicates a section of her report on emerging craft trends to DIY craft. She cites Glenn Adamson as saying that "DIY craft is a trend in search of a label," but I would suggest that it seems to have become its own label. More importantly, she points out his appreciation for the "active verb-like quality" of the term "crafter" over the more passive sounding "craftsperson." Indeed, I contend that this active characteristic is a "key distinction between the DIY and studio craft realms" and that "the latter strives for professionalism, whereas the new crafters embrace vocationalism."[26]

What will be the impact of this upsurge of the DIY movement? Studio craft has fought long and hard for its professional status, its specialized institutions and marketplace of dedicated galleries. Some artists and fine crafts professionals feel that the influence of the commercial gallery world runs counter to postdisciplinary practice. Known primarily as a textile artist, Barb Hunt teaches in the fine arts program at the Grenfell Campus of Memorial University in Corner Brook, Newfoundland. Hunt, who received a diploma from the University of Manitoba and an MFA at Concordia University in Montreal, describes herself "as a crossover artist with a foot in both craft and art worlds." She positions the postdisciplinary shift in craft as "post modern, where working in a variety of disciplines is typical."

Her own art practice has encompassed dress patterns cut from steel that questioned gender construction, hand-knit antipersonnel landmines in pink wool, and bodies of work inspired by Newfoundland traditions of grieving in lace, nets, stones, and fabric flowers blown from windy cemeteries. Her most recent work, which integrates her concerns with grieving and war, is created from camouflage army uniforms.

It is intriguing to think about the impact on a craftperson's practice of patrons and institutions, which collect according to specific media. Hunt believes "the focus on one discipline was encouraged by the commercial gallery system and academic art history [as] a way of pigeon-holing artists and controlling them, and thus their market." Wouldn't it be ironic if the identities so many potters, glass artists, and textile artists have shaped with dedication over the decades were the by-product not just of their training, but of the market as well? Inversely, the absence of such a market may be useful in explaining postdisciplinary practice in Newfoundland and Labrador. If you don't have a strong market collecting a specific kind of object, there is no one telling you what to make.[27]

Will the DIY movement cause an erosion of connoisseurship and collecting of studio craft? Connoisseurship actively rejects populism. It is a world based on labels, maker's marks, signatures, and exotic materials based on standards of research and documentation. In contrast, the DIY community is inherently populist and democratic. I suspect that studio craft or fine craft and DIY craft will remain at opposite sides of the court, like opponents in a tennis match, or be complementary opposites that inform and influence each other. They are unlikely to cannibalize each other. One will not replace the other, as they fulfill different functions.

One of the most intriguing features of sloppy craft—and this certainly represents an overlap with DIY craft—is that it is craft that exists beyond the walls of both commercial and public galleries, museums and teaching institutions. As an instance of this, I would point to the 2010 KnitCambridge project, where artist Sue Sturdy wrapped an entire city bridge with knitted samples donated by more than 1,000 volunteer knitters. Sturdy wanted to get as many people as possible involved and do something "that would put a smile on people's faces." She reported that they got pieces from across Waterloo Region, Owen Sound, Toronto, BC, the south-western US and even New Zealand. The purpose of the project was to remind local residents of their city's connection with the textile industry. With so much of Canada's textiles being imported today, many residents who lived in cities with once proud textile manufacturers are now largely unaware of their city's textile past. A small army of volunteers was required to take down the knitted wraps off the bridge. They next washed and cut the pieces into scarves, afghans, and blankets, which were donated to the Cambridge Self-Help Food Bank and The Bridges, a Cambridge homeless shelter. Other pieces were given some finishing touches and were auctioned off at the Tie One On Party. The proceeds of the auction went to support the Cambridge Centre for the Arts.[28]

FIGURE 6.1 *Sharon Kallis, The Ivy Canoe, 2008, community weaving. English ivy, woven into a boat structure for a small urban pond to increase a habitat for ducks and birds, 20 ft. long, photographed by artist, 2009.*

Sloppy craft, like craftivism (a neologism for craft + activism), often refers to craft with a developed social conscience that strives to support ethical practices, be they environmental, ecological, or in terms of social justice. Winner of the prestigious Lillian Elliott Award (2011), fiber artist Sharon Kallis jokes that she bastardizes traditional craft techniques but for a good cause. A Vancouver-based artist, she has collaborated for the past few years with environmentalists, ecologists, and community members to "forge a human/landscape relationship of stewardship and attention. Her creative process is driven by the twin desires to bring community involvement into the local management of invasive species, and to use ancient textile processes to turn the harvested plant materials back into a form that will support the re-establishment of native flora and fauna."[29]

Sharon Kallis likens her work with communities and natural environments to quilting bees: "everyone has a part to play and a piece to make." Rather than working with fabric squares cut from recycled clothing, Kallis and community volunteers start the project by harvesting what nature sheds—dried grasses, flowers, pods, weather-damaged branches—to form a bank of natural supplies with a seasonal palette. What they make is determined by what is available and, equally important, by what is needed. Kallis has sprung to prominence for her use of invasive species to create installations that actually assist native plants and their environments to flourish. For the *Ivy Project*, Kallis worked with volunteers from the Stanley Park Ecology Society who had pulled almost five hectares of invasive English ivy that was dried and then netted, crocheted or spool-knitted into nurse logs and bio-netting to hold eroding soil in place long enough for new native growth to return (see Plate 15). Kallis also "basket bombs"—teaching volunteers how to weave baskets which are then left in park environments, one of many instances where, for Kallis, "nature is our final collaborator."

Another collaborative project, both with the surrounding nature and local residents, involved Kallis working with locals to reclaim a river by harvesting willow in Missouri. Kallis explains, "I enjoy being a tourist and helping people to see their environment with fresh eyes. In exchange I learn about their relationship with the landscape and how it changes with time." Working with volunteers, "I never know how many I will get or who they will be," and this variety of harvested materials allows Kallis a certain freedom. She travels to residencies with little more than a few cutting tools, good working gloves, and a camera. But this is a part of her working philosophy that she sees as being distinctly Canadian: "There is a uniqueness to everyone's mark and what they make even if we do the same action. It's like the saying about Canada being a mosaic. We are a part of the ecology and it is important that we don't dominate it."[30]

This more democratic approach to craft is greater than self-expression for a special interest group or individual. This is an approach to craft that resonates with the times, one that links craft practice to many wider concerns of making in the twenty-first century. This is craft that embraces many social currents: think global/act local, feminism, gender politics, social justice, and ecological concerns. Sloppy craft and postdisciplinary craft are both tied to the aesthetic goals of the individual maker. In contrast, craftivism is group-driven and more akin to politics. It has the potential to become a craft movement that is democratic and grassroots-driven.

Focus on the democratic nature of group crafting rather than on the artistic ego of a singular, individual craftsperson recalls the Japanese ideals of Wabi Sabi, which preaches humility and observance of nature. The Wabi Sabi approach to ceramics, popularized by Soestu Yanagi (1889–1961) and Bernard Leach (1887–1979), could be summarized as the "perfection of the imperfect."[31] Humility was evident in the selfless approach, or anonymity, of the maker—highlighted by the title of Yanagi's book, *The Unknown Craftsman*, first published in English in 1972. Writing about Yanagi and *mingei*, or Japanese folk craft, Larry Shiner defines its Buddhist aesthetics as "non-dualism in life and art and the beauty of irregularity, simplicity, and humility [or] natural material, natural processes, and an accepting heart." Shiner also observes that "Yanagi was never enthusiastic about the artist-craftsperson, whom he saw as pursuing an individualistic aesthetic rather than resting 'in the protecting hand of nature' like the folk-craftsperson."[32]

It is perhaps ironic that this "perfection of the imperfect" fed into the abstract expressionist tendency of many artist-craftspeople. In his essay *The Fate of Craft*, Shiner notes that by the 1960s, the larger craft community in the United States was divided into the craft-as-art party and the pro-craft party, or the more traditional segment of the larger craft community. He traces the craft-as-art party's roots to the post-Second World War influx of craftspeople into university art programs. There, craftspeople studied alongside fine art students where "they absorbed the excitement of the new art movements."[33] Arguably, the craft-as-art party are those craftspeople most inclined to adopt a postdisciplinary practice, while the pro-craft party are those who choose instead to pursue a material-based practice.

But what of the craftivists and those who practice sloppy craft? It seems that behind every yarn- or basket-bombing crowd of amateurs and volunteers there is a textile or fiber artist as organizer and agent provocateur like Sue Sturdy or Sharon Kallis—in other words, a trained professional with a university degree. I think that the larger craft community has grown a third party to add to the craft-as-art party and the pro-craft party. This is a party of socially engaged public members who are interested in being more than a passive audience or a collecting public. In many ways, postdisciplinary and sloppy craft is heir to the spiritual and utopian or moral dimensions of both Ruskin's and Morris's visions for craft. This is seen in the recycling and upcycling of the postdisciplinarians and in the social values of the craftivists. These craft movements have broken down the often rural walls of the studio craft movement. Craft is no longer confined to the rural closet. Finally, we have a craft movement that the general, largely urban, public can care about.

Notes

1   The NeoCraft conference proceedings are amply documented in an excellent book, *NeoCraft Modernity and the Crafts*, Sandra Alfoldy (ed.) (Halifax: Press of the Nova Scotia College of Art and Design, 2007).

2   See Textile Museum of Canada website, http://www.textilemuseum.ca/about/, and the Gardiner Museum, http://www.gardinermuseum.on.ca/ (both accessed July 26, 2014).

3   Larry Shiner, "Craft," *The Encyclopedia of Aesthetics*, Vol. 1 (Oxford: Oxford University Press, 1998), pp. 450–3.

4   Gareth Williams, "Tales of the Unexpected," *Crafts* 219 (July/August 2009): 50.

5   See Nova Scotia College of Art and Design University's webpage on academic programs, http://nscad.ca/en/home/academicprograms/undergraduate/default.aspx (accessed July 26, 2014).

6   E-mail correspondence with Sandra Alfoldy, August 14, 2012. Thanks to Debra Campbell, Registrar, for confirming the start-up date of the IDS degree.

7   See NSCADU's webpage "Expansion and Growth in the New Century," http://nscad.ca/en/home/abouttheuniversity/past-present/21st-century.aspx (accessed July 26, 2014).

8   Glenn Adamson, *Thinking Through Craft* (London: Berg, 2007).

9   At 83.3 percent according to a 2007 Newfoundland and Labrador Stats Report.

      The Holley quotes and these statistics come from research material gathered and first used in my "No Holds Barred Creativity, Post-Disciplinary Craft in the Small Community," *Studio Craft and Design in Canada* (Fall/Winter 2011–12): 26–9.

10   Liesbeth den Besten, "Deskilled Craft and Borrowed Skill," *Think Tank, a European Initiative for the Applied Arts 5 (SKILL)* (2008), http://www.thinktank04.eu/image/papers/2008_LiesbethdenBesten.pdf (accessed July 26, 2014).

11   Jen Anisef, *Tracing Emerging Modes of Practice: Craft Sector Review* (Toronto: Ontario Arts Council, 2010), p. 5, http://www.arts.on.ca/AssetFactory.aspx?did=7095 (accessed July 26, 2014). Thanks to Denis Longchamps for first bringing this report to my attention.

12   In my own research, when I Googled "Knitting on-line group," I encountered 6,490,000 results in 0.31 seconds.

13   See https://www.ravelry.com/about as well as http://en.wikipedia.org/wiki/Ravelry (accessed July 26, 2014).

14   Sal Humphreys, "The Economies Within an Online Social Network Market: A Case Study of Ravelry," Conference proceedings, Australian and New Zealand Communication Association 09 annual conference: Communication, Creativity and Global Citizenship, Queensland University of Technology, Brisbane, July 8–10, 2009.

15   Gillian Reagan, "Web Site for Knitting Nuts Has New York Needlers in Stitches," http://observer.com/2009/02/web-site-for-knitting-nuts-has-new-york-needlers-in-stitches/ (accessed July 26, 2014).

16   Gareth Williams, *Telling Tales: Fantasy and Fear in Contemporary Design* (London: V&A, 2009). Published to coincide with exhibition of the same name at the V&A Museum, July 14–October 18, 2009.

17   Editorial (no writer specified), *Crafts* 20 (July/August 2009).

18   Pacific Northwest College of Art (PCNA) News, Portland, Oregon, October 10, 2009, http://pnca.edu/news/4090 (accessed July 26, 2014). See also www.portlandart.net/archives/2009/10/lots_of_lecture.html (accessed July 26, 2014).

19   These examples are drawn from the following sources: Denis Longchamps used Francois Houdé's Ming Series in his Universities Art Association of Canada 2012 presentation; the Philadelphia Art Alliance show, The Sitting Room, September 24, 2010 to January 3, 2011, used Jennifer Angus in the context of postdisciplinary and sloppy craft; while I have discussed Ryan's work and her Nativity in particular in my blog: http://gloriahickeycraftwriter.blogspot.ca/2011/12/modern-nativity-by-rachel-ryan.html (accessed July 26, 2014).

20   Waking Dreams was a solo show of Rachel Ryan's multimedia work at The Craft Gallery in St. John's, NL, September 17–October 30, 2011.

21   Some writers claim that craft has conquered the art world by rejecting the constraints of function, tradition, and the vernacular. Gareth Williams cites Grayson Perry as an example of this triumph, pointing out that the potter won the UK's coveted Turner Prize in 2003. See *Crafts* (July/August 2009): 51.

22   Bruce Metcalf, "Replacing the Myth of Modernism," *NeoCraft* (Halifax: NSCAD Press, 2007), p. 20.

23   Ibid., pp. 6–7.

24   Gloria Hickey, "Craft in a Consuming Society," in Peter Dormer (ed.), *The Culture of Craft* (Manchester: Manchester University Press, 1997).

25   For a good discussion of the role of professionalism in contemporary Canadian craft, see Sandra Alfoldy's *Crafting Identity, The Development of Professional Fine Craft in Canada* (Montreal: McGill-Queen's University Press, 2005).

26   Anisef, *Tracing Emerging Modes of Practice*, p. 10.

27   *Studio magazine* (Fall/Winter 2011–12): 29.

28   Ray Martins, "That's a wrap," *Cambridge Times*, September 8, 2010, http://www.cambridgetimes.ca/news/local/article/871111--that-s-a-wrap (accessed July 26, 2014).

29   Her recent collaborative projects are described on the Brandford Elliot Awards webpage, http://brandford-elliott-award.com/BEA_SharonKallis.html (accessed July 26, 2014).

30   For more on Kallis's work in the context of Canadian identity, see my "Gentle Giant," *Surface Design Journal* (Fall 2011): 11.

31 Soetsu Yanagi, *The Unknown Craftsman: A Japanese Insight into Beauty* (Tokyo and New York: Kodansha International, 1989), http://en.wikipedia. org/wiki/Yanagi_S%C5%8Detsu (accessed July 26, 2014).

32 Alfoldy (ed.), *NeoCraft Modernity and the Crafts*, p. 36.

33 Ibid, p. 37.

7

From Maria Martinez to Kent Monkman: Performing sloppy craft in Native America

Elizabeth Kalbfleisch

When the editors of this book inquired if I might be interested in contributing to the discussion on sloppy craft from my perspective as a scholar of Canadian Aboriginal and Native American art, I leapt at the opportunity.[1] On the face of it, through my contribution, I might advance a defense of highly skilled, tribally specific Aboriginal art practices while providing a cautionary finger-wagging at the rather breathless enthusiasm for this new aesthetic practised by a handful of white, urban artists. Except this was not the chapter I wished to write. Sloppy craft, the neologism attributed to artist Anne Wilson by the esteemed contemporary craft scholar Glenn Adamson, describes a range of postdisciplinary, often textile-based, practices in which refinement and studied tradition is exchanged for an unkempt and often kitschy embrace of amateurism.[2] Though the term has not yet been used in this context, certain contemporary Aboriginal art practices can in fact be usefully theorized as sloppy craft, chief among them the theatrical performance props of current art world star, Swampy Cree multimedia artist Kent Monkman (b. 1965).

Thus my chapter has two objectives: the first, to situate sloppy craft within the context of contemporary North American Aboriginal art by focusing on the relationship between postdisciplinary craft and performance in Monkman's work; the second, to contextualize the relationship between craft and performance through a brief examination of the history of Aboriginal craft demonstrators, thus testing the limits—and potential— of the still-emerging discourse around sloppy craft. For the latter goal, I will focus on the work of two twentieth-century Aboriginal artists—one major and one minor—Maria Martinez, celebrated Pueblo potter, and Anna Panadis, a lesser-known Abenaki basket weaver.

These two avenues of discussion are inspired by a recent essay by Valerie Cassel Oliver in which the author helpfully correlates craft and performance. She likens the rapid growth of sloppy craft as a postdisciplinary practice to a similar trajectory in the development of performance art in the 1960s and 1970s. She also compares public demonstrations given by craft practitioners to instances of performance art.[3] The latter is a point I will return to later; with respect to the former point, artists unmoored themselves from the constraints of the New York art establishment during this period. Through performance, artists narrowed the gap between the practice of art and the everyday, and between artist and spectator; by means of these innovations, artists rethought how and where art could be experienced. Cassel Oliver's analogy suitably describes the current postdisciplinary state of craft, where the boundaries of craft and art, popular and elite are becoming obscured, if not outright imploding. As Adamson describes it, postdisciplinarity is "not a border-crossing between discrete fields, but rather a situation in which such borders no longer really exist."[4]

More broadly, the level playing field of postdisciplinary art to which Adamson alludes equally reflects current Aboriginal artistic activity. Many of the most exciting Aboriginal artists working today in North America maintain postdisciplinary practices. Monkman, Rebecca Belmore, Shelley Niro, and Maria Hupfield, among many others, work in and move liberally between installation, performance, mixed media, and new media forms. Exploring—and achieving recognition within—multiple platforms is increasingly expected of contemporary artists, with Aboriginal artists being no exception. Yet within this large, often amorphous body of work, the artists cited above produce components or entire works, the roots of which reference a craft tradition. *True Grit, A Souvenir* (1989), an early work by Belmore (Anishnaabe), is a self-portrait of the artist depicted on an oversized stuffed cushion stitched from several different chintz fabrics and finished with gold fringe. It alludes to issues surrounding women's handicraft, cultural commodification and Aboriginal self-representation. The narrative of Niro's (Mohawk) video, *Honey Moccasin* (1998), culminates in a fashion show of clothing made to replace stolen powwow regalia. These new articles of clothing represent a DIY aesthetic, with Fruit Loops cereal and lollipops standing in for the more traditional and predictable beads and feathers, and were exhibited alongside the video in the Canadian Museum of Civilization exhibition *Reservation X* (1998). More recently, Hupfield (Anishnaabe) has produced some handcrafted sculptural objects, such as *Travel Bag* (2013). The bag, hand-sewn from industrial grey felt and filled with felt reproductions of various personal technological devices, references Joseph Beuys, Anishnaabe bandolier bags, and handicraft endeavors.

Monkman easily fits within this cohort of artists with diverse practices. He is best known as a studio painter, having first received widespread recognition in the early 2000s for his large canvases that rework familiar images of art history to address Aboriginal representation, queer sexualities, and cross-cultural encounters in the colonial landscape. Yet the artist's practice of art historical redress extends to multiple media, notably film, installation, and performance, genres that Monkman frequently explores. Working across genres, too, is Monkman's alter ego, Miss Chief Eagle Testickle, a globe-trotting time-travelling transvestite beloved by fans of the artist's work. Miss Chief appears in Monkman's paintings, films, and performances and has inspired installations. Her glamorous costumes and accessories are integral to her character, which drives Monkman's interventionist artworks.[5] The ultra-feminine, campy hybrids of luxury consumer goods, pan-Indian finery, and DIY handicraft donned by Miss Chief are highly suggestive of a sloppy craft aesthetic. Understanding the significance of these objects obliges an exploration of both the postdisciplinary landscape of contemporary art and craft as well as the particular history of handicraft (and performance) in the intercultural relationships between Aboriginal and settler peoples.

Art historian Todd Porterfield describes Monkman's red vinyl high-heeled boots, *Cree Leggings* (2011), laid out in a glass vitrine as part of the exhibition, *Kent Monkman: My Treaty is with the Crown* (2011), as relics.[6] The exhibition, held at Concordia University's Leonard & Bina Ellen Art Gallery in Montreal in 2011, included many references to colonial history and material culture, especially with the inclusion of multiple nineteenth- and early twentieth-century objects borrowed by the artist from the collections of the McCord Museum of Canadian History and the Montreal Museum of Fine Arts.[7] As seen through Porterfield's lens, the boots assume an historical aura and invite slippage between the fraught categories of "traditional" and "contemporary," and "Aboriginal" and "settler," as well as complicating visitors' expectations for viewing collected examples of Aboriginal dress. Described as relics, the over-the-knee boots, embellished down the back length with a strip of beadwork and small tufts of hair, could also be seen as relics—in the sense of remnants—of past performances in which they were worn by the artist as Miss Chief. However, positioning Monkman's performance props as relics alone falls short of articulating their full value as autonomous, contemporary artworks, and specifically, crafted objects.

While it is not unusual to display props along with other performance ephemera in order to reconstruct a performance, Monkman's performance props have become art objects in their own right. They have been presented, for example, in several recent thematic exhibitions, including *Shapeshifters, Time Travellers and Storytellers*, a groundbreaking exhibition of contemporary Aboriginal art at the Royal Ontario Museum in 2007 (see Plate 16); *Fashionality: Dress and Identity in Canadian Art* at the McMichael Canadian Art Collection in 2012; and *Changing Hands 3: Art Without Reservation* at New York's Museum of Arts and Design, also 2012.[8]

Perhaps the most famous of these objects is *Louis Vuitton Quiver* (2007), worn by Miss Chief in several performances and videos (see Plate 17). Monkman has also represented versions of the quiver in his paintings of Miss Chief: *Study for Artist and Model* (2003) features a similar quiver, slung casually against Miss Chief's easel as she paints a young, nude cowboy pierced by her arrows and trussed to a tree. Later paintings, like *The Good Samaritan* (2010) and *Two Spirits* (2011), include a Louis Vuitton "LV" patterned handbag, stuffed with colored feathers among Miss Chief's effects. In *Charged Particles in Motion* (2007), the artist depicts Miss Chief commanding a dog sled, patterned with the same "LV" motif, with two matching cases stuffed within. While some articles in these paintings can be viewed as prototypes for further objects yet to be materialized in sculptural form, the use of repetition serves to further identify these specific "hacked" and hybrid objects not only with Monkman's performance character, Miss Chief, but with the greater objectives of Monkman's practice.

By means of this ubiquity, *Louis Vuitton Quiver* has become an emblem of Monkman's practice and, importantly, a signifier of the cultural mash-ups the artist presents. Like the Plains animal skin back quiver (and staple of stereotypical Cowboys and Indians warplay) from which it takes inspiration, *Louis Vuitton Quiver* is crafted from leather. Here, emblazoned with candy-colored renditions of the ubiquitous designer logo, the quiver complements Miss Chief's glamorous persona. The quiver's function also complements this persona when Miss Chief arrives on horseback in pursuit of "European males" in the 2005 performance *Taxonomy of the European Male* and related film *Robin's Hood* (2007), in which she engages in a bow-and-arrow shooting contest with literary and folk characters Robin Hood and Friar Tuck.

Although the context of specific performances animates the object, the object nonetheless maintains its meaning as described above, indeed sees it enhanced, when it is put on view. The nature of its display at the Royal Ontario Museum provides another turn on the notion of a status-building, coveted consumer object as one out of reach to most. While the public viewed *Louis Vuitton Quiver* as part of an exhibition of contemporary art, this museum more habitually dedicates its public galleries to more traditional material culture, ethnology, and natural sciences. In that setting, the museum object finds itself divorced from its original cultural context, and with it, its original function eradicated: the (museum) quiver is now to be observed and revered, but no longer used.

Adornment conveys social codes. When performances rely on dress to the extent that Monkman's do, adornment provides a platform through which identity can be negotiated, indeed performed, in the public sphere.[9] *Louis Vuitton Quiver* enforces the hybridity produced by intercultural encounter that Monkman implies broadly in his work by drawing on both Aboriginal and European aesthetics. Moreover, as Monkman himself has expressed, *Louis Vuitton Quiver* evokes not just the hierarchies of wealth in today's globalized consumer culture, but those established through trade networks between settler and Aboriginal people in the colonial era.[10] The fact that the "LV" Louis Vuitton logo Monkman presents is often copied and associated with counterfeit designer goods further alludes to the history of appropriation of Aboriginal culture by the dominant population, a theme explored extensively by Aboriginal artists over the past three decades and which for many remains emblematic of North America's intercultural and colonial history.

Appropriation, representation, and history (and specifically art history) loom large as overarching themes in the artist's practice. As one art historian summarizes, "Above all, Monkman's works are chronicles of negotiation—with history, with power, with race, with desire, with self-hood ..."[11] Framing the artist's explorations of these themes as negotiations is highly apposite, given the benchmarks of this discussion on sloppy craft. Monkman's engagement with sloppy craft stands as one further example of negotiation, inviting questions over what negotiations the artist takes on by delving into the milieu of crafted objects. Artists who incorporate sloppy craft into their practice often do so with an intent that extends beyond its "sloppy" aesthetic; rather, engaging in sloppy craft for its refusal of the boundaries of studio craft and "high" contemporary art. As sloppy craft exists in a kind of liminal space relative to craft and art discretely defined, Monkman's production and use of performance props as sloppy craft objects portends an appropriation *and* negotiation of those germane fields of craft and art. While the schematic separation of art and craft has been contentious for artists overall, such divisions have historically been further problematic for Aboriginal artists who struggled to have their art accepted, valued, and displayed as contemporary art rather than ethnological specimen, the latter more typically aligned with craft.

Other Aboriginal artists create works that, in kind with those made by Monkman, challenge the limits of traditional craft practice and cultural expression. Like Monkman, both Lisa Telford and Jaime Okuma craft shoes; however, their work hardly represents a deskilled or sloppy craft aesthetic. Telford's *High Heels* (2007), a pair of ladies' pumps deftly woven from red and yellow cedar bark fibers, reflects her mastery of Haida basketry and her commitment to the continuity of this culturally specific textile art.[12] And while Miss Chief would doubtless love to wear the beaded Christian Louboutin open-toe booties, *Adaptation* (2011), made by Okuma, as craft objects, they differ categorically from the bead-embellished footwear that Miss Chief habitually dons. Okuma, an artist of Luiseño and Shoshone-Bannock heritage, has beaded since early childhood; she studies clothing and beadwork in historical photographs of Aboriginal people, drawing especially from the color and forms of Blackfoot regalia for her beaded dolls and more recently, flamboyant footwear.[13] The red-soled designer shoes that Okuma beads over evince a similar-statused desirability as, for example, a Louis Vuitton leather handbag. However, the nature of the

artist's intervention with the source object differs from Monkman's interventions. Further, the obvious skill Okuma brings to her beading differs
from the DIY workmanship which codes Monkman's use of (readymade)
commercial products and handicraft materials. The strips of machine
loomed beadwork with which Monkman adorns the heel, sole, and vamp
of *Beaded Moccasins* (2007), a pair of strappy red platform sandals, as well
as their intended use in performance, position his work amidst a different
order of cultural and material references (see Plate 18).

As practices of art diversify and greater slippages between fields and
disciplines occur, the concept of deskilling comes into play. Artists luxuriate
in the freedom to "call themselves whatever they wish" or, more pointedly,
practice freely what forms of art they choose.[14] Craft practitioners may
still find themselves excluded from this fluidity, dependent still on their
training and material practice. Relative to mainstream art, sloppy craft
is usually understood as a "calculated sloppiness," where artists without
specific training gamely take up home crafts.[15] Yet as critics have pointed
out, this represents more than a devolution of skill. Indeed, often these
artists are technically skilled but rather than showcase it, choose to privilege
the affective dimensions of home craft. Sloppy craft pays homage to the
benchmark feminist works of Miriam Shapiro and Judy Chicago, as well
as to Mike Kelley, whose installations evoked a kitschy amateurism and
inspired the moniker of low or abject art.[16]

While the nature of the finished footwear differs, Telford and Okuma
share with Monkman an interest in the intercultural history and traffic
in Aboriginal handicraft. Though she is highly knowledgeable of finely
woven Haida cedar clothing, Telford also drew inspiration from nineteenth-
century basketry shoes in the collection of the Burke Museum of Natural
History and Culture which were made as curios for the era's active tourist
trade.[17] Okuma's beaded booties implicitly reference the popularity of
Aboriginal novelty beadwork amongst Victorian settlers as well as the
spectrum of objects, workmanship, and attendant value attributed to the
practice of Aboriginal beadwork writ large, a spectrum comprising minor
trinkets for the tourist trade and more substantial items made for cultural
use. In a more general manner, Monkman also references the history of
Aboriginal intercultural handicraft through his performance props by
means of allusions to less skilled crafted components and a non-Aboriginal
market for inexpensive facsimiles of Aboriginal material culture. Of all the
works discussed here, *Dream Catcher Bra* (2007) brings this notion into
sharpest focus.

Monkman's *Dream Catcher Bra* also belongs to Miss Chief's arsenal of
costume-props, yet as a craft object it signifies in a different way to that
of the *Louis Vuitton Quiver*. *Dream Catcher Bra* comprises two bead and
feather-trimmed dream catchers, linked together and featuring sinew ties so
as to be fixed around the wearer's back in the manner of a string-bikini top.
Like the quiver, part of the object's charm is its juxtaposition of cultural

signifiers. Yet in a more pointed way, *Dream Catcher Bra* highlights the concurrence of high and low as it plays out in a particular contact zone between settler and Aboriginal cultures. The dream catcher may indeed have Ojibway roots. Early twentieth-century American ethnographer Frances Densmore describes the protective amulet hung over a baby's cradleboard and consisting of a small hoop, strung with twine or wool to resemble a spider's web so as to "catch everything evil as a spider's web catches and holds everything that comes in contact with it."[18] Capitalizing on this innocuous, feel-good message, the dream catcher, often embellished with dangling feathers and beads as seen in Monkman's version, emerged as a pan-Indian saleable handicraft in the 1960s and 1970s. Produced by Aboriginal and non-Aboriginal people alike, it has remained popular ever since with tourists, New-Agers, and "Indian enthusiasts." If the dream catcher holds any significance today it is as an example of the appropriation and commodification of Aboriginal culture, distilled to a most vapid state.

In crafting *Dream Catcher Bra*, *Louis Vuitton Quiver*, and indeed *Racoon Jock Strap* (2007)—a male undergarment fashioned from a reclaimed racoon pelt trapper hat—Monkman implements a postdisciplinary strategy of, as Johanna Drucker would call it, affectivity and entropy. By means of his affective gesture, the artist lends new meaning to existing mass produced goods, injecting them with some "human" life and rendering them active. "Affectivity," she writes, "takes what looked like matter already formed and uses it as simple matter to give rise to another level of organization and structure."[19] By contrast, in a tandem gesture of "entropy," the artist wrests source objects (a handbag, a souvenir ornament, and a fur hat) from their habitual context of production and circulation, negating their "usefulness" so they can no longer be consumed in that state.[20] They are repurposed as merely material, in this case as leather, hoops, and fur.

In fashioning *Dream Catcher Bra*, Monkman reappropriates the dream catcher from its dubious cultural purgatory, repurposing and redefining it. Made by Monkman and worn by Miss Chief, Aboriginal objecthood is *returned* to the dream catcher. While the artist's repurposing evokes today's post-Indian cultural mash-up, it does so by acknowledging the roots of this object as a cheap and fairly disposable handicraft.[21] Thus in referencing a spectrum of personal adornment that includes the contemporary and the traditional, the knock-off and the "authentic"—the proverbial "fluffs and feathers" (as Iroquois curator Debora Doxtator called this juxtaposition)[22]—Monkman gestures at the presence of this very spectrum in the history of Aboriginal art and craft. In addition to referencing cultural appropriations of indigeneity by settlers, his "deskilled" objects evoke Indian handicrafts—inexpensive souvenir-style items made not for Aboriginal use but for sale to settlers—and the historical place of these handicrafts in the intercultural sphere.[23]

Cassel Oliver, in the essay I referred to at the outset, highlights the "anti-establishment" origins shared by sloppy craft and performance art. She brings to light a second commonality by invoking craft demonstrations, whereby practitioners share their skills and techniques with other artists and the general public at regional festivals and World's Fairs—live events used to market specific craft objects but also to keep viable and disseminate the forms themselves. Necessary though this may be, these demonstrations often reinforce stereotypes around practitioners and their crafts as consumables. Cassel Oliver poses the question, "What if we step away from the concept of craft practice as demonstrative and into the dimension of craft practice as performance art, in which process is viewed as spectacle and workshops and collaborations function as participatory events in which the object is not just created but also used as an expressive element within a performance?"[24]

Cassel Oliver's analogy is particularly compelling when considered in an Aboriginal context. The alignment of craft with performance suggests a relationship in Monkman's work that has heretofore remained unaddressed by scholars, just as it evokes an important aspect of the intercultural history between Aboriginal artists and settlers. Monkman does not make his props during performances, as Cassel Oliver suggests of craft practitioners when making her analogy, and as do other contemporary artists seeking to unite craft and performance.[25] However, his performances reanimate them and moreover draw attention to the history of Aboriginal handicrafts I have already alluded to by means of the history of Aboriginal craft demonstrations. Craft demonstrators comprise but one aspect of the long history of Indian performances mounted for enthusiastic settler and European audiences. Scholars now liken nineteenth-century performers with troupes like Buffalo Bill's Wild West as the forerunners of today's Aboriginal performance artists.[26] However, the more performative aspects of Aboriginal craft demonstrations have not been examined in this light.

No doubt the most notorious Aboriginal artist to develop a profile as a craft demonstrator is San Ildefonso potter Maria Martinez (c. 1887–1980). Martinez reached theretofore unparalleled acclamation in the early decades of the twentieth century for her revival and refinement of Pueblo blackware pottery and, more broadly, for revitalizing San Ildefonso's pottery industry. The pottery she made collaboratively with her husband Julian elevated Pueblo pottery from curios collected by anthropologists and tourists to statused Modernist objects, proudly displayed in the homes of America's elite collectors.

Martinez is also famous for the persona of the artist, or more accurately, the image of the artist associated with the work. This notoriety is at odds with the Pueblo people's decidedly unindividualistic approach to pottery production, where the community of origin (such as San Ildefonso) is considered a more appropriate identifier of a specific work than is the individual artist responsible (such as Martinez). The large volume of photographs of Martinez making and carrying pots remains part of a public visual record, tying the art inextricably to the artist. These images aestheticize, domesticate, commodify, and feminize Pueblo culture and, in the words of scholar Barbara Babcock, position the artist as an *olla maiden*, the Spanish term for the clay vessels she produced.[27] Martinez herself commented on the public's interest in observing her in the act of making pottery and of photographing her doing so:

> And I would say, some Indian ladies they don't like [non-Indian] visitors, and they don't like anyone watching them making pottery. But me, I don't care. Summertime they find me outside making [pottery] ... I let them see, and if they want they can take picture. After what I think ... Big buses come, school buses. I go out and shake hands. Young kids, if they want to take picture, "Oh let them take." I don't mind.[28]

Martinez did not object to being photographed in association with her work, even at home, as it satisfied a public appetite for a living artist, an "authentic (Indian) maker" animating the work. As scholars have pointed out, Martinez recognized the economic benefits attention on her brought to her community.[29]

Despite the preponderance of still photography, however, Martinez's representation of her artistry was not static. She demonstrated pottery production in several documentary films, the camera following her as she methodically animated each stage of the process.[30] Moreover, Martinez's reputation grew as she performed pottery making at every World's Fair from 1904 until the Second World War, with appearances at St. Louis, San Diego, Chicago, and San Francisco. Scholars often cite that a mere six hours after her marriage to Julian, the couple set off for St. Louis.[31] They were invited to the 1904 World's Fair to demonstrate dance; however, Martinez found herself crafting "little pots" for onlookers, thus marking this event as the first public occasion she performed pottery making.[32] She and Julian also famously lived at the New Mexico Museum from 1909 to 1912, where, from 1911 onwards, they demonstrated their craft for visitors in the museum's courtyard.[33] Arguably, the emphasis on the stages of pottery production detailed in the films and live performances have the effect of demystifying the process of craft production, just as the relationship between Aboriginal artist and settler spectator reiterates those fantasies of *Indianness* highlighted above, fantasies that accompanied the public spectacles of the previous century's performing Indians. Nevertheless, as scholars have argued with regard to those earlier performers, Martinez maintained, indeed cultivated, agency as an artist, a craftsperson, and a Pueblo person via these craft-based performances.

While many forms of craft are associated with the private sphere, American scholar and curator Namita Gupta Wiggers makes the point that craft has always existed in a range of locations, both private and public. Wiggers notes that in recent decades, art practices have moved "out of the white cube" and into the street, the art fair, and the home.[34] In this respect,

FIGURE 7.1 *Jesse Nusbaum (photographer), Maria Martinez demonstrating pottery making in the patio of the Palace of the Governors, Santa Fe, 1912. Courtesy of the Palace of the Governors Photo Archives (NMHM/DCA), Negative #61764.*

art and art discourse has something to learn from craft, as these spaces speak to the practice and dissemination of craft. Martinez's craft performances took place in public settings: in the museum yard, at fairgrounds, and outside her home on the San Ildefonso Pueblo. The attention paid to Martinez as a public performer supports the view that these performance activities played a large role in her ascent as a successful and well-respected artist (and not just a marketable one). While Martinez achieved exceptional notoriety, meeting several US presidents and visiting the White House, countless other Aboriginal artists toiled in obscurity, participating in demonstrations as much about promoting and selling their craft as about performing *Indianness* for settler spectators. In 1948 and 1949, for example, the Canadian Handicraft Guild contracted Anna Panadis, an Abenaki basket weaver from Odanak, Quebec, to work as a crafts demonstrator at the Canadian National Exhibition (CNE) in Toronto.[35] The Guild had a special interest in the preservation of Aboriginal craftwork, expressing concern that "the remaining Indian handicrafts of the country are in such danger of dying out."[36] To encourage the practice and sale of traditional crafts and to educate the Canadian public, the Guild staffed its CNE booth with Aboriginal demonstrators.

To secure Panadis's participation, the Guild worked with the Handicraft Section of the Welfare Service, part of the Canadian government's Department of Indian Affairs. The Department spearheaded handicraft programs on reserves across Canada as economic stimulus, including a basketry program at Odanak, Panadis's central Quebec reserve. These government-run handicraft programs maintained a rather more pragmatic focus with regard to Aboriginal handicraft than did the Canadian Handicraft Guild. Panadis agreed to the Guild's terms for the 1948 CNE: eight days' work over ten days at $10 a day, plus train fare. This amounted to more than 64-year-old Panadis earned at Odanak making baskets to sell through the on-reserve program. However, once her expenses were deducted, she took home considerably less. Somewhat disillusioned, she wrote to Kathleen Moodie, the head of the government handicraft program, with whom she shared a friendly rapport:

> If I had known all the details about this trip to Toronto before they put out advertisements on the basket demonstration I probably would have preferred to stay home and make ... baskets quietly but my word is given and I never back out on anything no matter how little money will [remain] on my wages after all is over. I will stick to my promise in the old Indian way ... And who knows, this demonstration will probably give us a chance to have more orders for the shop—and the workers.[37]

For Panadis, the utmost objective of the demonstration remained the sale of craft, whether via the Guild at the CNE or through her regular activities at

FIGURE 7.2 *Alfred Irving Hallowell (photographer), Anna Panadis, Odanak, Quebec. Courtesy of the American Philosophical Society, Alfred Irving Hallowell Papers, Mss.Ms.Coll 26, F259.*

Odanak. As with Martinez, she was concerned for the economic well-being of fellow artists in her community.

At the CNE, Panadis worked with sweetgrass, a material rarely used for the baskets she made as part of the government initiative. Its high cost and limited availability made sweetgrass a less practical choice for these projects which depended on steady customer orders and affordable finished handicrafts. At this time, large "Jardinières" were especially sought after, as were sewing or knitting baskets in garish shades of pink, pale blue, yellow, and mauve. Once back in Odanak, Panadis was hoping to complete an order of four dozen Jardinières each week for five weeks. That non-organic pastel color scheme held little appeal for the Guild. Active Guild members, in particular Alice Lighthall, who chaired the Indian and Eskimo Committee, disagreed with the privileging-of-sales-over-cultural-integrity directive maintained by the Indian Welfare programs.[38] Lighthall expressed this view on multiple occasions, including in a 1951 letter to H. M. Jones, then superintendent of the Welfare Service responsible for the handicraft programs:

> The Canadian Handicrafts Guild is especially interested in preserving the traditional native craft-work of the different tribes. We, therefore, would strongly urge that any effort being made by the Department for these Indians should promote their own individual hand-work rather than introduce stereotyped patterns and mass-production methods. There is no surer way of killing the charesteric [sic] art-sense of a people that [sic] to vitiate their efforts by alien teaching. Nor is there any quicker way to kill the market for good Indian work, that [sic] to flood it with inferior products. Such things as (1) machine sewing (2) the use of bought leathers (3) foreign basketry materials (Chinese cord, etc) lower the value of Indian craft-work.[39]

Lighthall emphasized in Panadis's case that at the CNE she work exclusively with "Indian materials."[40] The sweetgrass basket contrasts with the colored one woven with cheap and durable imported Chinese cord, a material which in name and appearance signaled cultural incongruity to the tradition-centric Guild members and their patrons. Lighthall's strong preference for the most "traditional" of materials and styles was all the more pronounced within the performance context of the CNE. By this action, the identity of the artist colludes with the crafted object to produce an "authentic" experience for the spectator. As Leah Dilworth describes the context of artists in the American Southwest, "As represented in the spectacle, the Indian artisan produced not only collectible objects but also authenticity, which was located in the primitiveness of Indian hand labor."[41]

Panadis's performance of "Indianness" began before she sat down with her sweetgrass at the CNE grounds. As instructed beforehand, Panadis pinned a seven-inch strip of pale green, bright yellow, and red beadwork to her clothing as she disembarked the train so that the local Guild

representative assigned to escort her would recognize her. Not only does
the beadwork place the onus of identification on Panadis rather than on
her "host," but it does so in a highly culturally scripted manner, whereby
Panadis is identified through this crafted tag as *Indian*. The Canadian
Handicrafts Guild made use of this same strategy of identification to more
extensively situate the artist in relation to a recognizable Indian identity
by pressing for more information with regard to her Abenaki name and
lineage. Through Moodie, the intermediary, they asked that Panadis "find
a good [Indian name] if you have not already got one."[42] Panadis disclosed
that her father was a hereditary Grand Chief and that her Abenaki name
translates as Straight Arrow: "When I was young, I was so straight that my
father called me by that name so I just adopted it. Now that I am getting
old and my shoulders and back start to stoop, I have to keep reminding
myself to walk straight as much as I can, or else my name will change to
crooked-arrow."[43] Moodie further embellished this narrative, reporting to
the Guild that "[Anna's] forefathers are 'The Abenakis of St. Francois du
Lac', who fled from the attack of Rogers' Rangers 'leaving behind them
their sweetgrass carrying baskets and all their goods'."[44] With that, sweetgrass, her more traditional medium, is assimilated into Panadis's personal
and cultural narrative, as well as a broader Canadian historical narrative.[45]
Her labor is assimilated along with this account; even in the downtown
Toronto fairground, this suggests a kind of cultural return.

Clearly Martinez and Panadis did not enjoy the same postdisciplinary
privilege of Monkman and his contemporaries to move freely within a field
of cultural production uninhibited by borders and labels. My intention is not
to reclassify the objects of their production, collectively or individually, as
sloppy craft. However, connecting the refined and valuable blackware pots
crafted by Martinez to Panadis's "make-work" Indian handicrafts through
their shared history as crafts demonstrators underscores the performative
tenor to Aboriginal crafts in the intercultural sphere. Moreover, it histori-
cizes the performance context of contemporary sloppy craft as practiced
by Monkman, as this sphere is still one in which the artist works, albeit
decades later. Monkman has been described as shrewdly appropriating
forms of contemporary media "as effective weapons of empowerment and
force" to intervene in a colonial narrative.[46] Unlike those earlier artists,
Monkman obscures the crafting of the object as a barometer of (Indian)
artistic accomplishment and identity by not including the practice of
making as part of his performances. Rather, it is by means of his skilled
performances that his reputation as an artist is honed, with the crafted
objects serving as aide-mémoires to an artistic and performative past as
experienced by predecessors like Martinez and Panadis. Monkman injects
a new political dimension to contemporary sloppy craft as an Aboriginal
and intercultural form of expression, and one in the vanguard of postdisciplinary craft.

Notes

1   The term "Aboriginal" usually refers collectively to the indigenous peoples of Canada, and includes First Nations, Inuit, and Métis. It is not frequently used in the United States, where "Native American" still predominates as an equivalent term. For the sake of brevity, I use "Aboriginal" throughout, even when making reference to indigenous peoples throughout North America. The term "Indian" is rarely used today by settler scholars; I use it here when it is historically relevant or when referring to a settler-driven stereotype. The term "settler" is employed interchangeably with "non-Aboriginal."

2   Glenn Adamson (ed.), *The Craft Reader* (London: Berg, 2010), p. 586. See also his first book on craft theory, *Thinking Through Craft* (London: Berg, 2007).

3   Valerie Cassel Oliver, "Craft Out of Action," in Valerie Cassel Oliver (ed.), *Hand + Made: the Performative Impulse in Art and Craft* (Houston: Contemporary Arts Museum, 2010).

4   Adamson, *The Craft Reader*, p. 586.

5   While this chapter does not allow me to describe at length the full, contextual works of art in which the costumes and props I discuss are used, these works have been written about extensively elsewhere. For more on Monkman and his Miss Chief character, see David Liss, "Kent Monkman: The Wild West Lives Again!," in *Kent Monkman: The Triumph of Mischief* (Hamilton: Art Gallery of Hamilton, 2008), pp. 103–6; Cathy Mattes, "An Interview with Miss Chief Eagle Testickle," in *Kent Monkman: The Triumph of Mischief*, pp. 107–10; David McIntosh, "Miss Chief Eagle Testickle, Postindian Diva Warrior, in the Shadowy Hall of Mirrors," in *Kent Monkman: The Triumph of Mischief*, pp. 31–46; David McIntosh, "Kent Monkman's Postindian Diva Warrior: From Simulacral Historian to Embodied Liberator," *Fuse Magazine* 29:3 (2006): 12–23; and Tina Majkowski, "Gypsies, Tramps, Half-Indian, All Queer, and Cher: Kent Monkman Defining Indigeneity Through Indian Simulation and Accumulation," in Nancy J. Blomberg (ed.), *Action and Agency: Advancing the Dialogue on Native Performance Art* (Denver, CO: Denver Art Museum, 2010), pp. 103–27.

6   Todd Porterfield, "History Painting and the Intractable Question of Sovereignty," in Michèle Thériault (ed.), *Interpellations: Three Essays on Kent Monkman* (Montreal: Galerie Leonard & Bina Ellen Gallery, 2012), p. 92.

7   While these museums are located mere blocks from each other (and from the Leonard & Bina Ellen Gallery where the Monkman exhibition was mounted), they have quite different collections and mandates: the McCord is a small museum with settler and Aboriginal material culture in its collection, while the Montreal Museum of Fine Arts is an institution with more traditional fine arts holdings and limited works by Aboriginal artists.

8   Each of these exhibitions has been significant for the institutional or disciplinary challenge presented. *Shapeshifters, Time Travellers and Storytellers* challenged the Royal Ontario Museum (and its visitors) with

multimedia contemporary art, a departure for a museum whose mandate is the study and exhibition of natural history and world cultures. The McMichael, which hosted *Fashionality*, more typically mounts exhibitions of twentieth-century (settler) Canadian painting than it does material culture, especially of a contemporary nature. Finally, while the Museum of Arts and Design has a craft-based mandate and exhibits current work, the *Changing Hands* series of exhibitions, of which this was the third, presented materially and ideologically diverse practices of Aboriginal craft, thus at an institutional level bringing Aboriginal craft into conversation with other contemporary craft practices.

9   Jayne Wark, "Dressed to Thrill: Costume, Body, and Dress in Canadian Performative Art," in Tanya Mars and Johanna Householder (eds), *Caught in the Act: An Anthology of Performance Art by Canadian Women* (Toronto: YYZ Books, 2004), p. 87.

10 *Eighth Fire*, Episode 1: "Indigenous in the City," Canadian Broadcasting Corporation, Toronto, January 12, 2012.

11 Jonathan Katz, "Miss Chief is always interested in the latest European Fashions," in Michèle Thériault (ed.), *Interpellations: Three Essays on Kent Monkman* (Montreal: Galerie Leonard & Bina Ellen Gallery, 2012), p. 18.

12 Lisa Telford, "Intertwining: Learning for the Future from Our Past," in Robin K. Wright and Kathryn Bunn-Marcuse (eds), *In the Spirit of the Ancestors: Contemporary Northwest Coast Art at the Burke Museum* (Seattle: University of Washington Press with the Bill Holm Center for the Study of Northwest Coast Art, Burke Museum, 2013); Kathryn Bunn-Marcuse, "In(tension)al Enchantment," *FiberArts* 36:4 (2010): 52–3.

13 Dottie Indyke, "Jaime Okuma," *Southwest Art* 30:12 (2001): 60–2.

14 Adamson, *The Craft Reader*, p. 586.

15 Adamson, "When Craft Gets Sloppy," *Crafts* 211 (2008): 36.

16 Elissa Auther, "Sloppy Craft: an Introduction," *Fiberarts* 37:3 (2010): 38–9; ibid.

17 Telford, "Intertwining."

18 Frances Densmore, *Chippewa Customs. Bulletin 86* (Washington: Smithsonian Institution Bureau of American Ethnography, 1929; reprinted, Saint Paul: Minnesota Historical Society Press, 1979), p. 52.

19 Johanna Drucker, "Affectivity and Entropy: Production Aesthetics in Contemporary Sculpture," in Glenn Adamson (ed.), *The Craft Reader* (New York: Berg), p. 593.

20 Ibid., pp. 593–4.

21 Often used as a term of self-identification or differentiation, post-Indian seeks to avoid a singularly racialized or essentialized cultural identity. Post-Indian identities encompass various and varying relationships to and perspectives on indigeneity and its expression and often comprise a wide range of contemporary cultural influences.

22 Debora Doxtator, *Fluffs and Feathers: An Exhibition of Symbols of*

Indianness, A Resource Guide (Brantford, ON: Woodland Cultural Centre, 1992).

23 Trudy Nicks, "Indian Handicrafts: The Marketing of an Image," *Rotunda* (Summer 1990): 14–20.

24 Cassel Oliver, "Craft out of Action," p. 11; Adamson, "Perpetual Motion," pp. 21–5.

25 These "performance-craft works" are the focus of Nicole Burisch's discussion, where crafts produced during performance works "function either as props or documentary records of past events and thus open up new ways of thinking about the relationships between craft objects and actions, makers and audiences." See Nicole Burisch, "Craft Off: Performance, Competition, and Anti-Social Crafting," *Cahiers métiers d'art / Craft Journal* 5:2 (2012): 92.

26 Elizabeth Kalbfleisch and Aldona Jonaitis, "Native Performance Art: 'The Medium is Wide Open'," in Veronica Passalacqua and Kate Morris (eds), *Native Art Now! Developments in Contemporary Native Art* (Indianapolis, IN and Norman, OK: Eiteljorg Museum and University of Oklahoma Press, forthcoming).

27 Barbara Babcock, "Marketing Maria: the Tribal Artist in the Age of Mechanical Reproduction," in Brenda Jo Bright and Liza Bakewell (eds), *Looking High and Low: Art and Cultural Identity* (Tucson: University of Arizona Press, 1995), p. 125.

28 Richard Spivey, *Maria* (Flagstaff, AZ: Northland Press, 1979), p. 59.

29 Martinez taught pottery making to other women, enhancing San Ildefonso's reputation as a center for Pueblo pottery. While Martinez herself continued to produce the most sought after work, other members of the community also profited from the sale of their pottery. See Margaret D. Jacobs, *Engendered Encounters: Feminism and Pueblo Cultures, 1879–1934* (Lincoln: University of Nebraska Press, 1999), pp. 49, 175; Spivey, pp. 1–3, 53. Additionally, much has also been made of Martinez signing her name to pots made by other San Ildefonso potters, a practice that increased the value of these pots. See Alice Marriott, *Maria: The Potter of San Ildefonso* (Norman: University of Oklahoma Press, 1963 [1948]), p. 243. While this revelation caused some initial controversy, scholarly consensus is now that the practice reflects the Pueblo belief in the community identification prevailing over the individual; this attribution allowed the community to profit from the collector/ consumer's interest in Martinez. See Jacobs, pp. 87–8; Susan Peterson, *The Living Tradition of Maria Martinez* (New York: Harper and Row, 1989 [1977]), p. 92.

30 Films all based on historical footage and include: *The Hands of Maria: Maria Montoya Martinez, The Potter of San Ildefonso* (prod. J. Donald McIntyre with the Kansas City Museum of History and Science, 1968); *Maria and Julian's Black Pottery* (dir. Arthur E. Baggs, Jr., 1977); *Classic Maria Martinez: Native American Pottery Maker of San Ildefonso* (dir. Rick Krepela, 1999); *Notable New Mexican: Maria Martinez* (New Mexico PBS, 2006).

31 Spivey, *Maria*, p. 22; Babcock, *Marketing Maria*, p. 137.

32 Spivey, *Maria*, p. 22.

33 Susan Peterson, *Maria Martinez: Five Generations of Potters* (Washington, DC: Smithsonian Institution, 1978); Spivey, *Maria*, p. 34.

34 Namita Gupta Wiggers, "Craft Performs," in Valerie Cassel Oliver (ed.), *Hand + Made: the Performative Impulse in Art and Craft* (Houston: Contemporary Arts Museum, 2010), p. 28.

35 The Canadian National Exhibition, popularly known as "The Ex," has been an annual event since 1879, with its roots in a fair held in Toronto in 1846. See John Robinson, *Once Upon a Century: 100 Year History of the Ex* (Toronto: J. H. Robinson Publishing Ltd, 1978) and Oswald C. J. Withrow, *The Romance of the Canadian National Exhibition* (Toronto: Reginald Saunders Publisher, 1936).

36 Alice Lighthall, letter to H. M. Jones, July 11, 1951, Canadian Handicraft Guild.

37 Anna Panadis, letter to Kathleen Moodie, August 20, 1948, Canadian Handicraft Guild.

38 Kathleen Moodie, letter to Anna Panadis, June 5, 1948, Canadian Handicraft Guild; Lighthall, letter to Kathleen Moodie, 1940.

39 Lighthall, letter to H. M. Jones.

40 Lighthall, letter to Kathleen Moodie.

41 Leah Dilworth, *Imaging Indians in the Southwest: Persistent Visions of a Primitive Past* (Washington, DC: Smithsonian Institution Press, 1996), p. 125.

42 Moodie, letter to Anna Panadis.

43 Panadis, letter to Kathleen Moodie.

44 Kathleen Moodie, letter to Ruth Home, May 27, 1948, Canadian Handicraft Guild.

45 Moodie here refers to the 1759 attack on the Abenaki settlement of St. Francis by American colonial "frontiersman" Robert Rogers and his Rangers, on behalf of the British army as part of the French and Indian War.

46 Liss, "Kent Monkman," p. 103.

PART THREE

Sloppy craft in practice and pedagogy: A conversation

The third part of this book brings together opinions, regarding the phenomenon of "sloppy craft", of five maker/teachers who have taught, created work, and exhibited in North America, the British Isles, Europe, Southeast Asia, and Oceania. These voices are crucial to the "sloppy craft" debate as they emerge from the teaching frontlines of post-secondary art educational institutions where the students' individual creative visions meet contemporary and traditional art and craft approaches to mediums, skills, and ideas. Teachers negotiate this territory, bringing to bear on these elements their own experiences of practice and exhibition. As each of the contributors points out in various ways, their teaching role is to strike a delicate balance among these parameters, taking into consideration concept, material, skill, exploration, and professionalism. In this section, they consider whether "sloppy craft" within the classroom is amateur, an inability to skillfully resolve the material with the concept, a step in the learning process, or a strategy to merge material practices with new concepts.

The roles of craft in education, skill in craft education, and craft in art education have been ongoing pedagogical concerns for decades, certainly in Britain and the United States. Glenn Adamson has traced the debate regarding the value of craft education in the United States, noting that for elementary and secondary education it originated in the late nineteenth century and was played out throughout the twentieth. On the one hand, craft education was understood as a moral imperative because it created better individuals; on the other hand, it prepared students to take an economically productive place in society. The moral benefits of acquiring craft skills were pitted against the monetary ones, suggesting class distinctions.[1] As for post-secondary education, Adamson proposes that Josef Albers's teaching at Black Mountain College in North Carolina in the 1940s "eschewed the transmission of pre-established technique ... [and] exposed his students to a continuous experience by process, by which they would acquire skill in the most generic sense."[2] He also notes that "Albers approached teaching not as transmission of a discrete set of skills, but rather as an opportunity to give students the sense of what it was like to be skilled at all."[3] Adamson observes that Albers's teaching philosophy subsequently produced "leading conceptualists" as well as those "deeply involved in craft theory and practice."[4] As our contributors suggest, these two strands of making continue to dominate art school pedagogy today, but they also question if and how "sloppy craft" can or even does bring them together.

During the post-Second World War years in Britain, Tanya Harrod notes the codification of art education within the education department meant the marginalization of craft in contrast to painting, sculpture, textiles, graphic arts, and three-dimensional design. Craft struggled for its place, often sneaking in through the back door under these categories, but was ignored as a valid classification in itself. As skills became marginalized in the art schools, highly skilled craftspeople assumed the role of technicians.[5] The workshop movement, where tacit knowledge was privileged over formal training, was led by practitioners of the interwar years and their followers of the post-Second World War years, who struggled to counteract this exclusion. As our contributors observe, teachers today are very preoccupied by concerns for the preservation and transmission of tacit knowledge within post-secondary art school environments that place increasing emphasis on conceptual approaches and even digital technologies.

Some of the issues the maker/teachers raise regarding the current twenty-first-century debate and practice of "sloppy craft" and its relation to skill include: How does a teacher mediate the tensions arising from craftsmanship and skill pitted against intellectual and material freedoms? Can the emergence of "sloppy craft" be related to the structure of institutional teaching such as restricted class time, the lack of concrete purpose for works produced, expectations of a limited-time craft education, integration of multiple mediums, and students' value of craftsmanship? Is "sloppy craft" really a pedagogical problem or does it illustrate an attempt to successfully resolve technical and conceptual challenges, where success is redefined as knowledge about a way of working rather than object refinement? What is the relationship between concept expression and technical mastery? Do the traditional disciplines in art/craft practice have any significance today? What is the relationship between the emergence of "sloppy craft" and post/interdisciplinarity? Is skill-based craft obsolete, or is it necessary to nuance the importance of skill when addressing the integration of craft media and practice into the world of fine arts? How does each artist understand their own work in terms of "sloppy craft" and post/interdisciplinarity? Each contributor brought their own particular concerns and viewpoints to these issues, seen through the lens of their individual philosophies, institutional experiences, and practices.

Because of the post-secondary fine art institutional affiliations of these maker/teachers and their own positions within the craft and art worlds, the relationship between professional preparation and amateur or DIY craft expressions, that several chapters explore, has remained largely unexamined from an educational perspective. Maker/teachers involved in art education and art therapy programs would be a welcome addition to this discussion, and, as suggested by Alfoldy, Macdonald, and Hickey, could contribute much to exploring the opportunities for, and even perhaps limits of, sloppy craft. The contributors to Part Two also raise the important issue of production spaces, whether they be the home, the studio, the community hall, rural or urban areas, fairgrounds, or even academic and craft institutions. Tied to these are marketing spaces through galleries, museums, or the Web, articulated by contributors to both Parts One and Two. The third part adds another kind of space to these: the post-secondary fine arts and crafts academic institution.

Most conversations also often involve some kind of laughter. In fact both McBrinn (through Judith Butler) and Alfoldy bring up the matter of laughter as a strategy to confront serious issues such as gender and art/craft hierarchies and their points of convergence. Auther and Speaks and Longchamps present works by Faught and Craste, respectively, that express the sloppiness of craft and the craftiness of sloppy, works that often elicit laughter as a first response. Whether self-deprecating, making a comment on the absurdity of life, or reaching out to create social bonds, humor is an essential element in sloppy craft conceptual works or in DIY amateur practices associated with sloppy craft. For teachers struggling within post-secondary educational institutions to imbue their students with tacit knowledge and/or conceptual tools, the potential humor of sloppy craft might very well go unrecognized. Sloppy craft *is* a funny term: strange, illogical, partially self-deprecating, perhaps mocking, but without a doubt one that comments on both the silliness and seriousness of life. This humorous absurdity, however, has sobering consequences as those working with craft materials and techniques engage with the market. This engagement is an essential consideration for these maker/teachers as they prepare their students, which might explain the lack of laughter in the particular conversation that follows.

Auther and Speaks suggest that sloppy craft involves the hyperbolized flaw that is so exaggerated it no longer can be considered a flaw. In order to arrive at such intended exaggeration, the maker must have attained some important level of tacit knowledge from exercises of skill, involvement in processes, and manipulation of materials, and an audience must be able to recognize the use of hyperbole through a familiarity with the those skills, processes, and materials. This is what Longchamps refers to when he speaks of sloppy craft as pushing boundaries through the mastery of techniques. The teacher/makers in this section are tasked by their institutions to impart enough tacit knowledge to their students so that they can be aware of it as a potential expressive and conceptual tool.

Makers are often invited to contribute artist statements and images to texts that look at their work within a thematic context that includes the production of other makers; however, they are rarely consulted regarding issues seen as the purview of art and/or craft theorists, historians, or critics. The editors are convinced the maker/teacher constituency is crucial for taking into account all the voices that both frame and are impacted by the notion of "sloppy craft." Resolution of issues was not the aim in bringing these various ideas forward; rather, this part has been structured as a dialogic space where a wide range of viewpoints could be aired. As such, the particular voice of each contributor has been retained in the question response document, formulated as a conversation, and the accompanying chapters. Some writers have adopted a more academic voice, whereas others approached the topic conversationally. The three chapters that conclude this section enlarge upon specific concerns of the contributors, and again the editors respected the particular format adopted by each writer.

This third section was inspired by a paper delivered by Eliza Au at a University Art Association of Canada conference session, "Postdisciplinarity and Sloppy Craft—A Critical Engagement." Au's chapter has been adapted from that paper. In eliciting the views of the maker/teachers who subsequently contributed to this "conversation", the editors circulated the issues Au raised along with Glenn Adamson's essay "When Craft Gets Sloppy." Each contributor then submitted their considerations in a format in which they felt most comfortable. Conor Wilson presented essays inspired by each question. Jean-Pierre Larocque provided brief replies to the questions, subsequently explored in a May 2013 interview by Susan Surette; these were merged for the purpose of this "conversation." Kelly Thompson replied in writing to the questions, while elaborating upon her own experiences in her chapter, "Weaving practice and pedagogy." Peter Wilson initially engaged with the project through his chapter "Sloppy craft: As related to ceramics," which was later followed up with remarks regarding topics he felt important and that have been compiled into the "conversation". The editors feel this format respects the varied backgrounds of the contributors, allowing each to engage with aspects of "sloppy craft" in ways they felt to be most productive.

Notes

1 Glenn Adamson, *Thinking Through Craft* (Oxford and New York: Berg, 2007), pp. 78–80.

2 Ibid, p. 84.

3 Ibid, p. 86.

4 Ibid, p. 87.

5 Tanya Harrod, *The Crafts in Britain in the 20th Century* (London and New Haven, CT: Yale University Press for the Bard Graduate Centre for Studies in the Decorative Arts, 1999), pp. 221–43.

Notes

8

Sloppy craft and interdisciplinarity: The conversation

Conor Wilson (CW); Jean-Pierre Larocque (JPL); Kelly Thompson (KT); Peter Wilson (PW)

Editors: Do you think skill-based craft is obsolete, or is it necessary to nuance the importance of skill when addressing the integration of craft into the world of fine arts?

CW: *All* craft production is skill-based and, as such, it will never be obsolete, unless we believe that in the future, somehow, it will be neither necessary nor desirable to use our hands and minds to make things well. Making things by hand, if you are fortunate enough to be able to create "free" conditions in which to make, is immensely rewarding for the individual maker. The importance of developing and maintaining an *enjoyable* production process was brought home to me when I first read *Flow*, in which Mihalyi Csikszentmihalyi explores the idea that human happiness is dependent on the development of the ability to control inner experience in the face of uncontrollable external conditions. Csikszentmihalyi develops his theory through a study of the concept of "*flow*—the state in which people are so involved in an activity that nothing else seems to matter; the experience itself is so enjoyable that people will do it even at great cost, for the sheer sake of doing it."[1] Craft making is a good example of flow activity, which is broadly analogous to the Taoist concept of the "totally free and purposeless journey," signified, loosely, by the word *yu* (to wander, or a wandering). "Chuang Tzu believed that to *Yu* was the proper way to live—without concern for external rewards, spontaneously, with total commitment—in short, as a total autotelic experience."[2]

Socrates (as recorded in Plato's *Apology*), who was roughly contemporaneous with the figure who has come down to us as Chuang Tzu, also had a high regard for the "hand-artists" (*kheirotékhnai*), who, unlike most others, actually possessed the knowledge required for their practice. However, he seems to have turned Chuang's idea on its head in the creation of a hierarchy that places the love of knowledge above doing. Western philosophy dealt craft another blow in Immanuel Kant's *Critique of Judgement* (1790), written, perhaps uncoincidentally, in the middle of the period we know as the Industrial Revolution. In establishing the disinterested, autonomous character of art, Kant placed it in opposition to labor, or craft, which is "satisfying only for the payoff which results and not for the mere activity of making itself." Art, conversely, "is free from any interest in the existence of the product itself."[3] The fine artist, the *genius*, is gifted with the ability to channel the beauty and sublimity that are found in "purposeless" nature. This could be read as a mirror image of the Eastern conception of skilled making as purposeless, a route to "the Way," which, for Chuang Tzu, is synonymous with "Nature" and "Heaven."[4]

Marcus Boon draws attention to a rather more worldly interpretation of Kant's claim of the "mere activity of making itself" for art:

> In his essay "Economimesis," Jacques Derrida talks about how for Kant, the productions of the fine arts of poetry or painting are separated from the world of crafts because the latter has an obvious economic incentive attached to production, while the poet and painter produce apparently without regard to such economic considerations. Derrida shrewdly notes that this separation of poetic and painterly production from the "lower" world of the craftsman is itself economic, and part of an overall system of exchanges which Derrida calls "economimesis"—the inextricably mimetic quality of all formulations of economy.[5]

Kant's opposition between art and craft was entrenched through the theory and practice of modern art. John Roberts locates the beginning of a process of negation and deskilling in the conditions of late nineteenth-century European capitalism, when advanced modernist artists, such as Gustave Courbet and Edouard Manet, generate a "crisis around painterly craft": "As advanced modernist artists seek to define and resist what they see as their threatened or marginal cultural status, the priority—the *modernist* priority—becomes: *how, with what materials, and to what ends* does the artist labour?"[6]

Roberts argues that it was Friedrich Nietzsche who first recognized that "the modern artist does not just inherit and transform tradition, but is compelled to shatter it, blast it apart, remake it, and as such remake it again."[7] Negation became the determining framework of modern art and it was Marcel Duchamp who systematized the shift through his early ready-mades, which "reorder the way hand and eye have, traditionally, determined the form and content of art ... The immediate outcome of this shift is that the deflationary content of art is subject to the thoroughgoing dismantling of the metaphysics of the hand, of handicraft, of the handmade."[8]

Despite the hugely influential teaching methods of the Bauhaus, the flowering of interest in craft making as the basis for a new way of life in the 1960s and 1970s, and all manner of complex overlaps between art and craft thinking, there can be no doubt that "the crafts," in opposition to the cult of the new of contemporary art, came to be characterized within modernism (and postmodernism) as functional, traditional, old. Craft was, and still is, to some extent, associated with social conservatism and individual therapy.

If negation and deskilling are broadly accepted as central to modernist art practice, I accept that their place in contemporary art practice is not uncontested. My concern here is to think through a sense that art theory in the modern and postmodern periods focused on the radical potential of *art* to embody opposition and to reflect change, as opposed to the artist's practice as a *way of life*. I think that within the craft field a confusion, or a tension, has developed between a conception of craftsmanship as a way of life and the idea that, in order to prosper, craftsmen must shape their thinking and their products to fit the demands of the (better funded, more exciting) art world. It was established many years ago by Duchamp, Warhol, Arthur Danto, et al. that art can be anything, but, obviously, craft will only be accepted as art if it is framed according to the rules of contemporary art practice. This happens rarely, in the UK at least, but Edmund de Waal has shown that it can be done.

In his introduction to the "Craft in Theory" section of *The Craft Reader*, Glenn Adamson writes that "what seems important now is not whether craft can be defined as a sphere within art. More pressing is the more objective question of whether art institutions are willing and able to make space for craft-related thinking, as part of the subject matter for which they have been responsible all along."[9] Clearly, art institutions are now willing, in certain circumstances and, in courting them, it is less a question of nuancing the importance of skill than considering carefully how the skill is theorized and presented (or maybe that is what is meant by nuancing). But perhaps we should be less concerned with the institutions and more concerned with process, with the potential of craft's difference. We might co-opt and adapt a Groysian *aperçu*: "Art becomes politically effective only when it is made beyond or outside the art market—in the context of direct political propaganda."[10] It is curious that the postmodern pluralism that took hold in response to neoliberalism (and spawned the cynical/rich celebrity artist) has also weakened modernist hierarchies to the extent that "integration of craft into the world of fine arts" could be seriously discussed. It is equally curious that the strong position of craft (or the applied arts) within higher education, despite, or perhaps because of, its separation from fine art, has been weakened under those same socio-political conditions.

Political propaganda aside, interest in craft within other disciplines—philosophy, anthropology, sociology—might just give us the confidence to reclaim craft as a vital, separate field with a strong social, ethical, and political history: a useful platform for individual development and collective resistance to a dominant free market ideology that will promote insatiability all the way to environmental catastrophe. Peter Hughes has been writing about the value of craft for some time: "By collapsing, to greater or lesser degrees, the distinction between the mind and the body, object and subject and, ultimately, the material and spiritual, craft represents a challenge to the dominant conceptual framework of our civilisation."[11] Later, in the same paper, he writes about the importance of the Arts and Crafts Movement as a social and political movement that attempted to address the question of what constitutes the "good life." The "good life" here refers to a philosophical tradition that, in the West, dates back to Ancient Greece. It is concerned with a life that is at once fulfilling and lived in a manner consistent with one's values, as distinct from a life of material abundance or one that is free from fear or effort.[12]

More recently, in *The Art Kettle*, philosopher Sinéad Murphy makes a withering critique of art that purports to be oppositional, while drawing attention to the radical potential of craft:

> [W]hat [William] Morris also saw was that an existence "free" of the stuff and skills of existence is one for which possibilities for creativity, for originality, for resistance, are gradually dissolved, not simply because those who are free to think, create and invent, cannot follow through in practice on what they have thought of, created and invented ... but rather that they *cannot think, create, and invent*. The degradation occurs at the level of creative possibilities, and not simply at the level of their realization ... [T]hat which we now think of as life—all those things that we now regard work as "freeing us up" to do: read, paint, shop, travel, think—is also alienated, from the educative, the enlightening, incubation that is *craft*.[13]

JPL: The conversation about Art versus Craft has turned obsolete if not sour a long time ago but it is not over. I address the issue obliquely by transporting the conversation to other fields apparently not as mined. Who is questioning the craft of writing, or guitar playing, or cooking? The craft of making films? I ask students: Would you download this piece if it was a song? No? Why? Would you explain it? Would you dance to it? So you are learning to play the banjo? Are you skilled? So, no, teaching how to make things is not obsolete.

There are vocational schools where you can train for 12 months to throw pots. This training will make a decent thrower out of you but it will not make you think like an artist. It is not about skills; it is about what you make with the skills. Loose throwing or precise throwing on the potter's wheel—each approach stands for something; each is a visual statement. Is sloppy craft sloppy because the teaching of craft has reached a low point? Or is sloppy a prevalent attitude which stands for something?

To consider the first option, I would say that the teaching of art is uneven. There are great schools for craft, well rounded programs which prepare and nurture artists. There are also terrible places. In a beginners class you will see a lot of sloppy craft that is part of the process of how we learn and how we improve skills. That work is just evidence of what you've been learning and how you have been improving. As for the second option: there is sloppy because the artist cannot do better because of poor training and uninformed choices. Then there is sloppy as just another type of mark making: precise throwing, loose throwing, sometimes mixed together which requires some skill; deliberate marks, accidental marks, the whole array of mark making. In that context a sloppy mark is just a piece in a wider vocabulary used by artists. It does stand for something though. Consider sloppy or precise or virtuoso guitar playing. We perceive each differently.

As an artist you're making a pot or sculpture out of clay or any craft-related material. You're going to use all sorts of marks, and out of all this collection of marks you manage to say something. I remember when I was at Alfred University, there were people who threw loose pots, and there were people who threw pots that were crisper and tighter. Sometimes a war erupted between the two approaches. Personally I always thought the richer pieces were those that actually integrated the loose and tight together. That doesn't mean one is better than the other, but rather it stands for something else. It's not like an attitude; it's a way of experiencing yourself that comes out this way. Accordingly we might look at sloppy as the attitude of a new generation of maker, which might be the case because we see them painting as well as in the craft area. We just have to look at what it stands for, what it means. It may stand for a sort of ambivalence or it may be a way of saying, "Yes I'm making things, but I don't care in terms of a general trend or attitude." But I tend to look at "sloppy" as a part of a vocabulary. A lot of people may look at a painting by De Kooning, for instance, and think my kid could do that. Well the fact is that he struggled for over a year on a lot of those very important paintings. You look at paintings like *Excavation* or *Attic*, where even after one year of his working on them, they looked very sloppy. In this case such sloppiness stands for a philosophy, for things that could happen.

KT: Ask a painter or a musician this question—each has a craft. For me it is an obsolete question, unless broken down and defined more. Refer to Richard Sennett's book *The Craftsman*, where he talks about skill and training. There will always be a continuum of skills and valuing of those skills—what is more interesting for me in craft or art is what is being communicated; does this do so in a moving way with relevance to a wider context?

PW: The art and craft movement is a business like any other, and artists/designers look to minimize costs and maintain quality. The global economy relies on this specialization and cost differentials. Designers in all areas of endeavor, artists to instrument-makers, fashion houses to Apple Inc., all utilize these strategies. The global economy relies on specialization and cost differentials. The notion of "sloppy craft" has no place here.

A variant on this is that many individual artists find they require specialist skills for specific part/s of an item and outsource this section of the production to specialist craftspeople who are paid for their labor and skills. This is commonplace in the ceramic industry in Jingdezhan, China, where local artisans market their skills to foreigner artist/designers who flock there in droves.

There are still, however, many individual practicing artists who prefer to control every aspect of their own small-scale output and promote the individuality and uniqueness of their work. Having worked with trainees in the past, I now prefer to work alone, responsible for all phases of my production. William Morris and John Ruskin would have been proud of these artists for holding fast to the principles of the nineteenth-century Arts and Crafts Movement, albeit with different technology to assist the processes.

Editors: Do you think postdisciplinarity is possible, and if so why or why not? Do the traditional disciplines in art practice have any relevance today?

CW: I have written at length on this subject before,[14] so will try to condense my thoughts here and identify any changes in thinking. It seems to me that "postdisciplinarity" is one of those slippery, over-broad terms that people take up too readily, but that *are* used in an attempt to define real change. Clearly, the boundaries between disciplines are much more porous than they once were, but they have not disappeared and I doubt that they will. How could we organize an art school, let alone the wider university, without discrete programs that relate to specialist bodies of knowledge? Can we have "postdisciplinary" programs nestled amongst the other, disciplinary, programs? The fact that artists draw on knowledge and media from increasingly diverse sources and that we see this reflected in production (and teaching) in art schools does not amount to postdisciplinarity. Could a philosopher teach you how to make shoes? A glass blower how to write a poem? A mathematician how to dance? While the results might be intriguing as interdisciplinary experiments, students want to be taught by tutors who have specialist knowledge of, and significant experience in, the fields in which they hope to practice. Yes, those fields are less narrowly defined—if we leave aside the rest of the university and focus on art and design, it could be argued that there are now only two disciplines: fine art and design. There are significant areas of overlap between the two, but they still have broadly separate literatures, social networks, exhibiting structures, museums; even, I would hazard, psychologies.

Pedagogy in the applied arts or crafts disciplines is based on the development of knowledge and skills through making and material investigation. While concept and context are important elements, assessment is still largely based on the *quality* of finished, discrete objects. The relevance of skills and specialized material knowledge might be debated, but they are still the primary reference point for UK-based graduate and postgraduate programs. This approach to pedagogy is distinct from the dominant approach in schools and departments of fine art. Process and materials are central here as well, but production must be justified in relation to current thinking on what constitutes the discipline, whether it be sculpture, painting, photography, moving image, or print. "Concept" arises from a dialog between personal vision and shared/contested understanding of what it means to be an artist, now.

> Tradition in contemporary sculpture is a frequently ironised thing, a counterweight: the use of classical materials serving often as a shorthand for unbridgeable distance from a grand and idealised past.[15]

This is from a recent essay on sculpture. Such ironizing seems pointless, even detrimental, to forms of craftsmanship that accept traditional, material-specific specializations, but makers aiming for genuine art/craft hybrids must be prepared to define disciplinary status through questioning.

My direct experience has been in four UK art schools, all of which are university faculties, apart from the Royal College of Art, which has independent university status. Each deals with disciplinary structure in their own way, but, despite the emergence of new multimedia, or multidisciplinary hybrids, they still tend to offer programs that are more or less based on traditional disciplines. Some art schools have made a clear structural change in centralizing fabrication facilities, increasing access to equipment and knowledge that was once department-based. A fine art student, for instance, might learn how to screen print, or weld, make a video, or throw on the potter's wheel in order to make elements for an installation, or just because this form of production suits her purposes. A ceramics student could do the same, if he existed.

This last is a slight exaggeration, but ceramics in the UK, particularly at graduate level, has contracted alarmingly over the past 20 years. Some excellent multimedia programs have been created to meet the changing needs of students (or universities, or government), but I would love to see those universities recognizing the value and difference of the traditional applied arts areas—ceramics, glass, furniture and woodwork, textiles, jewelry and metalwork—and grouping them under the discipline of craft. Should we sit back and watch while our higher education system is reshaped as a result of "market forces"? Do we always have to escalate to the fashionable, facile post in response to the complexities and problems of the now?

The structure of the Royal College of Art offers a useful model—it has a School of Design, a School of Fine Art, and a School of Material. For me, the future of the programs within the School of Material lies not in becoming more like fine art or design, but in their embrace of craft. But, crucially, along with a celebration of our own way of doing things—of learning and generating knowledge through making—we should offer genuinely interdisciplinary teaching, so that those students who want to take craft skills into design or fine art contexts understand the rules and have a knowledge of the social networks of those contexts.

JPL: Mixing disciplines is exciting, but interdisciplinarity benefits from strong disciplines. The reality is that it takes years to become a good video artist. It takes time to develop as a writer or a painter or mixed media artist. It is no different. Most artists are invested in the materials they use and tend to gravitate to materials that best convey their ideas.

Western instruments were banned during the Cultural Revolution in China. As a result, a whole generation of musicians never learned the violin. The mandate of an art school is different from the Whitney Biennal. A teacher is not the curator of the year asserting what is relevant in any given year; our mission is to nurture talents and make it possible for all sorts of artists to develop without biases towards any approach. Nurturing diversity is the fun part and offering the newest approach alongside strong traditional disciplines is the better option. What new generations of artists will do with it all is their business. Let's not interfere or edit their choices. Who is to say what will be relevant?

It seems to me that it is impossible to have interdisciplinarity without having disciplines. I've seen some departments that so badly wanted to be doing what other schools or other areas of the schools were doing that they basically abandoned their materials. It's a dead end, and those areas were usually shut down after a few years. It has happened in Canada. I think the stronger the disciplines, the more you can talk about interdisciplinarity. It seems to me there are a lot of people who seem to be wishing that we could forget all the disciplines: an artist just comes in and says, "I've an idea, and I'm going to go to a preparation shop and have it made over there." A lot of sculpture departments are following that model and they have for a long time now. Therefore in classes they talk about ideas, look at proposals, and students go to the preparation shops to get technicians to have them do what they have to do. As long as the idea is served, it does not matter whether they actually made it or if someone else made it. I am not sure that this is the model that can work with ceramics. I wouldn't speak for anybody else, but I think that certainly for ceramics, it's a dead end.

KT: Traditional disciplines in art practice have relevance for those who wish to pursue them. Not all see this as interesting for them while others do. I think another debate could be added, in which the disciplinary practice of an artist might slowly evolve or change, but the content and approach shifts. Is this a disciplinary or methodology shift?

Editors: What do you think of the pedagogical approach explained by Anne Wilson where "[t]echnical skills are presented and taught quite rigorously, but not with an emphasis on fine-tuning high skill as the goal. The concept is the goal"?

CW: The desire to move away from the "fine-tuning [of] high skill" is understandable. In an address to the architects of the German Werkbund, late in his career, Theodor Adorno, that most subtle of aesthetic philosophers, cautioned, "if the fittingness of the means becomes an end in itself, it becomes fetishized. The handworker mentality begins to produce the opposite effect from its original intention, when it was used to fight the silk smoking jacket and the beret."[16] However, the separation of "technical skills" and "concept" is troublesome for me. The way something is made—its facture—cannot be separated from its meaning. Skilled making—an intimate engagement between body and material—is as *deep* as any other form of art production. Rather than taking the stability of craft production for granted and importing personal "concept" in the name of individual expression of an often vague "artiness," I would rather see us interrogating fundamental questions relating more to production than the individual: What are "materials" and where do they come from? Why make by hand in a so-called postindustrial age? How might hand skills relate to established and emerging production technologies? Why develop skills within a deskilling paradigm? Why specialize in a single material when artists work in an increasingly broad range of media? These questions (along with many others) seem to me to be essential to the generation of disciplinary discourse.

Adorno acknowledged that clear distinctions between art and craft, the purpose-free and the purposeful, are not easy to draw. More important to this discussion is what is necessary or superfluous to each individual work, whether originating from art or craft practices. Each activity "requires a precise understanding of the materials and techniques at the artist's disposal" and "the difference between the necessary and the superfluous is inherent in a work, and is not defined by the work's relationship—or the lack of it—to something outside itself." Furthermore, the imagination of the individual artist has limited purchase on "the wordless question posed to it by the materials and forms in their quiet and elemental language."[17] It is the business of the individual work to make its case in whatever context is chosen for it by a producer who should be armed with an understanding of that context.

JPL: Art schools are full of dos and don'ts—no doubts. They turn over every 20 years. The current model is that the concept is the goal. The implied message is that ideas are most important. The interesting question of how an idea or an experience is actually embedded into materials is not much discussed. This dominant model does not favor craft, not that the previous modernist model did either. The current perception is that making objects is passé; skills are irrelevant and not significant for the culture. We are promoting the artist as a generator of concepts that any skilled fabricator can build from blueprints. The ideal is the post-studio artist developing ideas on a laptop on a flight from São Paulo to London via Basel: the artist as director. Film directors do not make costumes or build sets; they approve. There is nothing wrong with this model. But there are problems with this model being the dominant one. One way out of this paradox is to first question how the discourse on the body is so often generated by artists who do not use their body to make art. Or why artists using their bodies or their hands are not included in the discourse. Granted, this is a caricature. Interdisciplinarity is indeed exciting, with new possibilities, but it is not the only way to be an artist. We should be careful not to turn it into another orthodoxy (*orthos doxa*: the only one way).

Craft is rooted in tradition in the sense that cooking and playing the guitar are traditions, carried over generations. This does not mean that craft is inherently conservative. On the contrary, the history of craft is also the history of inventiveness. Craft is about what begins to happen once humans feel safe and secure: they begin to embellish the shelter. Craft is about how to make things, but it is not mere fabrication. Craft can indeed be the guardian of prescribed ways of doing things, be it cooking or embroidering or representing, because craft is dependent on a social consensus. Tradition is, however, renewable or it will die. Any tourist market can confirm that. Where tradition stops breathing and embracing inventiveness you encounter products without soul, things made from a recipe for selling. Then we might as well enter the manufacturing practices of the industrial age or revisit the sweatshops of Asia where millions of highly skilled workers repeat the same alienating task. An artist will use craft differently. Think guitar player, musicians, merging mind and body as a felt experience.

Art schools are not teaching craft any more, but we are training artists to use materials associated with craft, which is still problematic because of the biases towards the baggage surrounding craft and art as categories. This is a challenging situation for a material craft-based department. Many do compromise. When I took over the Ceramics Department (Concordia University), students lacked basic skills but they had been allowed to make videos about clay. This is a problem. We want interdisciplinarity but we need to establish disciplines to do so. The previous faculty were uncomfortable with calling themselves ceramicists. As a result the ceramics area was on life support. We have managed over five years to change that situation.

I believe that the better informed you are, not only about the ideas around you but about your materials, the more options you have later on. For instance, I'm pushing my students in one assignment to work large, because many of them will try to avoid it at all costs. They never want to work large because they think they cannot do it. By working with them I prove to them they can and help them. They become convinced they can make it. And then they discover that they can acquire any skill they want, and later on that will enable them to work the way they want. They now have the skills to work larger if they want to. I think schools should equip students with the potential, and what they make of it is the student's business.

An art school must reflect whatever attitude and approaches are happening outside. Keep in mind that this is ever changing. We have all sorts of students coming in. We have from the most conceptually oriented to the ones that need to put their hands on the material. We have to make it possible for everybody to become the kind of artist they have to become. And because of that, I think that probably we have to split the schools into what we call traditional approaches, such as drawing and painting and material-based areas, and conceptual approaches. Then you can sometimes have a conversation between the two, and let students feel their way between or within a combination of the two approaches.

KT: This is a similar approach to that taken at Concordia University in the Fibres and Material Practices program. We are not a technical school, nor is it possible in the time frame available to train students to a high level. Some choose to revisit particular processes and become very competent within a discipline, while others take advantage of the "pick and mix" educational opportunity to choose a variety of courses. Having both options is great; not all students know what interests them prior to getting to university since they may not have been exposed to some subject areas. If students want to gain more intense technical skill training, there are other places better suited for that.

PW: A traditional training system in common practice since the Middle Ages was the atelier system. Taking one common example from Japan, trainees would work and learn from the master, often living with the master's family, helping around the house, tending the vegetable garden, as well as working in the pottery, sweeping the floors, and preparing the clay. When, after several years of practice, the trainee's work was deemed to be of an acceptable standard, they would produce what was required which was then marketed as the master's. In essence, sloppy craft stands in opposition to apprenticeship. The mastery of skills, through whatever means (perhaps apprenticeship), forms the basis of any art form. However, much more rigorous intellectual input is required to create artworks from mere technical facility. As Picasso said, "Anyone can draw like Rembrandt but it has taken me a lifetime to learn to draw like a child." It is very much about our ideas and how we develop them in creative ways.

The apprenticeship system is still available but it is rare as most potential artists and craftspeople opt for art education in post-secondary institutions, which has evolved and changed dramatically over the last two decades. The model of long studio hours of directed study in making saleable things proved to be unsustainable. As the popularity of ceramics declined throughout the 1990s, competition for students became fiercer, and as student numbers dwindled, funding became problematic. Courses were rationalized. In the late 1980s, for example, there were 36 art schools in Australia, all offering degrees in specialist ceramics programs. Janet de Boos, former head of the Australian National University Art School Ceramic Department, has discussed how internet technology has made "hands-on" disciplines, such as ceramics, available to students who would not normally have access to them on campus, and also facilitated lecturers to work from home super-vising students, in turn opening up opportunities for employment of artist teachers who are remote from the educational institution.[18] As part of this transition and a new range of performance criteria for staff, the teaching paradigms have changed, reflected in less face-to-face teaching time and largely leaving the responsibility for the development of these initial "craft skills" to the students. These skills require a lifetime of learning, refinement, experimentation, and development, to which any craftsperson will attest, and this is just the beginning—poor skills means poor quality work.

Editors: Do you think sloppy craft, understood as "my-kid-could-do-that aesthetics," is just a "bid for success in the contemporary art world"?[19]

CW: Sloppy craft is art. If the maker understands the game he is playing, then the pejorative phrase, "bid for success in the contemporary art world," becomes meaningless. Josh Faught clearly understood the game he was playing, which was one defined by the rules of contemporary art practice. His "sloppy craft" is craft only in as much as it is produced within a perceived disciplinary boundary and, perhaps, through the use of materials that are considered as traditional craft materials. Christopher Frayling remarked:

> Matching this social movement of some craftspeople into the art world, there is a parallel movement the other way round as "some artists look for new media in which to explore a current expressive problem." This new breed of artists produces standards that are "aggressively non-utilitarian" and the organisation of their work remains within the art world proper. "It becomes a virtue not to display conventional craft virtuosity, and the artist may deliberately create crudities either for their shock value, or to show that he is free of that particular set of conven-tional restraints." ... And the previous generation of craftspeople is likely

to become enraged at this invasion of their world. When these twin processes happen—craftsman enters the art world, while artist hijacks craft—"for most of the people involved, the experience is much more one of choice among alternative institutional arrangements and working companions than of creative expressive leaps."[20]

JPL: Since when is being an artist supposed to be about fitting in? The question about sloppy craft really is: what does it stand for? All beginners make sloppy craft. The rest has to do with an individual's sense of finish. De Kooning worked for two years on *Excavation*, a painting that could be understood as "my kid could do that," but a trained eye will immediately see the difference between "sloppy" because you cannot do better and "sloppy" as standing for an idea. It takes precision to paint ambivalence.

Precise, slick, hasty, sketchy, smooth, rough, textured: it all stands for ideas and feelings like mark making for a painter or marks on clay. So does sloppy.

There is a craft to playing a musical instrument whether you are Yo-Yo Ma or Keith Richards. Writing is above all about a voice, but there is certainly a craft to writing.

I am not a fan of Charles Bukowski, but he certainly made sloppy writing convincing.

I think it's a valid way of working. The use of sloppy and how we respond to it depends on the culture at any given moment. Sloppy seems recently to be happening a lot. I hear it a lot from my colleagues in painting who say their students are producing a lot of sloppy painting, but it is beyond student work; it's an attitude.

The bad art goes beyond the sloppy; it's just not good. But we're not allowed to talk about quality—that's another big taboo. But I do feel, as someone who experiences art, that there's a lot of stuff out there that I feel is not very good, or not very engaging or not very interesting—and once in a while, something that is absolutely wonderful. And I think it's the same with the crafts. There's a lot of bad craft around, and sometimes there's a craft piece that is just an amazing thing. And so, from that point of view, it doesn't matter what you call it, it's about being something outstanding, whether it's craft or art. And that sort of takes care of that problem, you know.

KT: No—this is a particular aesthetic and historical choice. The example of Josh Faught for this debate I find very interesting as it seems to overlook the fact that many of the things he does, he does well, but that the overall impression does not fit the "tidy" craft or singular studio craft definition or model of past practitioners who don't venture beyond one media. Choosing to juxtapose diverse elements seems to have more of a pop/collage reference, a craft mash-up, rather than being badly made. But I have only seen his work in reproduction or online, so that adds a different filter. Maybe they are really messy or sloppy!

PW: There is ambivalence with the term "sloppy craft" that needs clarification. With special relation to ceramics, a discussion of the influence of Zen Buddhism is relevant here because it has had a profound influence on ceramics in particular. It has permeated every thread of Japanese culture for the last four centuries. Its underlying philosophy/religion is a strong appreciation for the natural world, such as the unevenness of the mountains and the beauty of natural textures of stone and rock, and admiration of a humble work ethic and humility that flows through to daily life. In many areas of Japan this sensibility is evident, particularly in ceramics, for example in Hagi, Shigaraki, and Bizen and much of the folk pottery (Mingei). The terms *shibui* and *wabi-sabi* reflect this quality of the humility of daily life, of unevenness, of uniqueness. Other valued attributes include the asymmetrical and intimate, suggestive of natural processes, unpretentiousness, simplicity, modesty, earthiness.[21]

The question then remains: because of this seemingly raw and natural beauty inherent within this aesthetic, does the work imply a lack of craft skills when compared, for example, with a perfectly made and executed equivalent object? Clearly an appreciation of Japanese (and Korean) ceramics is useful here, but the works do not reflect sloppy craft or a lack of craft skills.

Editors: Can sloppy craft only have relevance if we move beyond traditional disciplinary boundaries, and what are the difficulties in doing this?

CW: We should be wary of reification. Sloppy craft is not a concrete thing, but a term that attempts to pin down a varying set of responses to ever-shifting social/epistemic contexts. If there were no disciplinary boundaries, the term "sloppy craft" would not have been coined.

JPL: When I took over the Ceramics Department of Concordia University (Montreal) six years ago, they were letting students do video in ceramics. There were people teaching the medium at that time who felt almost ashamed of being ceramists; they wanted to be called something else: artists. There is a pottery school here in Montreal where they don't call their students potters any more—they call them designers. I find that's a big problem. There is not a problem with being called a designer, but there might be a problem with this attitude of being ashamed of who you are and what you want to do. I think it's a big issue. The other issue is that everybody wants to be an artist. I think in the craft community this is related to status. And there is real bias against craft. But I'm not sure if this is how the battle will be won. I think that the reality is that there's a lot of bad art around, and there's some great art.

KT: Too much importance is placed on sloppy craft in this context, as a contrast to traditional boundaries (what is meant by this anyway?). It cannot be singular or separated from many other issues that shape choices for craftspeople or artists. There are swings in contemporary art as well, and I think a greatly overlooked area is the role of fabricators in a range of practices. Fabricators are highly skilled craftspeople, often artists in their own right, working for a salary. Acknowledging this relationship does not always sit comfortably with some artists. This could be an interesting follow-on conversation—or a future research project?

PW: You see in the work of ceramic artists Peter Voulkos, Don Reitz, and Paul Soldner, to name a few, distinctly innovative ways of working with clay. The works show a sense of scale, energy, and force, suggesting they have attacked the clay, built multiples, carved into it, and then subjected the work to harsh *anagama*-type firing processes (specific wood-fired, tunnel-like kilns) in the case of Voulkos and Reitz.

Jean-Pierre Larocque's works, for example, highlight an innovative way of using the unique textural qualities of clay to create surface and textures within large-scale works.

These are three of many possible examples of innovative engagement with clay, materials, and firing processes, and on first observation there may appear to be a lack of precisely finished pieces. However, the works need to be placed within the broader philosophical context of the art world, and abstract expressionism (in the cases of Voulkos and Reitz) had its influences here, as did the qualities of Zen. The makers' skill and understandings of the processes and explorations of the materiality of clay suggest anything but sloppiness in their art-making.

Editors: Do you think the concept of "sloppy craft" could be applied to your own practice?

CW: In a recent interview, Glenn Adamson defined craft as an activity practiced by "a person with deep knowledge and commitment to the production process, who applies that by hand to a purposeful result."[22] Adamson diplomatically channels Kant and Adorno, without committing to the "function" word. Sôetsu Yanagi was more direct. In his 1927 essay, "The Way of Craftsmanship," he asks himself,

Q. What is the particular kind of beauty in crafts?

A. Beauty that is identified with use. It is beauty born of use. Apart from use there is no beauty of craft. Therefore, things made that do not stand up to use or that ignore utility can barely be expected to contain that kind of beauty.[23]

If craft is seen predominantly as a way of doing, something that Adamson explored in *Thinking Through Craft* (2007), a relation to function is not essential. If we are talking about the historical category of "the crafts," then, I believe, that relation is, somehow, essential. Either way, craft is a highly specialized, skilled form of production, involving an intimate bodily knowledge of a (usually narrow) range of materials and related tools and equipment. Craft production is stable and based on repetition—to the point where the maker doesn't have to think about what they are doing. This is the point—doing something over and over and over again results in the ability to make unself-consciously, the body-mind released from the tyranny of concept; the tyranny of uncertainty, of self-criticism. I have done enough making to understand this at a bodily level—I play with it, but have never remained committed to a particular means of production or set of forms long enough to achieve a full uncoupling.

Craftsmen are supremely confident in their physicality, in their ability, and, in my experience, are rarely interested in questioning the basis of what they are doing, as artists (of a certain kind) are expected to do. I have always been interested in maintaining and exploring a sense of uncertainty, contrasting it with specialist knowledge and skills, so I have tended not to refer to myself as a craftsman. One way that I characterize my practice is as a mixture of craft and bricolage. It would be simplistic to say that the two constitute a straightforward binary, but craftsmen and bricoleurs seem to represent distinct psychological types. Perhaps I am just confused, but this seems to satisfy a need for stability and chaos, planning and spontaneity.

> [T]he "bricoleur" is ... someone who works with his hands and uses devious means compared to those of a craftsman ... His universe of instruments is closed and the rules of his game are always to make do with "whatever is at hand", that is to say with a set of tools and materials which is always finite and is also heterogeneous because what it contains bears no relation to the current project, or indeed to any particular project ...[24]

JPL: I am a maker and I consider that how something is made has everything to do with what it means. I was trained as a painter and went to two art schools. That's why I became interested in ceramics because I saw that what was taught in the painting department was something I could do by myself at home, actually. Nobody ever told me how to mix the different mediums together, the ratio of turpentine and dammar varnish. We never talked about that because it felt as if it were beside the question that was always about the content.

I work intuitively. I get interested in all sorts of marks. The question is always: what else can I do? Titian at 75 was painting with his fingers. I don't think he was thinking sloppy; but no trick in his book was off-limits. "Precise" and "sloppy" are only problematic if they do not stand for something.

I work long in my work to make a piece that feels like it made itself.

I strive to keep the freshness of a sketch even on pieces I continue for months. It is the feeling I am after. It is not the same as sloppy. I see my work as a conversation with material, a conversation between equals, so to speak. I'm aware that for a lot of artists, whether they do craft or art, the process is different. My approach is empirical. I know some artists who do have a vision, and they go about making that vision visible in the material. Personally I can't do that; I have to jump into it and discover my ideas as I make. I may have a loose idea when I begin, but, basically I make like a jazz musician improvises on a theme. I'm interested in something that retains the freshness of a sketch.

As a maker I'm attentive to the "poetry" of making; that's the part that excites me the most—the poetry of making as a place where the whole language of making, based on skill and craft, is loosened up to service something a little wilder than working from a blueprint.

KT: Probably not—I guess I am too old school, traditional in my aesthetics.

PW: The essential craft skills are fundamental to my own practice. While much of my work in ceramics is wheel-based, I appreciate a sense of understanding form, balance, weight, proportion, and how these elements combine with a glazed surface to create a crafted object. These qualities aren't stressed; they are inherent in the process; they are automatic. In themselves, the evidence of these skills does not equate to an exceptional piece of work because that relies on a range of other factors as well. It is the harmony of several key elements that make some pieces "sing" as compared to others.

The quote by Thomas Watson, founder of IBM, is pertinent here: "If you want to increase your success rate, double your failure rate."[25] This refers to the notion of practice, of persistent effort, of a work ethic. This development is a continuum, which over many years of learning-by-doing becomes intuitive, allowing other ideas to form and grow. An analogy would be the jazz pianist who spends his life practicing, learning harmonies, scales, chords, arpeggios, riffs, improvisations in every key, only to forget them all when he sits down to play as his imagination and ideas take over. The knowledge and practice is fundamental but until you "find your voice," the technical understandings and facility alone are relatively meaningless.

Finding your voice means what? It means: dedicated practice in your chosen areas; looking critically at your own and others' works, nature, the world; reading poetry, literature, reviews, catalogs, journals; accessing images; discussing exhibitions and artworks with friends; looking through museum collections; visiting galleries; traveling to other places; viewing architecture, fashion, paintings; being aware of art in all its forms such as music (classical in particular) and drama; developing your own opinions about the world, art, form, sculpture, painting, and knowing why. It means, then, setting a direction for your own work and developing ideas.

Editors: As a teacher and a maker, how do you consider the relationships among "fine craft," "sloppy craft," professional, and amateur?

CW: Derrida's analysis of Kant's privileging of fine art suggests an economic motive to the designation "fine craft." I prefer to stick with "art," "craft," and "design"—there are many overlaps between the three, of course, but also productive distinctions. I'm not bothered about distinctions between amateur and professional. There is good and bad, rich and thin work in all categories. The art world has as many levels as, if not more than, the craft world. Do we say that work that doesn't negate previous tradition is not art? What if the work is shown in leading galleries and receives critical acclaim? Do we accept that there will always be those who insist on the radical, transformative, oppositional potential of art, but also artists— many of them successful—who produce curious, or beautiful, or expressive objects for a market hungry for such qualities? The anxiety in the craft field over being associated with "non-professional hobbywork or even folk art"[26] has deep roots related to lack of attention, funding, and showing opportunities, but renewed interest in craft suggests that it might be more productive to hold fast, reclaim the word and explore and celebrate the useful differences between art, craft, and design.

JPL: It seems that I'm OK with sloppy craft, as long as it doesn't feel like a limitation; that it's not just a word that the writer is using to designate bad work. But if the novel is all sloppy, sloppy, sloppy, then you don't have anything beyond the sloppy.

Craft and craft-related materials are not necessarily the same thing. Ceramics or textiles are perceived as craft-based materials, but sometimes they are not about craft. They require craft for the making, but they may not celebrate craft, which is another thing. Craft is about how something is made in relation to its function. A lot of craft practices and forms come out of some tradition, and tradition can be strict and make you feel you have to obey how things should be made. There is craft that is very traditional, very strict, very contrived; and then there is craft that is very adventurous. We have to acknowledge that the world of craft is a big tent, where there are many different approaches. I believe that at some point you also have to question how things are being made and why you can only use a certain set of words, or certain ways of handling clay. What about the piece of clay that you just dropped on the floor? You immediately think, "Oh, this is just garbage," but you may look at it and say, "Wow, this is wonderful. I didn't think of making that, but, when it fell on the floor something happened to this clay that I may be able to use on a piece." You have to be open to what happens outside of the prescribed way of making something, to go beyond the accepted language. That's what artists always do. I am more interested in the poetry of material, and I think that can be found in the so-called crafts.

You look at a material and the material has a built-in set of parameters, what can be done with this stuff. It's probably the same if you're working with mixed media: what can be done with this stuff? How much of the vocabulary of the material will serve your ideas in the end? You know, that's really what it's about. Some people will explore that a lot more; some don't and it doesn't mean it's lesser art, just different.

Are you sure we can say "fine craft" as opposed to "sloppy craft"? I think that either the sloppiness in the crafted piece is a part of the vocabulary used to say something and it stands for something, or it's just a sloppily made piece. That is amateurish in my view and usually says I cannot do better and this is my limitation. You can usually see that. I think if we get into the territory I call the trained eye, like a trained ear for a musician that will hear subtleties between different interpretations, I probably see in a piece of ceramics that it is sloppy because the person couldn't do better versus part of the piece is interestingly sloppy in terms of the whole. That could be a fine craftsperson incorporating that element of sloppiness that an amateur cannot.

The dichotomy between the mind and the body in fine arts is stronger than ever; it didn't go away at all. And, in fact, in the visual arts we teach it. We're right back to saying the mind has the brilliant part: it has the concept and the ideas. The fabricator can be anybody. We're back to it, and the visual arts exemplify it. This may be linked to our culture, as we're not a culture where people work with their hands any more.

KT: I don't like boundaries or definitions unless grounded in the particular. Show me an example of work that you think fits each of these categories and we might then have a conversation based on the objects in front of us. Perhaps I'm too much of a practitioner rather than a philosopher.

PW: When I am judging ceramics prizes, I use a range of criteria: how well the piece has been resolved, taking into account if all the elements work in harmony; the object's complexity and uniqueness; and importantly, the expression of craftsmanship in the object, for I strongly believe that there is a craft base to every art form. I try to assess the artist's success in resolving these concerns and therefore consider notions of sloppy craft an impoverishment rather than an enrichment.

Editors: What do you think of the idea of interdisciplinarity in terms of your own practice as well as teaching?

CW: I have practiced and taught in art and design for over 20 years, more recently in critical and historical studies, but primarily within a ceramics context. The notion of interdisciplinarity is vital to both my practice and teaching—for me, it is a much more useful term than postdisciplinarity, and, as I said above, I would like to see more genuinely interdisciplinary teaching between the areas of craft, design, and fine art. Interdisciplinarity is an easy descriptor to claim, but less so to demonstrate. As Hal Foster wrote in 1998, before "postdisciplinary" had trumped "interdisciplinary" as the must-use term:

> Today so much work that purports to be interdisciplinary seems to be non-disciplinary to me. To be interdisciplinary you need to be disciplinary first—to be grounded in one discipline, preferably two, to know the historicity of these discourses before you test them against each other.[27]

My practice has always been fed by informal study in a wide range of disciplines, particularly sculpture, philosophy, and literature. Over the past four years of PhD research, I have explored and reassessed my making knowledge through a much more explicit and rigorous comparison with knowledge in these fields. Questions about documentation as product, the relationship between thinking, or concept, and imagination, between sites of production and display, between writing and making are explored through a skilled engagement with material.

Sometimes the various products of this practice seem like awkward hybrids, without an obvious home. I accept the situation as it is and my responsibility to frame the work in a way that is appropriate to my intentions. I increasingly use the term "craft" in my practice, but attempt to find methods for rethinking and re-presenting it—not in order to pass it off as art, but as a way of exploring what it is, as a way "to test itself against its own immanent logic."[28]

How might the conversation about material and skill and function intersect with current concerns in other disciplines? How might we use knowledge and methods from other disciplines to think through and communicate interactions between body, language, and material?

Picking up where I left off with postdisciplinarity, I would be thrilled to work for an art faculty that offered programs within three distinct, but intertwining disciplines—art, craft, and design; a faculty that offered formal interdisciplinary study between these three, but also between these and the other disciplines of the university. How exciting it would be to offer an interdisciplinary, practice/theory program (or module) in, say, functional crafts and political philosophy, or craft making and ecocriticism, or …

JPL: I am a maker. I believe that the way an object is made has everything to do with what it means. I consider making a language. A maker will articulate a material until it stands for something. I value how I experience art over what I may think of it. I am a painter, I make prints, I make ceramic sculpture, and I write stories.

KT: In my own practice, I think I am interdisciplinary in my subjects or content which shifts around; I have changed and used different approaches and technologies with weaving, but basically that is my medium. Where do you draw the disciplinary boundaries? For a personal response to this, see my essay in this section, "Weaving practice and pedagogy."

Notes

1   Mihalyi Csikszentmihalyi, *Flow: The Classic Work on How to Achieve Happiness* (London: Rider, 2002), p. 4.

2   Ibid., p. 150.

3   Douglas Burnham, "Immanuel Kant: Aesthetics," *Internet Encyclopedia of Philosophy*, http://www.iep.utm.edu/kantaest/ (accessed July 21, 2014).

4   Burton Watson, *Chuang Tzu. Basic Writings* (New York: Columbia University Press, 1996 [1964]), p. 19.

5   Marcus Boon, *In Praise of Copying* (Cambridge, MA, and London: Harvard University Press, 2010), p. 38.

6   John Roberts, "Art After Deskilling," *Historical Materialism* 18 (2010): 78–9.

7   Ibid., p. 81.

8   Ibid., p. 83.

9   Glenn Adamson (ed.), *The Craft Reader* (Oxford and New York: Berg, 2010), p. 34.

10 Borys Groys, *Art Power* (Cambridge, MA, and London: MIT Press, 2008), p. 7.

11 Peter Hughes, "Towards a post-consumer subjectivity: a future for the crafts in the twenty first century?" *Making Futures* 1 (2009): 217–23, http://makingfutures.plymouthart.ac.uk/journalvol1/papers/peter-hughes.pdf (accessed July 21, 2014).

12 Ibid.

13 Sinéad Murphy, *The Art Kettle* (Winchester, and Washington, DC: Zero Books, 2012), pp. 21–4.

14 Conor Wilson, "'You can use clay, but you can't do ceramics': Some thoughts on why ceramics isn't sculpture," *Interpreting Ceramics* 14 (2012), http://www.interpretingceramics.com/issue014/articles/02.htm (accessed July 21, 2014).

15 Martin Herbert, "The Broken Arm: Making, Unmaking, Remaking Sculpture," in *Thinking is Making: Presence and Absence in Contemporary Sculpture* (London: Black Dog Publishing, 2013), p. 28.

16 Theodor Adorno, "Functionalism Today" (delivered to the German Werkbund in 1965), *Oppositions* 17 (Summer 1979), in Glenn Adamson (ed.), *The Craft Reader* (Oxford and New York: Berg, 2010), p. 400.

17 Ibid., pp. 397–401.

18 Janet DeBoos, "Post-secondary art education in Australia," unpublished
    paper, "Education Panel," Australian Ceramics Triennale, Sydney, 2009;
    email to the editor, August 21, 2014.

19 Glenn Adamson, "When Craft Gets Sloppy," *Crafts* 211 (March/April 2008):
    38.

20 Christopher Frayling, "The Medium and the Message," in *On Craftsmanship:
    Towards a New Bauhaus* (London: Oberon Books, 2011), pp. 113–14.
    Frayling quotes Howard S. Becker, *Art Worlds* (Berkeley, CA: University of
    California Press, 1982).

21 Leonard Koren, *Wabi-sabi for Artists, Designers, Poets, and Philosophers*
    (Berkeley, CA: Stone Bridge Press, 2008).

22 Glenn Adamson (2013) interview for Blouin Artinfo, http://blogs.artinfo.com/
    artintheair/?s=MAD+glenn+adamson&x=67&y=14 (accessed July 20, 2014).

23 Sôetsu Yanagi (1927), "The Way of Craftsmanship," in Adamson (ed.), *The
    Craft Reader*, p. 168.

24 Claude Levi-Strauss, *The Savage Mind* (London: Weidenfeld & Nicolson,
    1966), pp. 16–17.

25 "Thomas J. Watson," BrainyQuote.com, Xplore Inc., http://www.
    brainyquote.com/quotes/quotes/t/thomasjwa209877.html (accessed August
    20, 2014).

26 Holly Hotchner and Nanette L. Laitman, "A Response to 'Tsunami
    Africa,' Glenn Adamson's Commentary on 'The Global Africa
    Project in the March 2011 issue of *Art in America*, Africa Talks,
    Museum of Arts and Design,'" http://gap.madmuseum.org/content/
    response-tsunami-africa-glenn-adamson%E2%80%99s-commentary-global-
    africa-project-march-issue-art-ame (accessed August 20, 2014).

27 Hal Foster, "Trauma Studies and the Interdisciplinary: An Overview," in Alex
    Coles and Alexia Defert (eds), *The Anxiety of Interdisciplinarity* (London:
    Backless Books, 1998).

28 Adorno, *Functionalism Today*, p. 396.

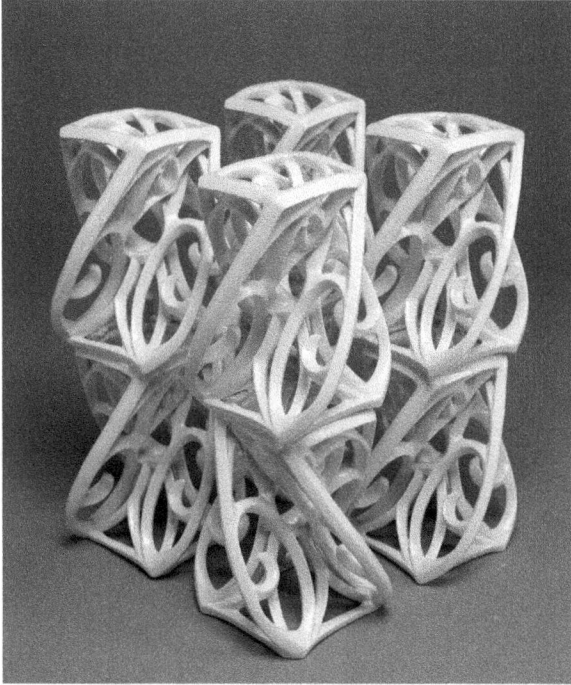

FIGURE 8.1 *Eliza Au, Twist (2013), cone 6 slipcast stoneware, 36 x 53 x 36 cm. Photo: Stephen Wilde.*

FIGURE 8.2 *Eliza Au, Basin #2 (2011), cast glass, 25 x 25 x 25 cm. Photo: Stephen Wilde.*

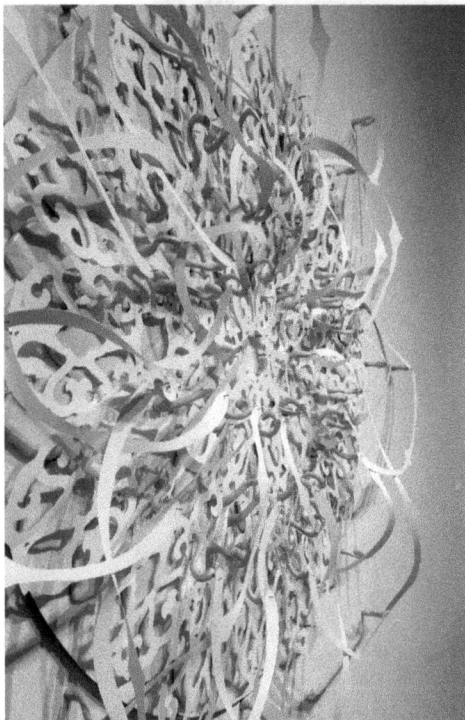

FIGURE 8.3 *Eliza Au, The Meditation of Order: Center Mandala (2009), cone 5 slipcast stoneware, metal and paper, 182 x 15 x 182 cm. Photo: Ying-Yueh Chuang.*

FIGURE 8.4 *Vue d'atelier/Studio view—Jean-Pierre Larocque, 2014. Photo: Bertrand Carrière.*

FIGURE 8.5 *Jean-Pierre Larocque, Figure #6, 2005–06, all figures between 96.5 x 70 x 40 cm. and 109 x 34.5 x 28 cm. Detail, front. Ceramic with glazes, multiple firings. Exhibited at Gardiner Museum, Toronto, June 23–October 9, 2006 in Jean-Pierre Larocque: Clay Sculpture and Drawings. Photo: Bertrand Carrière.*

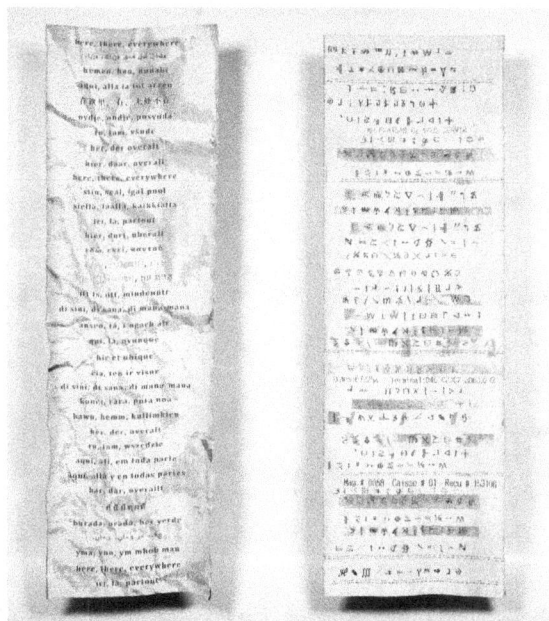

FIGURE 8.6 *Kelly Thompson, Translation (2013), 73 x 233 cm., and Tracking (2013), 76 x 228 cm., computer-assisted, hand jacquard woven, cotton and bamboo yarns. Photo: Richard-Max Tremblay.*

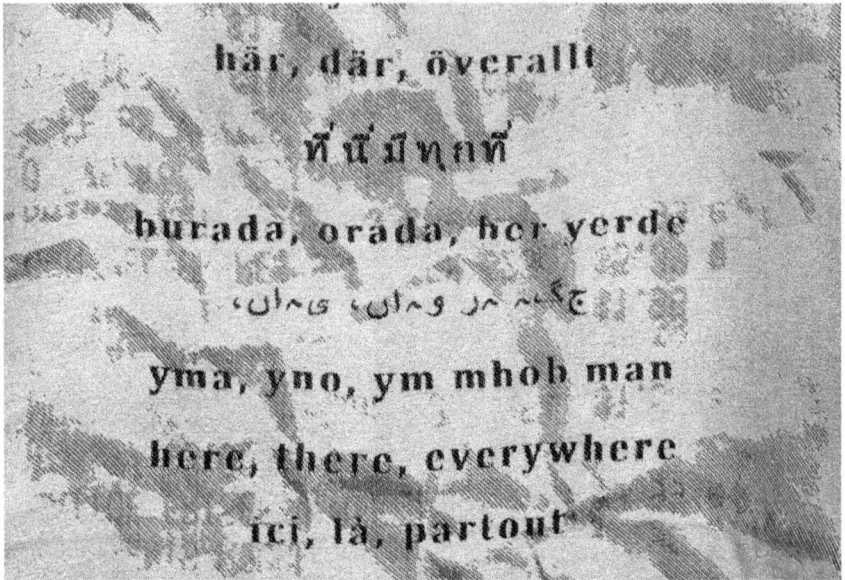

FIGURE 8.7 *Kelly Thompson, Translation (detail), computer-assisted, hand jacquard woven, cotton and bamboo yarns. Photo: Richard-Max Tremblay.*

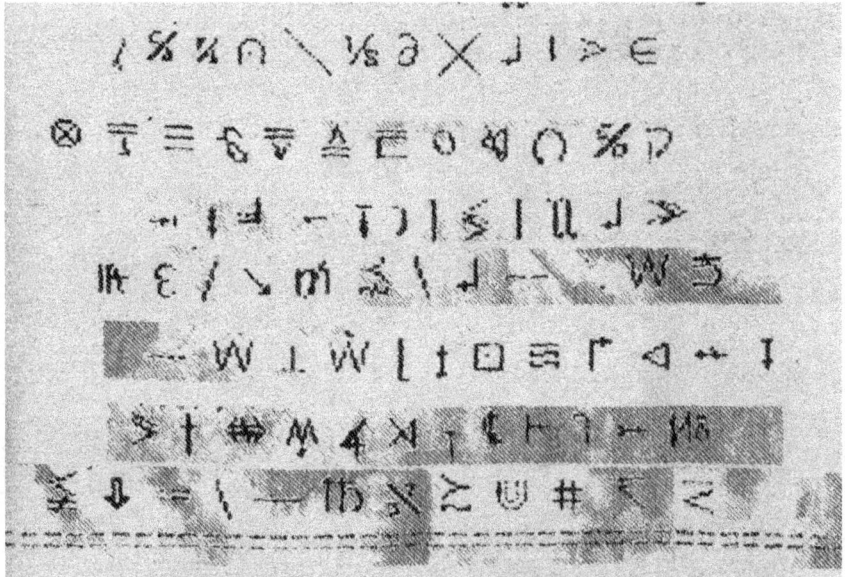

FIGURE 8.8 *Kelly Thompson, Tracking (detail), computer-assisted, hand jacquard woven, cotton and bamboo yarns. Photo: Richard-Max Tremblay.*

FIGURE 8.9 *Conor Wilson, Object_Text_Object (2013) (detail/video still), Royal College of Art Research Biennial (Disruption), Gulbenkian Galleries, Kensington, London. Multimedia installation (collaboration with Amanda Game). Objects, text, sound, dual moving image projection. Photo: Conor Wilson.*

FIGURE 8.10 *Conor Wilson, Residency installation, 2013 (detail/Bag_4 [punched bag & mallet]), Cranbrook Academy of Art, Michigan, USA. Clay, wood, text. Photo: Conor Wilson.*

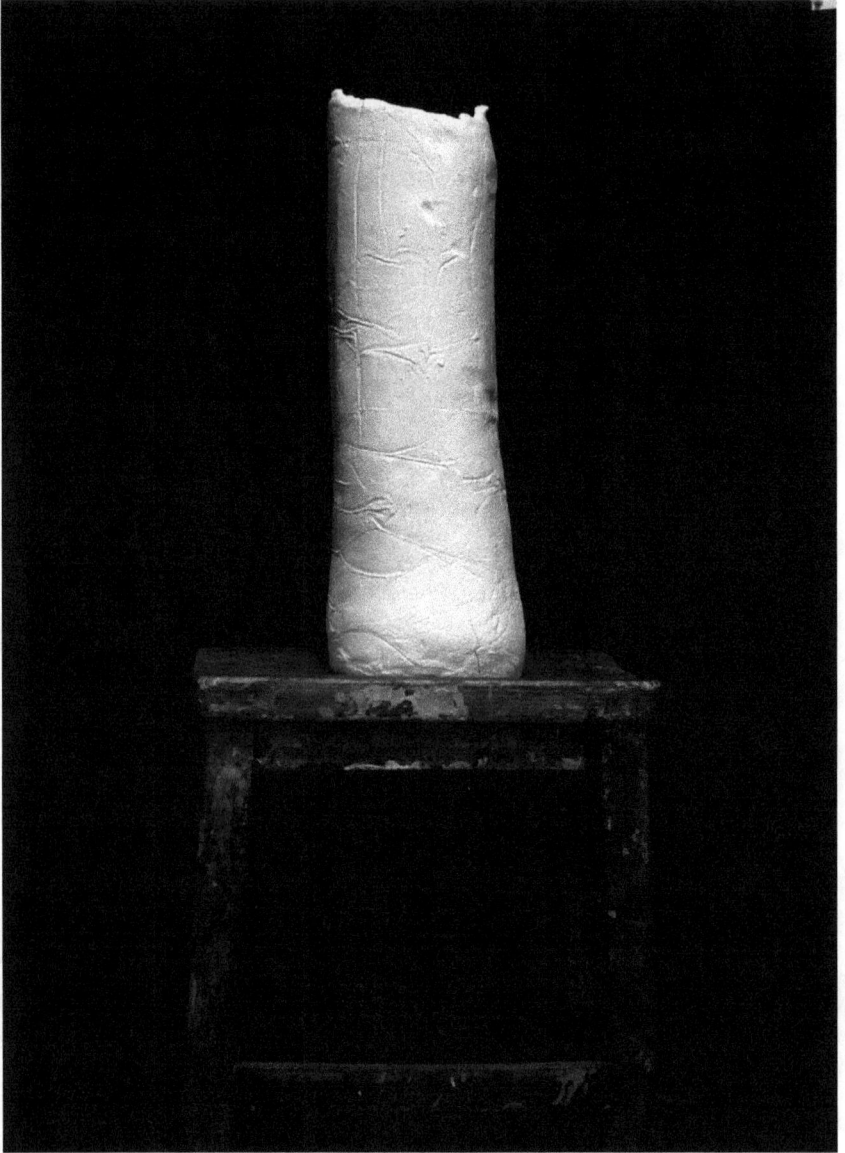

FIGURE 8.11 *Conor Wilson, One Bag, 2014 (detail), Royal College of Art, Hester Road Gallery, Battersea, London. Multimedia installation. Objects, text, sound, moving image projections. Photo: Conor Wilson.*

9

Teaching ceramics in an interdisciplinary environment

Eliza Au

I've heard it many times from several different people—"This grad show is really bad," or "After four years of art education, you'd think they could make something better." My experiences as a graduate student and consequently a sessional instructor have given me a broad perspective on such remarks, and on the expectations of a four-year craft education. I am concerned about the dilemma an instructor faces in trying to mediate the push–pull relationship between instilling the values of craftsmanship and skill versus those of intellectual and material freedom.

The dictionary definition of "sloppy" is "slovenly" and "careless," and when applied to a student`s project such negative connotations are usually an insult, especially in a craft context. Sloppy craft would be thus understood as work made with unintentionally poor craftsmanship compromising the purpose, quality, and value of the object. I have seen many sloppy craft projects presented in my classes, and I also admit, I have made a few "sloppy craft" projects in my student years. Before we start blacklisting sloppy craft as simply a poorly crafted object, we need to take into account that a sloppy craft object does not equal a failure in learning. Sloppy craft cannot be simply categorized as a problem before examining our perspective of the term.

I think of what is being produced on a spectrum: "sloppy craft" on one end, and "resolved craft" on the other. A maker needs to produce many "sloppy craft" projects before they can get to the "resolved craft" end. Craft education can be understood as a series of technical and conceptual hoops the student jumps through to arrive at conclusions that are eventually funneled into a resolved object. However, a resolved object is not necessarily equated with a "successful object," another loaded evaluative term in the classroom. A sloppy craft project can be successful as long as it fits the learning criteria. In the criteria I give my students, "success" is coming to conclusions about a way of working, rather than having a piece technically and conceptually finalized. An important issue is the connection between "sloppy" and "technical." From my own personal perspective and practice, the technical aspect of the craft of ceramics still holds a very central role in ceramic education. Knowledge of the medium and its processes contribute to its eventual conceptual and aesthetic outcome. Technical skill is a product of time and usually cannot be fully realized in the short period of art school education.

Having said this, educators within the ceramic field and other craft fields as well need to examine their expectations of students. Sloppy craft as unintentionally poor craftsmanship is produced in the classroom because of several factors: lack of time, perhaps because students are working on one or more jobs which cuts down on studio time; unreasonable expectations of a four-year craft education in which we cannot compare the craftsmanship of long-term and short-term practitioners; students' unclear concepts in their works that lead to use of inappropriate processes; integration of multiple mediums that brings into question students' abilities to create a resolved object; the value students accord craft objects and, in relation to that, the objects they have made.

Time is a key factor in the development of skill and the ability to go through the process of trial and error. For example, students in a three-credit studio course at the Emily Carr University of Art and Design in Vancouver, Canada, are required weekly to spend three hours of time in the studio outside of class. In order to complete at least two projects, this comes to, after class time, a total of 33 hours in an 11-week course for all the required tasks. These tasks might include researching the project, acquiring needed materials specific to the project, working in the studio, troubleshooting technical issues, loading and firing kilns, and installing the work for critique, and added onto this is travel time between home and studio. Full-time students would be taking at least two other courses with similar or heavier academic or studio loads, as well as working a part-time job. Unfortunately, this time squeeze is a fact of life in contemporary post-secondary art, craft and design institutions. What is apparent to me, however, is that as a teacher, I need to fit the maximum amount of learning in the minimum amount of time.

When discussing ceramic teaching, it is impossible to dismiss the issues of craftsmanship and the development of skill. By this, I mean the nuts and bolts about clay and glaze, and of learning how to throw and make a mould, and acquiring other techniques—all quantitative things that we can measure: either you know it or you don't. Considering the spread of time over work and school, what might be reasonable expectations for students to acquire these skills in a four-year art education, a relatively short period of time? Can we really suppose a freshly graduated art student to be an expert in their chosen field? Malcolm Gladwell, in his book *Outliers*, notes that neurologist Daniel Levitin maintains that "ten thousand hours of practice is required to achieve the level of mastery associated with being a world-class expert—in anything."[1] Ten thousand hours over a period of ten years means 20 hours a week for ten years. Taking into account that Levitin was talking about genius, we can downgrade it a bit and summarize it to mean it takes a lot of time to get good at something, more than that offered in post-secondary art school education.

Students are unclear about the purpose of their work, mostly because the curriculum has been broadened so widely. A class I recently taught at Emily Carr College of Art and Design was "Architectural Ceramics," and not "Brick Making" or "Tile Making," which are clearly technical classes. Every person who teaches "Architectural Ceramics" is going to assign completely different projects and introduce different methods of working, and their assignments are geared to have a very broad translation. On the one hand this forces students to think out of the box and explore their own interpretations, but on the other hand, by opening the floodgates of "freedom," students flounder when trying to choose the right processes to complete their assignments. It becomes very clear that process is integral to aesthetic: if you want something to look manufactured, you are most likely to cast your object, and if you want something to look handmade, you are more likely to throw or hand build your piece. Unfortunately, when each student has a goal tailor-made to his or her liking, there is no cohesive outcome of the course: every student has learned something different. This outcome may or may not be positive, depending upon the student's success in learning the targeted skill set.

Working in an interdisciplinary studio environment, where integration of materials is encouraged, brings up some pertinent issues for students and teachers. Each material, whether ceramic, metal, textile, and so on, has its own way of working. It is impossible for the student to master every craft in every medium they use. I see interdisciplinary studies as a double-edged sword. On the one hand, it promotes integration across mediums and fields, but on the other hand, it takes time away from gaining focused knowledge in one particular medium. Bruce Metcalf suggests this interdisciplinary environment has to do with studios becoming satellites: "every studio practice is reduced to being a service or a resource for students who come and go freely [with the consequence] there is no incentive for the patient accumulation of skills, and no particular value placed on tradition."[2] Interdisciplinary practices have a direct link to the discipline of ceramics looking towards contemporary art. Contemporary art normalizes making amateurish objects in Glenn Adamson's view (in relation to the exhibition *Unmonumental: The Object in the 21st Century*), and he notes that what is most common now "are found objects .... 'relational' situations requiring only rudimentary props, and of course, outsized sloppy sculpture."[3] I agree there is a trend towards students producing something in a ceramics class that could easily be mistaken for a project in an interdisciplinary sculpture class. Many of my students have included other media in their work as a major part of their projects, and to add to the confusion of mixed media, the ceramic parts of these projects are not readily apparent as "ceramic" but could be read as plastic, fabric, or some organic material.

How students value their work is a tough question. I've had a student ask me about his project, "If I fixed the crack, do you think I could sell it?" I think he is completely missing the point. As part of the educational process these projects are to be learned from and not taken as an end product. Students need to take what they learn and use it to propel their work into the next project. The question a student should be asking is not "What is the value of my work?" but "How do I make my work valuable?" Students tend to have a very short-term goal for their art, which often is the school sale or the dumpster. There is nothing wrong with the work ending up in those places, but there is something wrong when class projects are made for them. If the student's goal is to make something to sell for $20, they are going to make something that is worth $20. Too often dumpsters are filled with sloppy craft projects that are disposed of at the end of semester, while a few good ones could end up in the garden or kitchen cabinet. The question "What am I making this for?" is one that too often remains unanswered. Creating just for the grade rather than the learning process is extremely problematic. If what is being taught or what the student is to gain is not articulated clearly enough, the student produces garbage. A strong lack of student understanding regarding how their work is socially relevant accompanies an inability to form a direction towards a career.

Sloppy craft has its place in the educational development of the ceramics student. Judging only the end product is a superficial way of evaluating the "success" of an object, and fails to take into consideration previous projects, the processes, skills, and techniques that were learned, and how much trial and error was involved. I am not suggesting a drastic change to the current educational system within ceramics, but perhaps more of an awareness and re-examination of the idea of sloppy craft. To achieve a maximum return from time and energy invested in the course and studio requires a greater awareness of what project goals are and how they can be attained. If students are to find their own direction, as they should, their art education also needs to arm them with efficient practices. The current art and craft educational system has its pros and cons in these respects, and educators need to learn to work within the constraints of their own time and energy.

Suggested reading

Alfoldy, Sandra, *Crafting Identity: The Development of Professional Fine Craft in Canada* (Montreal and Kingston: McGill-Queens University Press, 2005).
Hickman, Richard, *Research in Art and Design Education: Issues and Exemplars* (Chicago: Intellect Books, University of Chicago Press, 2008).

Holly, Michael Ann and Smith, Marquard, *What is Research in the Visual Arts: Obsession, Archive, Encounter* (Williamstown, MA: Sterling and Francine Clark Art Institute, 2008).

Macdonald, Stuart, *A Century of Art and Design Education: From Arts and Crafts to Conceptual Art* (Cambridge: Lutterworth Press, 2005).

NSCAD Papers in Art Education 5 (Halifax: Nova Scotia College of Art and Design, 1990).

Sennett, Richard, *The Craftsman* (New Haven and London: Yale University Press, 2008).

Walling, Donovan R., *Rethinking How Art is Taught: A Critical Convergence* (Thousand Oaks, CA: Corwin Press Inc., 2000).

Notes

1   Malcolm Gladwell, *Outliers: The Story of Success* (New York: Little, Brown and Company Hachette Book Group, 2008), p. 40. Gladwell refers to Daniel Leviton, *This Is Your Brain on Music: The Science of a Human Obsession* (New York: Dutton, 2007), p. 193.

2   Bruce Metcalf, "Craft Education: Looking Back, Looking Forward," Distinguished Lecture given at the at the NCECA 41st Annual Conference, Louisville, Kentucky, 2007, http://www.brucemetcalf.com/pages/essays/craft_education.html (accessed July 26, 2014).

3   Glenn Adamson, "When Craft Gets Sloppy," *Crafts* 211 (March/April 2008): 38.

10

Weaving practice and pedagogy

Kelly Thompson

Intentions. Choices. Decisions. What is to be? Is craft seen as other? Is concern with materiality a handicap?

A critique scenario

A student presents their work on a wall. The critique format to which the class and professor have agreed is that the student presenter is not to speak initially; no clues are given other than the object, image, performance, or projection in front of us. It is the work of the class to "read" and discuss what is presented. To openly wonder ... To speculate, recognize, identify, and reference. Intentionality is tested, without the artist statement.

Warping, wind, wind, wind, turn. Threads slip, slide, wind. Tension but relaxed, winding. Repeat, back and forth. Count.

Today, what we are presented with looks like the leftovers of someone else's process: a series of approximately 100 threads, suggesting a warp, loosely parallel threads with some areas of intersecting threads at the end, familiar as the beginning of a weaving, then transitions, loose diagonal intersecting threads with very little holding it together. It is messy and sparse. There are three of these placed in relation to each other, as if having a conversation. All of the same black wool, with variations in length and details; one piece is pulled together with a large overhand knot at the cut ends.

Wind on, a different winding, different tools to encounter. Tools to encounter, observe, engage.

This is not a weaving class in which material choices, quality of selvedges, or other techniques may inform the immediate responses. It is an open project in an Advanced Fibers class. Skillful technique may not have been the student's goal. It tests instructor and students alike. Is this work about failure, frustration, or a sly poke? Is it a material response to Abstract Expressionism, a comment on deskilling,[1] or anti-craft statement? Or perhaps evidence of lack of time or care or motivation to complete the project as originally planned? How do we start to talk about it?

Weave. A back and forth action, intersecting. Lift, through, change, beat, lift, through, change, beat. Repeat. Intersections, structure, lines. Structure to surface. Repeat. Back and forth to objectness.

As professors, our familiar frameworks are tested constantly (or that is what one hopes for), but it can also challenge one's own aesthetic comfort levels and content or subject familiarity. The skill of the teacher is in handling the tricky situations to make the experience a relevant one for the class and the individual. Critiques are learning opportunities to allow space for possibilities, to question diplomatically, with responses and reactions as feedback. The presenter at the end can inform, defend, or acknowledge surprise or accuracy of the comments. It is not a space to make presenters cry, although that does happen at times (usually a symptom of a student's lack of sleep, stress, or anxiety, although I have observed brutal instructors who think challenging to the point of breakdown is a way for the student to make a breakthrough).

Discipline. Learned actions become a bodily knowing. Mind and body: choices, intentions, decisions. Repeat and practice. Discipline is contradictory, self-control, and punishment, regulation, subject, and instruct.

What is interdisciplinarity in the fine arts? Interdisciplinarity across fields is one thing, but within? Can this even be relevant? I understand interdisciplinarity when discipline specific knowledge (skills, traditions) might have particular relevance, while the approach to subject (methodology and content) may have great similarities. A biologist and an artist have different training, but the conversations can be relevant for each, a respect for experience. Am I an interdisciplinary artist because I weave cloth, but also print or project images on it? Do I need to perform it to be truly interdisciplinary? Is this relevant?

Has interdisciplinary become shorthand for using a variety of tools and processes?

Describing oneself as an interdisciplinary artist I believe is overused in contemporary profiles: are you really all those things at a professional level? Or perhaps it is necessary to avoid being boxed in. Either way, the discipline is art; why complicate or obfuscate? Call a tool a tool.

Through the internet we have access to many different dialogs, disciplines, and information, and a culture of skimming inevitably occurs during a research phase. In fact we are considered remiss if we don't keep up. Inevitably, material is read through our subjective eyes, the familiar items are selected or deleted as relevant to our current interests. The democratization of information available through the Web, and the current utopian wave of 3-D printing, the Maker movement, and personalized production, amongst other changes, is still contingent on economics. Because you can send an image of your dog and get it woven into a blanket, do you? Is that interesting to anyone other than your family?

If you outsource, does this make you interdisciplinary?

Interdisciplinary outcomes are common in art school contexts. Contemporary art and current education systems lead this way. What is acceptable within a fibers class? Is discipline specificity an issue? More important to me is: how and to what critical purpose is the content of the work communicated and related to the technique, material choices, or visual or cultural context in which it is presented? Is the labor your own and is that significant? What is the subject being addressed? Is there a social, political, personal, environmental or historical content? Does the work make us think or ask questions of ourselves?

Another critique scenario

The class is presented with a 1980s Madonna music video, with the artist dancing and lip-synching layered in front of the famous singer. It is funny, but as audience we are also slightly uncomfortable for the performer who does not have the body image, grace, or style of Madonna. It is awkward. The imposition or interjecting of self is very skillfully done, trying to blot out the original performer, yet with hints of self-deprecating knowing, a mimicry of familiar moves now performed for camera, honoring fame and adolescent influence, desiring to be but simultaneously humorously overtaking the main character. This mash-up demonstrates the use of multiple skills—camera, editing, music, blue screen, YouTube, dancing—while the content addresses self-awareness, body image, identity, DIY mash-ups, popular culture, repetition of observed actions, mimicry, and humor.

This is a self-portrait commentary in video, in a fibers class, her first performed video. What is the discussion to be had? Some might suggest we critique only the costumes as the fiber content, but this is the least relevant component in a culturally and personally rich project. Like many others, this student negotiated and embraced the complexity of interdisciplinarity without constraint.

Learning to do something when it is needed is familiar to humans, within or outside of formal education. Institutions may create syllabi for this learning, but the Web is a new site of learning. Teaching is democratized. David Gauntlett, in *Making is Connecting: The Social Meaning of Creativity, from DIY and Knitting to YouTube and Web 2.0*, suggests the Web creates opportunities, accessibility to creatively engage and collaborate, and this is healthy for a broader society. By implication, this form of creativity is political, enabling engaged individuals rather than feeding passive consumers. People can make a choice to make or do something on their own (DIY skill sharing, blog, music video) rather than just consume what is given from the big media or corporate culture. The Web is both a metaphor and means for fostering different kinds of interactions, craft activities, political organizing, networking, and communicating. [2]

Flexibility is required

As a tenured faculty member at Concordia University in Montreal, I am now into my third full-time teaching job at the post-secondary level, in three countries.[3] In addition, I have art degrees from two other universities in different countries again.[4] Some might say this is messy, restless, unreliable. I prefer to think of it as nomadic, an enriching educational experience. "Thompson's work speaks to the question put by Joan Borsa: 'how to be located but not fixed—how to have ground or position but continue to travel?'"[5]

Extract from my recent tenure dossier teaching statement

In fine art practices I believe students need to be self-motivated and drive their own creativity, rather than the instructors identifying the specific hoops students must jump through to get a good grade. Students gain marks when they demonstrate innovative and experimental outcomes, sustained engagement and commitment in making decisions—including technical and conceptual, and resolution of ideas as appropriate. Technical samples are treated differently than projects and are considered important exercises necessary for skill development. Providing opportunities to learn skills is part of my pedagogical approach; projects give the space for making aesthetic and conceptual choices, with or without applying the skills covered. Setting high standards and belief in the student's capability is vital to motivating and encouraging independent thinking.

Skills: Enabler of choices?

Richard Sennett in *The Craftsman* writes that "all skills, even the most abstract, begin as bodily practices," and secondly proposes that "technical understanding develops through the powers of imagination", closely linked to language to "direct and guide bodily skill."[6] He refers to craft as the skills involved in any professional, learned activity—whether a pianist, an operator of scientific instruments or computers, a surgeon's scalpel hand. I like this wider interpretation of craft.

In his introduction, Sennett states that:

> History has drawn fault lines dividing practice and theory, techniques and expressions, craftsman and artist, maker and user: modern society suffers from this historical inheritance ... But the past life of craft and craftsmen also suggests ways of using tools, organising bodily movements, thinking about materials that remain alternative, viable proposals about how to conduct life with skill.[7]

Memory is subjective, reconstructed, retold, fragmentary, often distorted. History pretends otherwise, but it is all these things too. Practice. Technology. Changes.

A shift occurred in my artwork when I started using a computer-assisted hand jacquard loom. The tools change and opportunities to work different ways emerge. Initially trained on standard four- and eight-harness looms, I have worked on a draw loom, mechanical dobby and then a computer assisted dobby, and a jacquard loom. All weaving requires a base technical understanding of the parameters one is working with: decisions get made about materials and loom set-up, which affect subsequent possibilities. With the jacquard, more time is spent on the computer than on the loom in producing work. The finesse is worked out through digital simulations and materially woven samples; it is essential to test densities and relationships of structures to ensure correct pattern proportions. Many of the jacquard looms that artists use require hand-throwing of the shuttle with weft yarns and beating the fell edge. This is something I still enjoy—the body–mind relationship of production. Industrial looms are fully mechanized, run by highly skill technicians, each loom with its own parameters but capable of fast production. However, gaining access for shorter runs is much more difficult than for digital textile printing.

Interdiciplinarity and Web 2.0

Chris Anderson, former editor of *Wired* magazine, says the Maker movement is the next industrial revolution: "Basically, the Maker movement is what happens when the Web meets the real world. It's the combination of the Web's innovation model with a new generation of computer-controlled desktop manufacturing tools that have a democratizing impact, much like the PC and the Internet did a generation ago."[8] He goes on to explore the broader implications of this digital revolution:

> When you upload a video to YouTube you are broadcasting and have the ability to reach billions of people. It blurs the line between the professionals and the amateurs. And we're seeing the same thing with manufacturing. If you design something on the screen and you 3D print it, are you manufacturing? No. You are prototyping.[9]

What is not addressed is the issue of the digital skills and equipment needed to get to that point, and the functional or critical awareness that the material form will live up to the virtual impressions—or as William Morris explains, the "'hope of product'—the achievement of having made something worthwhile."[10] The new labor force in this revolution are the technicians, fabricators, and online or outsourcing service personnel. Given the art economy, many of these skilled individuals are also likely to be creative artists or craftspeople, working to support their practice.

The concept of "open source" software and the Web as a communal space for sharing may be updating or renewing the idealism of the Arts and Crafts Movement, perhaps with a DIY democratic element that the original movement failed to achieve: "craft skills were valued for their own careful, individual, handmade beauty, not because they were supposed to be the skills of an expert elite."[11]

Luanne Martineau, in her thoughtful articulations on "reskilling" and analysis of John Roberts's "deskilling" in art, suggests that craft's relation to technology might be somewhat different than Gauntlett proposes. "[T]he current discussion of reskilling focuses on revisiting craft as a place from which to critique or react to the post-digital age of software-specific art and design, consumerism, condensed time, and globalization."[12] However, she also indicates the idealism and hope underlying much of the contemporary movement: "The role of craft within this moment of post-studio art practice is, in many ways, the articulation of a desire to locate a believable and sustaining continuity between medium, community, and message ... by seeking a more direct and intimate model of material and social engagement."[13]

Craft, craftsman, craftsperson, crafter, craftivist, studio craft, sloppy craft, amateur, professional, discipline, interdisciplinary, postdisciplinary, making, thinking, skill, reskilling, materiality, the material turn ...?

The chart is a shifting terrain. My position and practice, as always, is contingent, temporal, and localized.

Notes

1   John Roberts, *The Intangibilities of Form: Skill and Deskilling in Art after the Readymade* (London: Verso, 2007).

2   David Gauntlett, *Making is Connecting: The Social Meaning of Creativity, from DIY and Knitting to YouTube and Web 2.0* (Cambridge and Malden, MA: Polity Press, 2011).

3   School of Art, Otago Polytechnic, Dunedin New Zealand, 1988–2004; Goldsmiths, University of London (2004–8); Concordia University (2008–).

4   Bachelor of Fine Arts (Textiles), California College of Arts and Crafts, 1985; Oakland, CA, USA, Master of Arts (Visual Arts); Australian National University, Canberra, Australia (1994).

5   Leoni Schmidt, *Kelly Thompson: Locus Operandi*, Dunedin Public Art Gallery, New Zealand, 2001. Catalog published in conjunction with the exhibition.

6   Richard Sennett, *The Craftsman* (London: Allen Lane/Penguin Group, 2008), p. 10.

7   Ibid.

8   Chris Anderson interviewed by Vikram Alexei Kansara, "Chris in The Long View: Chris Anderson says the Business Revolution is the Next Industrial Revolution," *The Business of Fashion*, http://www.businessoffashion. com/2012/11/the-long-view-chris-anderson-says-the-maker-movement-is-the-next-industrial-revolution.html (accessed November 6, 2012).

9   Ibid.

10 Gauntlett, *Making is Connecting,* p. 41.

11 Ibid., p. 49.

12 Luanne Martineau, "Reskilling," *Esse* 74, Savoir-Faire (2011): 5.

13 Ibid.

11

Sloppy craft: As related to ceramics

Peter Wilson

*The boring truth is that the artist is more a labourer than
a visionary, albeit an inspired one. For every natural talent
there are a million honest toilers, all striving towards the light.*[1]

Each year, several thousand graduates emerge from art schools in Australia,
with many searching for a gallery in which to show and develop a market
for their work. The obstacles confronting these young artists are immense,
for even for those with a serious body of work, energy, and ideas, the
notion of getting their work noticed takes ingenuity, relentless time, effort,
and luck. Inevitably their vision takes a reality check as they are caught
between working in impoverished circumstances and meeting the costs of
living, and many succumb to the reality of having to postpone their vision.
The question remains as to whether graduates are equipped to survive as
artists, or is that an unrealistic expectation?

One factor within art schools is the lack of "studio time" in which
students can concentrate solely on the development of the craft skills of their
chosen field. Perversely, art schools within universities are constrained by the
requisite research outputs and administration of the lecturing staff. Hence,
good teaching (as evaluated by the students) is seen as a less important
outcome for tenured staff than research, and is subsequently reduced to allow
more resources to be allocated to the former. Actual face-to-face teaching
time varies, but it is a very small component of the overall course. It could be
argued, however, that the acquisition of these craft skills is the responsibility
of the students and that they should put in the extra time to develop them.

Similarly, understanding the materiality of their craft takes time and
cannot solely be developed during class time each week for a three-year

fine arts degree. A huge amount of additional time needs to be spent in the studio experimenting, learning throwing/forming techniques, designing work, taking risks with this, mixing glazes, stacking kilns, preparing the kiln for firing, firing, watching how others tackle the problems of making, developing understandings of form, and the list goes on. Discussions and critical analyses of artworks are also impacted by reduced teaching hours, as are an ongoing discussion about aesthetics, understanding the history and context of artworks, and examining collections of works as held in galleries and museums, a crucial part of any art program.

By way of comparison, a traditional apprenticeship in ceramics in Japan (or any other country) would require at least five years of diligent commitment, underpinned by a strong work ethic. The apprentice would become part of the extended Japanese family and assume the prescribed roles as befitting each year of the apprenticeship. For example, year one would entail cleaning the studio, preparing the clay, stacking kilns, gathering and preparing the wood for firing, mixing glazes from 8.00 a.m. until 6.00 p.m. each day, six days a week.

This degree of preparation for life as an artist is the antithesis to that of an art school graduate because it is a practice-based model requiring a much larger commitment than most people would be prepared to give. Modern life is a strong factor in the development of younger artists. By this I mean that people's brains are changing. The internet and computers are creating an evolutionary shift in the way people think. Information is at our fingertips and is external. No one seems to have time to think deeply anymore. Everyone is multi-tasking, skimming screens for instant information, spending hours superficially speed-reading—but where is the parallel explosion of wisdom? The artist needs imagination to develop work in order to not merely imitate that which is already there. The nourishment of the imagination requires an intrapersonal intelligence such that the enrichment of our senses and our ideas occurs regularly.[2] It may be through our contact with nature, through music, reading, or poetry. This is the wellspring from which we develop our work and is the basis of our replenishment along with our understandings of materials.

John Olsen, one of Australia's senior and pre-eminent artists, argues that there is a strong decline in painting standards. He doubts if artists generally are undergoing the long dedicated hours of isolation to achieve wondrous results. Few, he claims, seem prepared to spend decades struggling to reach a goal, as it is all about instant results, instant gratification. Olsen states that Tracey Emin's *Unmade Bed*, for example, contains no nourishment in its style of work to compel the viewer to linger and keep looking at it. In contrast, one would do so with a painting by, for example, Lloyd Rees (1895–1988), intrigued by how he solved visual problems, and return again and again to discover something profound.[3] Lucien Freud commented along similar lines after observing Damien Hirst's *Shark in formaldehyde*: "It's OK, it's clever, but after you've seen it once, there's nothing much to come back to ... it may be clever but is it worth the trouble? Where's the achievement? Where is the craft in these works?"[4]

For a ceramic artist like myself, there is a joy in the process of making. It takes the form of a conversation between the artist and the object, which requires a sensitive and nuanced dialog with the material: a little more height here, less weight at the foot, a more balanced lip, how will the glaze flow on this surface, a little broader in the shoulder—tickle me! Few of us embrace poverty, as *Sydney Morning Herald* art critic John McDonald explains, but for most artists, the pleasure of making exceeds the pleasure of making money.[5]

McDonald highlights the value of a strong work ethic as vital, along with the notion of a practiced hand, understanding the myriad complexities and nuances of color, texture, form, surface, and how they interrelate—all of which take time to develop. One is developing and trying new possibilities all the time.[6] The idea of an inquiring mind and experimentation is so fundamentally a part of the creative process. The resulting maker's body of work will provide evidence of the time spent in the studio resolving these problems, rather than on the luncheon circuit, socializing, feeding a virtual community of followers via social media with regular updates on Facebook and Twitter.

When John Ruskin, William Morris, and Charles Voysey founded the Arts and Crafts Movement in England in the nineteenth century, railing against the impoverished level of design, quality, and variety of the industrially produced goods at that time, I doubt they envisaged first, the strength, diversity, and longevity of the movement, and secondly, how the social circumstances would impact on contemporary craft practice a full century and a half later.

Notes

1   John McDonald, "Around the World Holiday Snaps," *Sydney Morning Herald*, February 18, 1995.

2   Howard Gardner, *Frames of Mind : The Theory of Multiple Intelligences* (New York: Basic Books, 2004).

3   Janet Hawley, "A Beautiful Life," *Sydney Morning Herald*, December 10, 2011, p. 14.

4   Martin Gayford, "Worshipping a Golden Calf," *The Spectator*, October 25, 2008, p. 45.

5   John McDonald, "When Publicity Trumps Probity," *Sydney Morning Herald*, September 27, 2008.

6   Ibid.

Postscript

Reprint of Glenn Adamson, "When Craft Gets Sloppy" *Crafts* 211 (March–April 2008)[*]

Young craftsmen like Josh Faught are at the forefront of the sloppy craft movement. Glenn Adamson discovers why the haphazard has become so hip.

IT'S A SCENE THAT REPEATS itself over and over again in art schools these days. The eminent professor of a craft-based department, visiting a student's studio, inspects the work in progress. What she sees is expressive. It's got personality. It is work that's clearly going somewhere. There's only one problem. It's really badly made.

That is exactly what happened a few years ago at the School of the Art Institute of Chicago. The professor was the textile-based artist Anne Wilson (recently featured in the Victoria and Albert Museum show *Out of the Ordinary*). The student was Josh Faught. But the conversation didn't go in the expected direction. Wilson was intrigued, not appalled, by what she termed her student's 'sloppy craft'. As she says of her department's pedagogical approach, 'Technical skills are presented and taught quite rigorously, but not with an emphasis on fine-tuning high skill as the goal. The concept is the goal.' To her, Faught's devil-may-care approach seemed perfectly acceptable. It was well matched to the content of his work, which explores the dynamics of individual and family dysfunction through a combination of personal and archetypal imagery.

---

[*]Reprinted with kind permission from Crafts Magazine. Minor edits have been made to this reprint to conform to Bloomsbury publishing requirements.

Faught, in turn, embraced the label – or at least the idea that 'calculated sloppiness' was a fair description of what he was up to. It aligns him, first of all, with a line of artistic thinking running back to the first Feminist artists, such as Miriam Schapiro, Joyce Kozloff, and Judy Chicago, who often employed homely crafts with which they had no particular expertise. The 90s fascination with low or 'abject' forms, in the hands of such artists as Mike Kelley and Sue Williams, is another point of reference for him, as are the fibre artists of the 70s – Magdalena Abakanowicz, Sheila Hicks, Walter Nottingham, and their peers – somewhat fashionable in their day, then deeply unfashionable as their work came to seem emblematic of a hairier, hippier, and more hedonistic time. The worm has turned again though, at least in Faught's eyes. In early fibre art, he sees a 'sense of restlessness, or even a sense of downright domestic hysteria at play.' His 2006 installation *Nobody Knows I'm A Lesbian*, with its haywire pileup of textile techniques and confessional imagery, returns to all three of these historical points of reference – Feminism, fibre art, and abjection. In doing so, it suggests just how unprocessed those moments are in the history of art-through-craft.

A cynically-minded person, however, could view Faught's work as a transparent bid for success in the contemporary art world, which has long made a point of embracing my-kid-could-do-that aesthetics. In the UK, Tracey Emin's hilariously bad embroideries and Sarah Lucas's casually thrown-together sculptures are notorious, but the trend is much broader than the (once) Young British Artists. The list of other prodigious talents from around the world who craft at least a little bit sloppily includes Ghada Amer, Rachel Harrison, Tim Hawkinson, Christian Holstad, Shinique Smith, and Franz West. The New Museum in New York has just opened its new building with *Unmonumental: The Object in the 21st Century*, an exhibition of mostly sloppy sculpture that is billed as 'conversational, provisional, [and] un-heroic'. And when the art world turns its gaze on traditional craft materials, as is the case with Rebecca Warren's (Turner Prize-nominated) or Grayson Perry's (Turner Prize-winning) ceramics, the sense is that it's not only OK but necessary for a contemporary artist to be amateurish. The lack of evident skill somehow implies the presence of concept. The same goes when avant-garde designers approach craft. This is a particularly noticeable development in the Netherlands, where the Droog collective pioneered a peculiar slick-sloppy aesthetic. Latter-day exponents include the clay chairs of Maarten Baas, the witty product designs of Chantal van Heeswijk, and the narrative furniture of Atelier Van Lieshout.

So why has the unkempt become so very stylish? Perhaps it's a matter of production values. If one wants to make sense of the bewildering visual cacophony of a major contemporary art fair (like Frieze or Art Basel), it's sometimes helpful to ignore how things look, and what they are supposedly about, and instead focus on how they are made. We are in an art boom, and faced with spectacular installations like those in Tate Modern's Turbine Hall, anything seems possible. But making things, it turns out, is still quite difficult. Indeed, the one thing that seems to bind the majority of contemporary art together is the lack of skill required to create it. What we have now, mostly, are found objects, outsourced fabrication, bad painting, big photos printed on expensive equipment, 'relational' situations requiring only rudimentary props, and of course, outsized sloppy sculpture. Seen in this context, perhaps what we're looking at in the proliferation of the sloppy isn't about concept at all. Maybe it's a response to the economics of art-making. For the lucky few with big-name galleries and patrons, fine craftsmanship and multimedia production are easily bought off the peg: but for those without financial backing, size and guts will suffice.

Like any contemporary artist, Josh Faught must negotiate these conditions of production. And yet his particular brand of sloppy seems, as Wilson intuited, to be going somewhere special. Faught's work puts a new spin on the always-interesting dilemma of why we value craft in the first place. There are as many answers to this question as there are ways of making, but one dichotomy seems especially crucial. On the one hand, skill commands respect. We value the integrity of the well-made object, the time and care it demands. Therefore, what we most want out of our craft is something like perfection. On the other hand, though, we value craft's irregularity – it's human, indeed humane, character. We want craft to stand in opposition to the slick and soulless products of systemised industrial production. In this frame of mind, we might care less for an immaculate object like a Fabergé egg than someone's first pinchpot, or a knitted jumper made for a grandchild.

Faught seems to come down on the latter side of this argument, hard. But it's not so simple. Like the artists that inspire him, he indicates a way out of the conundrum, a refusal of the false choice between the perfect and the affective. There are great differences between Sheila Hicks, Miriam Schapiro, and Mike Kelley, but all are similar in one key respect. They each separate themselves from the amateur even as they quote it. This is not only a matter of form – content does count here – but form is a big part of it. The swagger of Hicks's cascading braids, the historical layering of Schapiro's 'femmage,' the disturbing unpredictability of Kelley's collaged stuffed animals, all find correspondence in Faught's installations and sculpture, which are (formally speaking) anything but inept. This is, perhaps, the dirty secret of sloppy craft: there may be nothing so difficult to pull off convincingly.

I asked Wendy Maruyama, the great American furniture-maker, for her opinion about sloppy craft. She responded, 'I completely understand it's usage. Sometimes it's done well, sometimes it's done poorly and sometimes it pisses me off that some people do it poorly so well and get away with it!' Joshua David Riegel, a curator and critic in Brooklyn agrees. In work like Faught's, he says, 'there is a purposeful defiance of a perceived easy construction (belying our desire to equate "sloppiness" with celerity) and a consequent irreverence for easy consumption (in that expectations are turned on their head if not shattered altogether).'

In the post-disciplinary art environment in which students are trained today, a long-term investment in dedicated skills is less and less common. As Tanya Harrod noted recently, a line was crossed when instructors began teaching skills on an 'as and when' basis. Students learned how to do something – embroider a pillowcase, throw a pot, carve wood – only when they thought they needed to. Indeed, they might only do it once. No form of pedagogy could seem more appropriate to a culture that seems afflicted with attention deficit disorder, and at the same time obsessed with informal knowledge. Right now the quintessential art forms may no longer be physical objects at all but rather music video mashups and hypertext-rich blogs.

The DIY movement, currently at the height of fashion, is an obvious expression of this open-sourced culture, and the crafters' emphasis on community and gratification often results in a casual attitude to technique. This permissiveness has deeply penetrated art-school culture, fascinatingly blurring the line between hobbyism and professional endeavor. But as Sabrina Gschwandtner, author of the blazingly fresh book *KnitKnit: Profiles and Projects from Knitting's New Wave*, points out, there is more than one side to DIY. Some indie crafters work hard to perfect or at least improve their craftsmanship, precisely as a way of bringing the disputed strands of contemporary experience into focus. Knitting and other homespun craft activities are restless phenomena, susceptible to a huge range of technical, formal, conceptual, and political frameworks. 'We have to keep interrogating the boundaries of contemporary craft,' says Gschwandtner, 'so it doesn't remain at the level of "sloppy stitches"'. I suspect that Josh Faught, in some respects the quintessential product of a post-disciplinary craft education, couldn't agree more.

INDEX

www.ingramcontent.com/pod-product-compliance
Lightning Source LLC
Chambersburg PA
CBHW050429280326
41932CB00013BA/2047